WELFARE HOT BUTTONS: WOMEN, WORK, AND SOCIAL POLICY REFORM

Welfare Hot Buttons provides a comparative assessment of contemporary social policy change in three Western countries: Canada, the United States, and Great Britain. In this challenging work, Sylvia Bashevkin examines the effect of the social policies of three Third Way political leaders – Bill Clinton, Jean Chrétien, and Tony Blair – on the fate of single mothers on social assistance. She argues that despite seemingly progressive campaign rhetoric, the social policies implemented under each of these leaders were in many respects more punitive and restrictive than those of their neo-conservative predecessors in the 1980s. During this latter period social assistance policy moved toward selective targeting of work-tested and means-tested benefits to 'deserving' persons. Designed as tax or fiscal measures, these benefits helped to establish an individualized and marketized system of support that was directed toward rewarding 'working families.' In effect, single mothers in all three countries were now required to enter the labour force while their children were still young, and the social citizenship of childless people and of adults who did not or could not work for pay was severely compromised.

Bashevkin addresses a number of other contentious issues while exploring the implications of the erosion of traditional social welfare programs in Britain and North America. In its comparative approach and substantive analysis, *Welfare Hot Buttons* makes an important contribution to the existing body of literature on social policy.

SYLVIA BASHEVKIN is Director of the Canadian Studies Program and a professor in the Department of Political Science at the University of Toronto. She specializes in the areas of women and politics, public policy, and comparative politics.

ALSO BY SYLVIA BASHEVKIN

Toeing the Lines: Women and Party Politics in English Canada (1985, 1993)
True Patriot Love: The Politics of Canadian Nationalism
Women on the Defensive: Living through Conservative Times
Women and Politics in Western Europe, ed.
Canadian Political Behaviour, ed.
Women's Work Is Never Done, ed.

SYLVIA BASHEVKIN

Welfare Hot Buttons: Women, Work, and Social Policy Reform

UNIVERSITY OF TORONTO PRESS
Toronto London

UNIVERSITY OF PITTSBURGH PRESS

Toronto London
Printed in Canada

ISBN 0-8020-3716-X (cloth)
ISBN 0-8020-8517-2 (paper)

Printed on acid-free paper

Published in the United States in 2002 by University of Pittsburgh Press, Pittsburgh, Pa. 15260. A United States CIP record is available from the Library of Congress.
ISBN 0-8229-5799-X

National Library of Canada Cataloguing in Publication

Bashevkin, Sylvia B.
Welfare hot buttons : women, work, and social policy reform / Sylvia Bashevkin.

Includes bibliographical references and index.
ISBN 0-8020-3716-X (bound). – ISBN 0-8020-8517-2 (pbk.)

1. Public welfare – Canada. 2. Public welfare – United States. 3. Public welfare – Great Britain. 4. Single mothers – Government policy – Canada. 5. Single mothers – Government policy – United States. 6. Single mothers – Government policy – Great Britain. 7. Canada – Social policy. 8. United States – Social policy. 9. Great Britain – Social policy. I. Title.

HV31.B37 2002 361.6′5 C2002-901741-6

This book has been published with the help of a grant from the Humanities and Social Sciences Federation of Canada, using funds provided by the Social Sciences and Humanities Research Council of Canada.

The University of Toronto Press acknowledges the financial assistance to its publishing program of the Canada Council for the Arts and the Ontario Arts Council.

University of Toronto Press acknowledges the financial support for its publishing activities of the Government of Canada through the Book Publishing Industry Development Program (BPIDP).

Contents

Acknowledgments

For some time, this study has been nicknamed the *How Could They* project. My provisional or working title was offered only partly in jest, in response to enquiries from friends and colleagues about what I was working on. The phrase reflected a profound frustration and disappointment with the social policy directions of Third Way national leaders, particularly in the United States and Canada. As readers will note in the pages that follow, the passage of time seemed only to sharpen my sense of being let down.

Thankfully, in every respect other than the real-world political one, the experience of undertaking this study was positive and uplifting. I learned a great deal from activists and experts working on welfare reform issues in the United States, Canada, and Great Britain, and was inspired by the commitment of so many people to embattled ideals of equality and social justice. Given the constraints of contemporary research ethics, the more than 120 helpful interviewees who were willing to speak with me remain anonymous in this account.

The challenge of preparing a cross-national and cross-time study of social policy development was aided immeasurably by the contributions of a series of assistants at the University of Toronto, notably Cheryl Collier, Gina Cosentino, Tristan Fehrenbach, Joy Fitzgibbon, Jessie Fyfe, Helen Giddings, Genevieve Johnson, Jacqueline Krikorian, and Heather Murray. Research for the study was funded by a grant from the Social Sciences and Humanities Research Council of Canada (SSHRCC), and this book was published with the help of a grant from the Humanities and Social Sciences Federation of Canada, using funds provided by SSHRCC.

I am especially grateful for the ongoing interest of colleagues and students near and far. Since 1998, materials from this study have been presented at conferences of the Canadian Political Science Association, the Harvard University Center for European Studies, the York University Centre for Feminist Research, and the International Political Science Association, as well as at invited sessions at the University of Toronto, Queen's University, the University of Western Ontario, Canada House in London, Mount Allison University, the Hebrew University of Jerusalem, Tel Aviv University, the University of North Carolina (Chapel Hill), McGill University, City University of New York Graduate Center, and the School of Public Policy and Social Research at UCLA. For their kind hospitality at these various venues, my warmest thanks to Richard Simeon, Thelma McCormack, Keith Banting, George Perlin, Paul Nesbitt-Larking, Andrew Nurse, Arie Schachar, Hanna Herzog, Gary Marks, Antonia Maioni, Joyce Gelb, and especially Barbara J. Nelson. I genuinely appreciate the questions, comments, and suggestions offered by so many insightful listeners in all of these places.

Preparing the manuscript was made easier and more pleasurable by the cooperative efforts of many colleagues. Six contributors to a comparative volume on social policy development taught me a great deal about the field; they are Maureen Baker, Dionne Bensonsmith, Jane Jenson, Gwendolyn Mink, Selma Sevenhuijsen, and Leah Vosko. For their willingness to share important source materials, I am grateful to Gerard Boychuk, Ran Hirschl, Ruth Levitas, Ruth Lister, Don Moggridge, Alain Noël, Julie Simmons, Donley Studlar, and Kent Weaver. As chair of the Department of Political Science at the University of Toronto, Robert Vipond secured a half-sabbatical during which I wrote the first draft.

Virgil Duff, my editor at the University of Toronto Press, has been witty, helpful, and committed throughout the publication process. The referees who assessed the manuscript offered a wealth of constructive commentary in their reports. Early versions of some of this research were published in articles in the *Canadian Journal of Political Science* (March 2000) and *International Political Science Review* (October 2000). The text of the book is up-to-date through the end of 2001, and all monetary amounts are reported in the currency of the respective country.

Finally, I have once again benefited from the sustained support of a wonderful family. After so many preoccupying research ventures, my debt to my daughters and husband is simply incalculable.

All errors of fact and judgment remain my own.

WELFARE HOT BUTTONS

CHAPTER ONE

Introduction

At its best, meaningful social science research answers three fundamental questions. First, what happened? Second, how did these developments transpire? And third, so what? Of what larger significance are the patterns and events under study?

This book presents one of the first comparative assessments of contemporary social policy change in three Western industrialized countries: the United States, Canada, and Great Britain. It adopts as its starting point the following puzzle: If conservative political executives in these nations endorsed a serious rethinking and retrenchment of welfare programs through the 1980s, and faced eventual electoral defeat partly because of the stances they adopted, then how did their 'post-conservative' successors end up pursuing fundamentally similar or even more regressive policy directions? In addressing this question, we explore the conservative policy legacy in each country, the promises offered by 'post-conservative' elites in their campaigns to secure top public office, and the terms and consequences of these new leaders' decisions.

Our approach is premised on the argument that the climate of ideas in which policy debates unfold matters a great deal. The language or rhetoric employed by politicians and other opinion leaders helps to set the tone of public discussion, particularly in a field as riddled with highly charged social themes as welfare reform. What, if anything, is the 'proper' role of women in liberal democratic societies? What constitutes a successful family unit? Can paid employment be considered the *sine qua non* of contemporary citizenship? How, if at all, might governments help poor people? Addressing any one of these questions entails sifting through a veritable freight-load of ideological weights.

Over time, these contentious questions have become a crucial pivot of public debate in the United States, Canada, and Great Britain. Much of the controversy since the 1970s has followed from concerns over changes in women's lives and family structures. These, in turn, prompted worries in some quarters that the family unit, and perhaps even Western civilization as we knew it, were both in danger of imploding. One commonly cited barometer of change and, for some observers, decline was the rise of single mother households, particularly lone mother-led families at the bottom of the socio-economic ladder.[1] Cultural commentators as well as politicians from across the spectrum expressed varied sentiments toward this social category. They lamented and deplored its existence, empathized with and castigated its members, but rarely remained silent on the subject.

Particularly in the United States and Great Britain, conservative political rhetoric in the 1970s and following singled out lone mothers collecting public assistance benefits as a popular hot button target, and invoked this issue as a convenient shorthand for the frustrations and insecurities that 'middle-class taxpayers' or 'people who played by the rules' felt toward social outsiders. Efforts to target what critics on the political right viewed as the individual moral failings of poor single mothers served to undermine not only older materialist ideas about the bases of poverty and the purposes of government spending programs, but also the organized groups that held fast to a pro–welfare state outlook.[2] Rather than assessing how social policies could help ensure the provision of basic human needs including food, shelter, and care, new conservatives turned the discussion upside down to emphasize what they saw as the abject failures of the modern welfare state – above all, its creation of what was portrayed as a dependent underclass of morally deficient individuals. Composed primarily of lone mothers and their children, this underclass was, it was claimed, reproducing itself at an alarming rate, far removed from prevailing norms about the value of paid work. The challenge facing decision-makers who carried such an outlook was how to transform individual members of a dependent and normatively flawed substratum into self-sufficient and morally upright social contributors.

This study argues that progressive interpretations of poverty and inequality were marginalized or pushed on the defensive by important changes in the climate of ideas about social welfare. Women's groups and anti-poverty organizations faced a particularly difficult challenge, we suggest, in their efforts to maintain support for a materialist and structural (as opposed to moralist and individualist) understanding of the welfare state.[3] In the United States and Great Britain, and to a somewhat lesser extent in Canada, conservative political executives employed divisive language designed to isolate progressive social activists; by denigrating collective action on the left of the spectrum, these leaders helped to drive a wedge between feminist, anti-poverty, and other campaigners, on one side, and the boundaries of 'legitimate' political mobilization, on the other.

As some feminist activists were quick to recognize, women as a group and poor women in particular became critically vulnerable once conservative hot button rhetoric zeroed in on a presumed lack of personal responsibility and self-sufficiency among social assistance recipients. In more general terms, progressive interests were pushed on the defensive by the rise of pro-market, individualist norms celebrating the primacy of paid work, economic independence, and minimal government, which in turn undermined collectivist valuations of unpaid caring, human interdependence, and shared or mutual responsibility between state and society.

The conflict among these competing ideational frameworks was starkly revealed in debates over reforming welfare programs. If the primary carriers of the individualist perspective were politicians and policy experts on the right and centre of the spectrum, then their increasingly marginalized adversaries could be found among anti-poverty and feminist groups on the political left. These campaigners, while far from homogeneous even within single political systems, generally rejected the notion that single mothers on social benefits were morally deficient creatures in need of a sturdy work ethic. Unlike welfare state critics who cited increasing rates of paid work by mothers with partners and childless women as evidence that social assistance schemes were outdated and unsustainable, progressives tended to view the labour force circumstances of these various groups as vastly divergent. Their outlook was grounded in older materialist arguments that structural inequalities in access to caregiving, education, job opportunities, and income meant poor mothers living on their own with children experienced lives that were far different from those of their married or childless counterparts, and worlds apart from those of middle-and lower-class men.

Above all, structural analysts asserted both that raising children was very hard work – especially in the absence of adequate financial resources and the emotional support of a second parent – and that the independent role of single mothers in caring for their children stood as a significant social contribution in and of itself. Feminist campaigners thus highlighted the varied tensions contained in moralist rants against 'dependent' women, notably their opposition to the reliance of poor mothers on social benefits versus their celebration of the economic vulnerability of more affluent women vis-à-vis men.[4]

In the contested turf between these sides stood middle-of-the-road academic and policy experts who absorbed elements of both the moralist and structural views, and believed it was possible to broker a workable détente between them. As advisers to governments or bureaucratic appointees in their own right, these pragmatic 'fixers' sat at the crucial tipping point in Anglo-American welfare debates. Their attempts to craft and sell policy compromises, as the moralist freight train rolled further down the tracks, reflected the profound tensions inherent in welfare policy battles during the 'post-conservative' years.

The structural arguments of left-of-centre feminist and anti-poverty interests were grounded in five main criticisms of conservative leaders Ronald Reagan and George Bush in the United States, Brian Mulroney and (briefly) Kim Campbell in Canada, and Margaret Thatcher and John Major in Great Britain. First, progressive campaigners saw conservative social policy as focused primarily on drawing public funds out of what were already modest, residual, and heavily means-tested income support programs. Efforts to introduce rigid work requirements, reduce federal transfers in the US and Canada to lower levels of government, and require child-support payments by non-custodial parents were viewed as circuitous means of cutting already limited welfare payments.

Second, progressives alleged that conservative rhetoric, especially in the US and Britain, converted poverty from an economic condition into a cultural and – above all – a moral malady. So-called 'family values' discourse effectively defined single mothers trying to raise their children as 'irresponsible' deviants who deserved public humiliation and other forms of state-sanctioned punishment.[5] In the view of critics, negative talk about 'dependence' and 'irresponsibility' obscured the interconnectedness and interdependency that remain central to a democratic society, and neglected the fact that women's reliance on state benefits was in many cases preferable to their reliance on traditional forms of family organization.

Third, according to feminist and anti-poverty interests, conservative efforts to push single mothers collecting social benefits into paid work ignored significant problems of sex segregation and pay differentials in labour markets that were themselves restructuring, so that secure, stable, remunerative employment was more and more difficult to find. Welfare-to-work programs were unlikely to improve the economic circumstances of poor households for the simple reason that most single mothers 'cannot get jobs that pay better than welfare.'[6]

Fourth, critics claimed that pushing single mothers of young children into twenty or thirty or more hours of paid work per week denied the value of their unpaid child care and nurturing responsibilities, and ignored the fact that child-care programs were extremely limited in these three countries. Finally, in North America, the decentralist impulse behind conservative welfare reforms threatened to accelerate a 'race to the bottom' in these federal systems, where social assistance was already based on localized 'patchworks' made up of individual sub-national schemes.[7] Further decentralization, according to advocates on the left, risked undermining the already fragile idea of national social standards in federal systems.

To the extent that critics of conservative social policy prescribed core goals for 'post-conservative' leaders, these usually included ending cuts to already threadbare income support programs; resisting the use of moralistic discourse about welfare and single motherhood; paying attention to labour market issues of sex segregation and unequal pay in designing job training or placement programs; creating affordable, accessible, and high-quality child-care programs; and, in federal systems, refusing to cede more authority to sub-national levels of government.

If one overarching theme united these various counter-arguments, it rested in the notion of mutual or reciprocal ties between civil society and the state. Rather than agreeing with conservative claims that such connections worked in one direction only, whereby citizens owed this 'responsible' behaviour or that set of personal norms to an increasingly devalued state, progressives insisted that government was useful, necessary, and obligated to provide crucial enabling supports to both women and men for what T.H. Marshall and others termed social citizenship.[8] These supports included state responsibilities to regulate the labour market, or offer decent child care provisions, or assist people who were unable to work, as basic components of a two-way (rather than unidirectional) social contract.

When they ran for the highest political positions in their respective countries, Bill Clinton, Jean Chrétien, and Tony Blair seemed like balanced, compassionate campaigners who might fulfil at least some of the expectations of progressive campaigners. As politicians who claimed to borrow the best from a variety of ideological traditions, these leaders presented the public face of what became known as the Third Way approach to politics. At one level, they offered a compelling critique of conservative political executives then in office. George Bush, Brian Mulroney, John Major, and their fellow partisans were portrayed as too harsh, too extreme, too immoderate in their handling of the delicate mix of state and market forces that shape people's lives. Rather than dismissing the idea that society exists as an organic unit beyond the realm of individuals and families, as Margaret Thatcher had famously done, new leaders were anxious to talk about how they would bring communities closer together so as to renew a frayed social fabric.[9] In particular, Clinton, Chrétien, and Blair promised to rejuvenate public education and health programs so as to promote future economic growth.

At the level of rhetoric, proponents of the Third Way emphasized moderation and centrism as antidotes to the rough, tough 'market fundamentalism' of Reagan, Thatcher, and company.[10] Yet on another plane, they also suggested it was time to displace the unwieldy, statist, and rights-based preoccupations of left-of-centre interests. For example, Third Way leaders promised to respect traditional values including individual responsibility and local community autonomy. The initial electoral platforms of Bill Clinton, Jean Chrétien, and Tony Blair differed in their specific details, but all were shaped by a common thread that spoke to renewed social cohesion and, in particular, to a judicious rather than heavy-handed use of state levers to temper the rising clout of international market forces. At long last, voters in three major Anglo-American countries were told, they could look forward to a prosperous era featuring global capitalism with a more compassionate human face.

Just how balanced and moderate would Clinton, Chrétien, and Blair turn out to be? More specifically, how likely were these Third Way politicians to resist the rising clout of moralistic approaches to welfare reform? Would they pursue rhetoric and policies in this area that were measurably different from those of their conservative predecessors? Based on a careful assessment of two terms of the Clinton administration, two terms of the Chrétien government, and one term of the Blair government, we conclude that 'post-conservative' leaders elected to office beginning in 1992 failed to fulfil many of the expectations of progressive campaigners. Although their images may have seemed moderate because of an inventive rhetoric about the balanced middle path, social assistance policy realities under Clinton, Chrétien, and Blair were in important respects *more* punitive, more restrictive, and more obsessed with paid work than those of their predecessors. Structural and material approaches to poverty were hardly ascendant under their watch, as policy directions and, in some instances, elite discourse echoed and reinforced the tenets of a moralistic script. In the realm of welfare reform, in short, the Third Way during the period under study offered no warm, fuzzy blanket of traditional liberal or social democratic compassion. Rather, in most cases, it offered up a cold, hard slab of individualist pavement called market readiness.

Despite the differing social policy traditions of their countries, at least three shared directions characterized the welfare reform records of Clinton, Chrétien, and Blair. First, these leaders introduced or, in the US case, enriched a layer of what were effectively *work-tested social benefits*. Earnings supplements, family credits, and other payments directed primarily toward parents who were employed for pay expanded in such a way as to overshadow older means-tested and, in the British case, universal social benefits. Second, these work-tested benefits were largely developed and administered as part of tax or fiscal policy, rather than in the context of traditional social welfare programs. We therefore describe the 'post-conservative' approach to benefits as increasingly *taxified or fiscalized*, in contrast to the usual social program expenditure route that had been followed in older schemes.

Third, the growth of tax-based vehicles to target work-tested benefits to parents who were employed for pay contributed to an *erosion of social citizenship norms*. Rather than building a more robust regime of universal social engagement and rights, as campaigners on the left had hoped, Third Way efforts tended to define in more narrow terms the paid employment of parents as the *sine qua non* of post-industrial belonging. In so doing, these leaders effectively demeaned the unpaid caring work of millions of adults, overwhelmingly mothers, at the same time as they diminished the citizenship status of people without children.

Overall, we argue, Third Way social policies often focused on the selective targeting of work-tested and means-tested benefits to 'deserving' persons. Designed as tax or fiscal measures, these benefits helped to establish an individualized and marketized system of support that was directed toward rewarding 'working families.' As a consequence, the social citizenship of childless people and of adults who did not or could not work for pay was vastly compromised, while the low pay, limited mobility, and profoundly insecure nature of much of the paid work that was available – particularly for lone mothers – were conveniently ignored.

In explaining how and why Third Way leaders pursued directions that were fundamentally congruent with and, in some cases, more punitive than those of conservative elites, we propose two main arguments. First, we suggest that the actions of Clinton, Chrétien, and Blair on social assistance issues were shaped by a deep-seated political pragmatism that made them unwilling to challenge moralist claims. If conservative rhetoric had established via repeated assertion that dependence on state benefits was itself faulty, and that paid work offered the best cure for this moral malady, then Clinton, Chrétien, and Blair were prepared to operate within those parameters. Sustained emphasis on the electoral bottom line reduced the likelihood that they would vigorously reassert structural arguments, and hold off the moralist surge. Although 'post-conservative' leaders spoke more forcefully than did their predecessors about the obstacles to market self-sufficiency facing poor single mothers, only Blair was prepared to put significant sums of cash on the line to address material problems including limited access to child care.

Second, we maintain, Clinton and Chrétien were pushed to the right by resurgent conservative interests. Both North American leaders faced formidable new competitors during their initial campaigns for top office, notably Ross Perot in the United States in 1992 and Preston Manning (leader of the Reform party) in Canada in 1993. Strong fiscal pressures to cut taxes, reduce government spending, eliminate federal deficits, and bring down national debt levels emanated from Perot, Manning, and a chorus of sympathetic business interests. At the same time, US Republicans and Canadian Reformers articulated a fierce social conservative message about the need to reinforce traditional 'family values.' It was hardly surprising that significant cuts to social assistance programs along with harsh rhetorical attacks against single mothers coincided chronologically on the North American continent.

If a comparative accounting of the impact of changes in climates of ideas can be constructed, it would probably rank the United States as the site of the most severe effects, followed next by Canada, and then Great Britain. In the US, welfare debates were closely intertwined with racial stereotypes about fecund African-American women and a criminal underclass of African-American men. Bestial references to welfare recipients as alligators and wolves, employed in 1995 debates by Republican members of the US House of Representatives, marked a nadir in political discourse that had few parallels in the other two countries.[11] The content of 1996 welfare reform legislation signed by President Clinton went considerably beyond national–level provisions in Canada or Britain by imposing fixed time limits, rigid work requirements, and invasive social regulations on lone mothers who sought benefits. Indeed, the 1996 law was interpreted by some observers as marking the end of an already feeble American welfare state.[12]

In Canada, a somewhat more robust welfare state, the very significant withdrawal of federal funds from social programs that was announced in the 1995 budget coincided with a loss of national policy guidelines or principles that had prevailed for three decades. The supports for job training and child care that Liberals promised in their 1993 campaign platform failed to materialize, leaving poor women in Canada to face less generous, more punitive, and often more paternalistic welfare regimes at provincial and local levels. Yet despite the growing emphasis in Canada on paid work or work preparedness as a condition for receipt of benefits, the terms of moral regulation facing Canadian single mothers generally remained less onerous than those facing their US counterparts.

In Britain, arguably the most generous of these three welfare systems, government efforts after 1997 to move more lone mothers off benefits and into paid employment advanced well beyond those pursued in previous years. Yet decisions by the Blair cabinet to invest in income supplements, child-care credits, and other supports that would permit lone mothers to work for pay created more generous provisions than were available at the national level in North America. Moreover, the New Labour leadership demonstrated greater willingness to invest in educational upgrading than did US Democratic or Canadian Liberal elites, suggesting that the British Third Way on social assistance reform was distinctive on several levels.

Our response to the question of 'what happened' begins by tracing the legacy of conservative leaders who assumed office in 1979 and following. At the level of discourse, we pay particular attention to American and British language that vilified single mothers and social benefits, and argue that this rhetoric spilled over in significant ways to Canada as well. Single mothers on social assistance were increasingly identified as lazy, deceitful and, above all, personally irresponsible in their use of public funds to cultivate a life of leisure without paid work. In the hot button rhetoric of welfare state critics, poor women's 'dependence' was presented as a perverse by-product of misguided government programs. Women-headed households were also viewed as a potentially rich laboratory in which to test how closer state, confessional, or private sector supervision could rehabilitate the morally deficient. Not surprisingly, lone mothers along with the government programs supporting them and their children became bullseye targets on a deeply perforated social dartboard.

In terms of formal policies, chapter 2 highlights US Republican initiatives including the 1988 Family Support Act, Canadian Conservative decisions including the 1990 cap or lid on Canada Assistance Plan transfers to better-off provinces, and British Tory legislation including the 1991 Child Support Act. Taken as a group, conservative initiatives were designed to reduce social spending by governments, particularly in the area of welfare assistance, at the same time as they had the effect of pressing lone mothers to rely more on income from other sources, including paid employment and child maintenance payments from ex-partners.

Chapter 3 examines the campaign rhetoric and policy proposals of Third Way leaders in the United States, Canada, and Britain. Bill Clinton's talk of 'ending welfare as we know it' and 'providing a hand up, not a hand out' suggested metaphors about social assistance as a trampoline to labour market success, in place of the cushy hammock it had allegedly become. Following up on his view that 'welfare should be a second chance, not a way of life,' candidate Clinton argued for expanding tax-based incentives that would encourage adults to work rather than go on social assistance. The Red Book platform of the Chrétien Liberals spoke of 'investing in people' so that single mothers on welfare could 'find good child care for their children,' enter the paid labour force, and 'break the chain of dependence.'[13] Tony Blair's New Labour approach emphasized a similar theme of individual duty and fiscal prudence. Writing in 1996, Blair proposed to 'build second-generation welfare ... giving people a hand-up and not just a hand-out ... Welfare should be a springboard to success and not just a safety net to cushion failure.'[14]

How did these ideas play out in practice? Chapter 4 probes Third Way records in each country, and explains them with reference to a pragmatic political calculus by 'post-conservative' leaders. In the United States, the 1996 Personal Responsibility and Work Opportunity

Reconciliation Act signed by President Clinton reduced federal welfare spending by ending any legally enforceable right of individuals to collect social assistance, defining time-based benefit limits, and further offloading program responsibility via block grants to state governments. The 1996 Canada Health and Social Transfer replaced an older federal/provincial cost-sharing regime (under the Canada Assistance Plan) with a less regulated system of lump-sum transfers to the provinces, reduced funding for those transfers, and combined social assistance with health and education monies. Despite the Red Book promise on child care, no national program was set in place in this field. In Britain, the 1997 New Deal for unemployed youth was extended a year later to include a voluntary national scheme for single parents on income support. Unlike developments at the federal level in the US and Canada, the New Deal injected substantial sums of new national-level monies into job training, counselling, and child care to assist lone mothers on benefits, but offered fewer resources than were targeted toward other categories of people in Britain without paid work.

Chapter 5 probes the consequences of welfare reform developments in all three countries. At a quantitative level, it reviews the decline through the Clinton years of social assistance caseloads in the United States, and the increase in federal expenditures on income supports via the Earned Income Tax Credit. In Canada, caseloads also declined over time while federal spending on tax-based supplements to parents who were employed for pay rose. A parallel situation emerged in Britain after 1997, as the take-up of Income Support benefits dropped and spending shifted toward in-work earnings and child-care supplements. At a more qualitative level, chapter 5 uses data from interviews with more than 120 American, Canadian, and British activists and experts to explore the impact of these shifts on feminist and anti-poverty campaigning groups. It examines the expectations of progressives on the eve of Third Way victories, and evaluates their responses to the Clinton, Chrétien, and Blair records. Particularly in the United States and Canada, Third Way rhetoric and action seemed to isolate and marginalize campaigning interests, a pattern that spilled over in Britain to groups that defended social benefits for people not in paid work.

So what? Of what larger significance were conservative and Third Way records in this field? Chapter 6 argues that policy trends after 1980 helped to overturn what had been a fragile social contract in major Anglo-American systems. In particular, we maintain, Third Way leaders tipped an already precarious and uneasy weighting in these countries of social rights and individual obligations toward a seemingly inexorable stress on duties owed. Over time, the combined effects of narrowed social assistance eligibility, a glorification of paid work as the single unambiguous answer to welfare 'dependency,' and the growth of a highly administrative or regulatory approach to social policy suggested a new duty state was emerging to replace the residual liberal welfare state. How would this duty state operate? Who would pay the ever-increasing wage subsidy costs necessary to keep low-income workers in the paid labour market? Chapter 6 concludes by assessing possible responses to the growth of the duty state, including feminist proposals in the United States to pay a caregiving allowance to single mothers.

In evaluating American, Canadian, and British social policy developments, this account takes issue with several prevailing interpretations. Its main conceptual target is scholarship that presumes an entirely positivist, or normatively and ideationally detached, stance can be adopted toward questions of women, work, and welfare reform. This stream of analysis tends to ignore many crucial questions, including issues of public discourse and the treatment of women within it. In the discipline of political science, researchers typically ramp up an elaborate institutional explanation of why elites made the decisions they made, without examining in detail the values and rhetoric about gender, class, and race that helped to frame their actions.[15] At its core, the present study insists that welfare policy changes cannot be understood without reference to ideational climates about women and women's roles, including the language employed by opinion leaders within those contexts.

In empirical terms, this account calls into question Paul Pierson's influential assertion that Anglo-American welfare states were remarkably resilient in the face of a neo-conservative onslaught by Ronald Reagan, Margaret Thatcher, and their supporters.[16] We posit instead that when individual regimes are examined with reference to the discursive and programmatic treatment of poor single mothers, many of them from minority racial and ethnic backgrounds, the erosion over time of already minimal social assistance provisions stands out quite starkly. Moreover, evidence that hardy, well-entrenched progressive interests ensured a pattern of welfare state resilience is difficult to find. In our view, Anglo-American proponents of a structural or material approach to social assistance policy were hardly in a buoyant position after 1980.[17]

This study also interrogates the portrayal of Anglo-American welfare states as a homogeneous grouping. In *Globalization and the Welfare State*, for example, Ramesh Mishra argues that the decline of social policy standards in predominantly English-speaking countries was far steeper than in other post-industrial cases including Japan and continental Europe.[18] Although Mishra's basic conclusion remains convincing, it obscures important differences among Anglo-American systems in the nature and degree of downward movement. For this reason, the present study directs primary attention to social policy variation among Anglo-American countries, and urges further comparative research on this cluster of cases.

With reference to the women and politics literature, this account disconfirms expectations that more gender-sensitive public policy would necessarily follow from the presence of an active, mobilized female electorate, and from growing numbers of female decision-makers.[19] Neither the important role played by women voters in ensuring the election of the Clinton administration in the US, the Chrétien government in Canada, and the Blair government in Great Britain, nor the appointment of a handful of prominent women to senior policy positions in all three countries, seemed to ensure that these regimes would be consistently responsive to women's employment and caregiving realities. A number of female political elites, including avowed feminists, appeared complicit in the making of what were on the surface 'gender-neutral' policies, which turned out on closer inspection to be highly gendered or, at best, gender-denying. A key pivot of women and politics research, therefore, needs to be re-examined with reference to issues of class and minority status as these overlay and complicate the gender variable.

Above all, this study casts doubt on a core premise of leading Third Way advocates, including British sociologist Anthony Giddens.[20] Instead of breaking with their conservative predecessors, we argue, some of the rhetoric and many of the actions of Clinton, Chrétien, and Blair on social benefit questions were fully consistent with their Republican and Tory precedents. Hot button talk about welfare dependency became more muted, but hardly disappeared. Residual, means-tested programs tended to become more threadbare over time, and efforts to encourage single mothers to rely on some combination of new partners, ex-partners, or paid work (rather than state benefits) only accelerated. In North America, already devolved social assistance schemes became even more decentralized over time.

Most significantly, Third Way leaders often employed a moralistic rhetoric that defined personal responsibility as individual self-sufficiency in a free market economy. Like their predecessors, Clinton, Chrétien, and Blair tended to ignore the profoundly unequal outcomes produced by that economy. As British social scientist Ruth Lister observed, Third Way elites attempted the impossible – namely, 'to divorce the rights and responsibilities which are supposed to unite citizens from the inequalities of power and resources that divide them.'[21] This strategy glossed over fundamental social divisions involving gender, class, and race using a seemingly balanced discourse about cohesion and inclusion, as part of an effort to obscure any basis for exclusion other than failure to pursue paid work. The tendency of Third Way leaders to treat challenges facing low-income citizens as primarily individual rather than structural in origin served to reinforce the central message of a moralist approach. Poverty, to the extent that it was discussed, became associated with problems facing either 'blameless' children or value-deficient adults.[22] In short, Third Way welfare reform directions, when closely compared with their Republican and Conservative precedents, often reflected more similarities than differences.

No study of contemporary welfare reform debates can make sense unless it is placed in a longer-term context. In all three countries considered in this book, social assistance for lone mothers and their children was consistently meagre, means-tested, and stigmatizing even before conservatives came to power in 1979 and following. In Gøsta Esping-Andersen's terms, Anglo-American welfare states were weak, market-supporting, liberal regimes that contrasted with the more generous, market-usurping, universalistic systems of continental Europe.[23] The historic goal of cash assistance programs for lone mothers in the United States, Canada, and Great Britain was to offer basic income from public funds to substitute – at a very rudimentary level – for the earnings of an absent (and usually deceased) male breadwinner.

Designed with this purpose in mind, social benefits set in place by the mid-twentieth century enabled single mothers to stay at home to care for their dependent children, provided that they met stringent bureaucratic requirements. Social assistance programs geared toward single parents in Anglo-American systems thus developed overwhelmingly (often more than 90%) female client bases. Anglo-American welfare schemes were also characterized by low benefit levels, close moral regulation of the lives of mothers to ensure there was indeed no male breadwinner, and tight limits on eligibility to ensure that few additional resources existed for the family. These strictures and stigmas offered the baseline against which poor women organized welfare rights campaigns during the 1960s and following to challenge what they viewed as coercive, controlling, and stingy state benefits programs. Anglo-American welfare schemes, in short, imposed not only serious constraints on the lives of lone mothers, but also presented opportunities from time to time for political organizing and resistance.[24]

In the United States, arguably the most individualistic of the three political cultures under study, the program known as Aid to Dependent Children (later called Aid to Families with Dependent Children, or AFDC) was established in 1935 under the terms of the Social Security Act. Although it began as a shared-cost program in which the federal government paid one-third of expenses, state governments controlled the setting of eligibility rules and benefit levels within broad national parameters.[25] Until 1996, cash assistance payable under AFDC came with a series of linked benefits, including Medicaid health insurance and food stamp vouchers. Court decisions beginning in the 1960s limited the ability of states to impose tight moral strictures (including spouse-in-the-house rules) and required due process appeals procedures, but did little to raise the actual value of cash benefits.[26]Indeed, AFDC payments were not adjusted for inflation after 1972, meaning that by the time the program ended in 1996, 'combined AFDC and food stamp benefits were inadequate to take a family to even 80 percent of the poverty line' in most US states.[27]

The 1966 Canada Assistance Plan (CAP) established a shared-cost framework under which the federal government paid half of all qualifying expenditures for social programs and social services in the provinces and territories. CAP evolved during the same period as did universal health insurance schemes in Canada, which also used federal government funds to deliver provincial programs. Universal family allowances paid to mothers beginning in 1945 varied by province; family allowances were based on a per-child calculation that reached about $35 monthly for each child at the time that they were phased out in 1992.[28] As in the United States, sub-national governments enjoyed wide latitude in setting welfare eligibility rules and benefit levels as long as they remained inside the CAP national guidelines. Social rights litigation in Canada reached many of the same limits as it did in the US, including after the introduction of a Charter of Rights and Freedoms in 1982.[29] Welfare programs across Canada varied widely, but were generally viewed as somewhat more generous and less restrictive than their counterparts in the United States.[30]

In Great Britain, historically the most collectivist of the three cases considered here, the national cash assistance program created in 1966 as Supplementary Benefit, renamed Income Support in 1986, was offered in coordination with other means-tested programs including Housing Benefit (to help with rent payments) and Council Tax Benefit (to help with property taxes).[31] Britain introduced a universal family allowance called Child Benefit after the Second World War but, unlike Canada, did not dismantle this program as a national cash payment to mothers. Universal health care provisions in Britain were introduced in the 1940s, again by the central government. Because of unitary state arrangements, British social programs were extremely uniform compared with those in the US or Canada, even though some schemes including Housing Benefit were locally administered. Taken as a group, welfare provisions in the UK tended to be more generous and less restrictive than those in Canada and, in turn, the United States.

In an area that remains as normatively loaded as welfare policy, it is essential for readers to know where authors stand. At an early point in the research process, this writer was somewhat hopeful about the prospects for progressive, gender-sensitive social reform under Third Way leadership. Over time, however, developments in North America dimmed that optimism, even as it appeared that Bill Clinton's social policy rhetoric, for example, was somewhat more muted than that of his Republican predecessors. A more humane approach to poor women and their children may at some point eclipse the punitive strategies that dominated the period under study, as the limits of welfare reforms that ignore structural realities in the labour market, gloss over the limited availability of affordable, high-quality child care, and press moralistic hot buttons to demonize and demean lone mothers become more and more evident.

CHAPTER TWO

Conservative Legacies

For a variety of reasons, Anglo-American welfare regimes supporting lone mothers and their children were widely viewed as far from ideal, even during their ostensible 'golden age.' Progressives condemned what they saw as the social control dimension of income assistance programs, notably the invasive regulation of poor families by armies of social workers and other public employees. Many women who received welfare benefits resented the limited support offered under schemes that had originated in widows' pensions of the early twentieth century. Taken together, these criticisms of social control, meagre benefits, and the stigmatization of poor mother households shaped the agenda of modern welfare rights groups, which demanded an overhaul of existing assistance programs. In the United States, for example, the National Welfare Rights Organization (established in 1966) campaigned to end overnight man-in-the-house raids and to create a guaranteed annual income.[1]

On the other side of the debate stood conservative critics upset with what they saw as costly and socially misguided programs. This chapter evaluates their rhetorical as well as policy legacies in the United States, Canada, and Great Britain. Our purpose in probing the social assistance discourse and decisions of conservative political executives is to lay the groundwork for a comparison with subsequent Third Way patterns. Above all, we want to identify the parameters of a conservative record in each country in order to assess whether the language and actions of Bill Clinton, Jean Chrétien, and Tony Blair represented a fundamental continuity or break with these precedents.

The central thesis of this chapter is two-fold. On one level, we maintain, Republican and Conservative elites, particularly in the US and

UK, explicitly rejected progressive arguments dating from the 1960s that viewed benefits as inadequately low and the moral regulation of welfare mothers as inappropriate and overzealous. On a second plane, we suggest, conservative elites advanced a powerful counter-argument that advocated not only reduced social spending – whether because such expenditures were unaffordable from a fiscal perspective or because they were so generous as to be a disincentive for paid work – but also a renewed moral regulation of single mother households, including via compulsory welfare-to-work programs. Furthermore, American and British conservatives favoured vigorous enforcement of child support payments as a route toward lowering government welfare costs. Overall, Republican and Tory leaders set in motion a process of overturning the prevailing consensus in all three countries about the purposes of social assistance policy. By implanting a more punitive view of welfare programs and their beneficiaries in the mainstream of public debate, these elites made varied strands of anti-poor rhetoric legitimate, and were able to introduce diverse strategies at a policy level to advance their own agendas.

Our discussion opens with the US case, where presidential candidate Ronald Reagan's 1976 campaign speech about a supposed Chicago 'welfare queen' set the tone for much of the Anglo-American rhetoric that was to follow. Negative and harshly judgmental in tenor, Reagan's comments during his initial unsuccessful run for the presidency targeted two specific hot buttons concerning lone mothers and welfare. First, Reagan alleged in very direct terms that one particular woman on social assistance and, by implication, many others like her were fraudulent abusers of an overly generous public welfare system. Second, the equally powerful subtext of Reagan's discourse pointed to the deviant or outsider status of mothers on welfare; in the US context, 'they' – unlike 'us' – were members of racial minorities, living outside stable nuclear family households in decrepit inner cities, not engaged in acceptable forms of labour market participation. Reliance on government welfare checks, according to the Reagan world view, produced a perverse and often criminal form of 'social dependency.'

After 1980, President Reagan proceeded to pursue congruent directions at a policy level. He supported legislation designed to improve the enforcement of court-ordered child support payments by pressing absent fathers to pay up. The 1988 Family Support Act began the transformation of the AFDC program into a mandatory work-for-welfare scheme. As an initial step toward more draconian legislation signed by

President Clinton in 1996, the 1988 act was decentralist, work-oriented, and residualist in that it transferred power from the federal to state level, encouraged movement from social assistance to paid work, and placed limits or caps on federal welfare spending, all under the guise of welfare reform.

As leader of the Progressive Conservatives in Canada, Brian Mulroney was less ideological and more pragmatic than his US and UK counterparts. During his nine years as prime minister, Mulroney said little publicly about single mothers or welfare reform. His general preferences for an ambitious, highly productive, and competitive society in Canada, however, presented indirect evidence of Conservative views on social assistance schemes then operating under provincial jurisdiction with open-ended federal subsidies. Mulroney suggested that however important or, in his words, 'sacred' social programs might be, there came a point at which they were simply not affordable. Moreover, by working to build closer and more cordial relations with Canada's neighbour to the south through the Reagan/Bush years, and by pursuing a decentralist domestic agenda that promised greater powers for sub-national governments, Mulroney opened the door for the adoption of US-style welfare rhetoric by Canada's provincial leaders. By the fall of 1993, the social democratic premier of British Columbia, Mike Harcourt, was referring to fraudulent welfare recipients as 'varmints,' a colloquial term for vermin.[2]

One of the most lasting legacies of federal social policy during the Mulroney years was the 1990 'cap on CAP,' which imposed a ceiling on increases in federal transfers to Canada's three wealthiest provinces. By introducing a 5 per cent limit on subsidies in what had been an open-ended system, the lid on Canada Assistance Plan (CAP) transfers not only invited better-off provinces to reduce social spending, but also constrained the ability of the federal government to impose national welfare standards. In foreshadowing a subsequent decision to eliminate CAP by the Chrétien government, Mulroney's cap on CAP cut social expenditures, offered greater latitude to the provinces, and moved federal elites away from providing open-ended, intergovernmental cash transfers for which they could not take political credit. In effect, the cap on CAP was integral to a larger pattern by which Canadian social welfare policy became more decentralized, individualized, and driven by the cost/benefit calculus of decision-makers at all levels.

British Conservative rhetoric on the subject of women and welfare was in many respects parallel with that of US Republicans. Margaret

Thatcher frequently argued for a restoration of what she described as the Victorian virtues of stable home and family; her perspective maintained that welfare spending damaged traditional moral standards and threatened 'our whole way of life.'[3] Thatcher's key Tory mentor, Keith Joseph, was even more emphatic in his denunciation of fecund single mothers on income support who were causing 'our human stock' to degenerate.[4]

The 1991 Child Support Act represented the landmark social welfare legislation of the Thatcher/Major period. The act required absent fathers to pay child support, and deducted the full amount of maintenance payments they provided from welfare benefits paid to mothers. The legislation thus reflected important elements of a 'family values' or social conservative agenda, at the same time as it responded to fiscal demands for reduced government spending on welfare programs.

After probing the main lines of welfare reform rhetoric and policy in all three countries, this chapter concludes with a look at cross-national comparisons. To what extent was an observable conservative consensus on social assistance emerging through the 1980s? How did shifts toward greater decentralization of welfare policy in the two federal systems, the United States and Canada, play out at state and provincial levels? What sources of pressure seemed most likely to shape future developments in all three countries?

Hot Button Talk in the United States

With its populist approach to the subject of welfare's excesses, Ronald Reagan's finely honed rhetoric became a hallmark of American conservative opposition to social assistance programs and those who benefited from them. Reagan stressed the need for government to help only what he called 'the *truly* needy,' and insisted that others who could work go out to work.[5] As governor of California, Reagan instituted a series of reforms designed to stop what he later described as 'an endless cycle of dependency that robs men and women of their dignity. I wanted to see if we couldn't rescue some of those people from what FDR had called the "narcotic" of welfare.'[6]

Reagan framed his criticisms around moralistic as well as fiscal claims, weaving the two together in seemingly effortless, commonsense prose. The economic arguments were easy enough to make: in California, welfare caseloads had risen over time and, even according to Democrats, could not be sustained without a significant tax increase.

As a two-term Republican governor, Reagan said he was a tax fighter who refused 'to keep pouring more money into a bucket that was full of holes.'[7] Instead, he campaigned successfully for a clamp-down on waste and fraud through tightened eligibility rules as well as extensive computer checks of new welfare applicants and existing recipients.

It was at the level of moralistic rhetoric that Reagan excelled as a hot button politician. He claimed throughout his career that welfare was creating a corrosive dependency on public hand-outs. In his view, the downward spiral that destroyed families began with easy payments to teenage mothers, continued as welfare extended from generation to generation, and was only reversible if, for all those people conservatives defined as able-bodied applicants, work became a condition for receiving benefits.

This perspective was conveyed to the world through the use of powerful anecdotes, most notably one about a black woman in Chicago named Linda Taylor. In his 1976 presidential campaign speeches, Reagan drew on press accounts of Taylor's then-imminent welfare fraud trial by summarizing the details of her deceitful history: 'She has eighty names, thirty addresses, twelve Social Security cards and is collecting veterans' benefits on four nonexisting deceased husbands ... And she's collecting Social Security on her cards. She's got Medicaid, [is] getting food stamps, and she is collecting welfare under each of her names. Her tax-free income alone is over $150,000.'[8] Although subsequent research revealed that Taylor was not a teenager (she was 47 years old) and that she had been charged with defrauding the state of Illinois of $8000 (rather than $150,000) under four assumed names (rather than 80), the anecdote about what Reagan called the Welfare Queen reverberated widely. According to journalist David Zucchino, 'few voters paid attention to the facts. The image of the big-spending, lavish-living, Cadillac-driving welfare queen was by then thoroughly embedded in American folklore.'[9]

Just as Reagan's depiction of the wasteful excesses of welfare spending spread well beyond local campaign rallies, so too did his portrayal of the inherently deviant nature of single mothers. Reagan served as an effective popularizer of the New Right ideas of Charles Murray, who recommended eliminating the entire federal welfare and income support system in order to force recipients into paid work or marriage; George Gilder, who argued that welfare destroyed family life by removing the independent, wage-earning role of the man; and Lawrence Mead, who advocated strong and well-enforced work requirements to alter the values and behaviour of welfare recipients.[10] Women-headed welfare households were thus distanced from the ranks of the deserving or 'truly needy' once American conservatives represented them as a dangerous and growing underclass that owed its existence to misguided government decisions.

Reagan's depiction of Linda Taylor as a Chicago welfare queen captured the undeserving underclass notion in a nutshell. As explained by American social theorist Mimi Abramovitz,

> the *underclass* is defined as being composed of socially isolated people living in disorganized neighborhoods that are characterized by high rates of crime, hustling, drug dealing, school dropouts, and joblessness, as well as by high rates of female-headed households, teenage pregnancy, out-of-wedlock births, and the intergenerational receipt of welfare. The strong emphasis on behaviors that is linked to women's lives conveys the message that crime, drug use, school dropouts, teenage pregnancies are transmitted from one generation to another by women who head families without men at the helm.[11]

In short, even if the specific details of his portrayal may have been erroneous, the broad point of Reagan's rhetoric about Linda Taylor loomed large. His message invoked concerns over socially deviant outsiders and the threat posed by welfare mothers to prevailing middle-class norms about work, state, and family. Like many of his 'moral majority' supporters, Ronald Reagan insisted that government needed to shore up rather than undermine both traditional family organization and the work ethic.

The solution to welfare dependency as he saw it was to make benefits programs as unattractive as possible, including by forcing 'able-bodied recipients' into paid work. In 1971, Governor Reagan negotiated an arrangement with President Nixon that permitted the state of California to begin pilot workfare programs; these required welfare recipients to accept jobs as a condition for receiving public assistance. Reagan insisted throughout his campaigns for the presidency that the workfare experiments tried in California – an obvious welfare 'magnet' because of its attractive climate – could produce similar results elsewhere.[12] In his words, 'I attempted to tell Americans what we had accomplished in California to reduce waste and welfare abuse, and I proposed returning to states and communities direct control over a variety of federal programs such as welfare, aid-to-education, and housing, along with the taxing power to pay for them.'[13] In short, the Reagan approach highlighted tight controls on social spending, a renewed emphasis on work, and a willingness to let state and local governments design their own routes to welfare reform. Each of these priorities was driven home at a rhetorical level by unabashed moralizing about the need to defend traditional family values. If, in Reagan's own words, welfare had become 'a tax-financed incentive for immorality that was destroying the family,' then it was the job of the new president to reverse this dangerous tide.[14]

Reagan-Era Policies

Given strong support from some state-level leaders including Arkansas governor Bill Clinton, the welfare reform record of the Reagan White House was remarkably productive, if not necessarily effective in meeting all of its goals.[15] The president's team began by using the California model of altered eligibility rules to lower the uptake of benefits nationwide. Under the terms of the 1981 Omnibus Budget Reconciliation Act (OBRA), tighter rules denied welfare payments to more than 400,000 households, or more than 10 per cent of the families then on AFDC. Nearly 300,000 other recipients saw their benefits fall considerably.[16]

Part of this shift followed from penalizing low-income wage earners, either by removing them from welfare rolls altogether or by cutting their benefits, dollar for dollar, in line with their earned income. This provision flew in the face of competing arguments for looser earnings disregards, which claimed welfare recipients should face minimal benefits penalties if they took on paid work, and should feel encouraged to seek more paid employment.[17] The 1981 OBRA also made it harder for people to qualify for federal unemployment insurance benefits and failed to maintain the value of the Earned Income Tax Credit, introduced in 1975 as a way to assist low-income earners.[18] Reagan's insistence on offering economic relief to affluent households, combined with his refusal to adjust arrangements at the other end of the spectrum, led to a 'more than doubling of the tax burden for low-income households in the four years between 1980 and 1984.'[19]

President Reagan's preferred alternative to work incentives was work requirements. Although the 1981 OBRA offered states more opportunities to experiment with workfare, the 1988 Family Support Act (FSA) vastly broadened the chances that states would operate mandatory welfare-to-work schemes. In its effort to reduce social spending, enhance what conservatives defined as personal independence, and increase what they called parental responsibility, the FSA set out a Job Opportunities and Basic Skills Training (JOBS) program. As of October 1990, all US states would be required to have 7 per cent of AFDC recipients in JOBS programs; this figure was scheduled to increase to 20 per cent by 1995.

The Family Support Act identified the key target groups for training and education under JOBS as teenage mothers, adults on AFDC for six years or more, and mothers who were within two years of losing AFDC eligibility based on the age of their youngest child (this age varied from state to state). In other words, the policy was *not* aimed at short-term welfare recipients or others who were likely to move on their own toward paid work. As Catherine Chilman points out in her evaluation of the FSA, this legislation faced enormous hurdles at the implementation stage, 'central among them ... the targeting of probably the most difficult groups, particularly the long-term poor.'[20]

The JOBS approach followed logically from a conservative view of the character flaws of what were seen as personally irresponsible individuals. The terms of the FSA required that each eligible mother be assessed, monitored, and reported on with reference to her employability. What vocational or technical training did she need? (The FSA would not pay for studies toward a university-level degree.) In order to take on paid work, what were her child-care and transportation requirements? Using a 'capped' or fixed federal subsidy, states had to offer some combination of job search, job training, and community work programs as well as child-care supplements. Intensive management of each welfare-to-work candidate became an integral part of the JOBS strategy, and imposed considerable burdens on state governments. Other costly terms of the 1988 legislation included provisions requiring all states to extend AFDC to two-parent families, and to offer Medicaid coverage as well as child-care supplements to ex-AFDC recipients during their first full year of paid work.

Reinforcing the provisions of the 1984 Child Support Enforcement Act, the FSA compelled absent parents, the vast majority of them fathers, to pay child support, and increased the role of employers and courts in enforcing support payments.[21] The roughly one billion dollars collected for AFDC families under these provisions did not mean, however, that additional public funds were invested in job placement, employment training, or education activities.[22] Many states lacked the matching funds necessary to claim federal monies, which were themselves inadequate according to numerous observers, and had a difficult time meeting the varied costs of child-care subsidies, two-parent AFDC benefits, community service programs, and so on.[23] Not surprisingly, the FSA fell short of meeting President Reagan's stated goal, namely, 'real welfare reform ... that will lead to lasting emancipation from welfare dependency.'[24]

These shortcomings of the FSA, however, did not deter US welfare reformers. As Reagan's Republican successor, George Bush appointed a committed social conservative named Dan Quayle to the position of vice-president. Together, Bush and Quayle hammered away at what they saw as an irresponsible culture of single motherhood perpetuated by both government welfare programs and the laissez-faire social values of the American entertainment industry.[25] During his term in the White House, Bush promised to make it 'easier and quicker' for states to experiment with workfare and other reforms by using federal waivers to circumvent existing rules.[26]

State leaders were anxious to take advantage of Bush's offer. Wisconsin governor Tommy Thompson, for example, obtained a federal waiver in 1992 to experiment with the Parental and Family Responsibility Initiative, popularly known as Bridefare. Under the terms of this pilot program, benefit applicants living with their child's father were subject to looser welfare eligibility rules and earnings exemptions than if they lived on their own. This initiative, intended to encourage the formation of two-parent households, built on earlier waiver-based efforts during the Reagan years to ensure that all Wisconsin parents with children aged twelve weeks or older participated in mandatory workfare schemes.[27] Also during George Bush's term, states including Wisconsin and New Jersey requested waivers to experiment with child exclusion or family cap rules that limited welfare benefits for children conceived while their mothers collected AFDC payments.[28]

The Reagan/Bush legacy on welfare reform was vast and substantial, since it extended from heated rhetoric about dependency and welfare queens to the arcane details of subsidized job training schemes. At the point that Republicans lost control of the White House in 1992, three elements of their imprint were clear. First, government spending on welfare benefits in the United States was rising rather than falling. During George Bush's term as president, for example, state AFDC expenditures rose nearly $2.7 billion, while state Medicaid spending more than doubled.[29] Second, a broad discursive push by conservatives against welfare programs and single mothers showed no sign of disappearing. Third, the mandatory workfare emphasis of leading Republicans, with its refusal to invest in extensive training or child-care programs that could assist parents on welfare, was gradually becoming the dominant policy position.

Given the fiscal mess that resulted from economic recessions, upper-income tax cuts, and high-spending defence budgets during the Reagan/Bush years, it was questionable whether future presidents could find the funds necessary to finance a different approach to welfare reform – one that might have been grounded in material rather than moralist arguments. As well, it was difficult to see how new leaders could challenge the increasingly punitive climate of opinion concerning welfare that conservatives had worked to foster in the United States.

Brian Mulroney and the 'Sacred Trust'

In contrast to Ronald Reagan's feisty talk about welfare queens and benefits dependency, Brian Mulroney articulated a far more nuanced version of hot button rhetoric. Mulroney, in fact, was well known for his rhetorical support of social spending; during approximately ten years as a federal party leader and prime minister, he presented himself as a passionate champion of social programs who only grudgingly, reluctantly trimmed government expenditures. Top Canadian Conservatives thus cultivated a centrist, reasonable image during this period that said, 'We'd like to help everybody, but we just can't afford the high costs.'

The 'sacred trust,' one of the most vivid phrases used by Mulroney during the 1984 federal election campaign, set the tone for Tory discourse. When asked how the Conservative promise to eliminate the federal deficit by 1990 would affect domestic spending, Mulroney responded with a firm assurance that deficit-cutting would not endanger universal social programs. The latter, in his words, constituted a 'sacred trust, not to be tampered with' by deficit fighters in Ottawa.[30] He continued in this same vein by insisting that 'no social program at all, affecting anyone in need, shall be touched by a Progressive Conservative government.'[31]

Mulroney's attempts to allay Canadian voters about his intentions in power were reflected in comments made during a televised campaign debate with Liberal leader John Turner. Mulroney zeroed in on the issue of federal patronage jobs in his 1984 exchange with Turner, alleging that the Liberal leader's decision to appoint a raft of Trudeau-era partisans to various positions was not only offensive, but also expensive. In building up to his verbal knock-out punch against Turner's claim that he 'had no option' but to fill the jobs, Mulroney stated, 'The cost of that [patronage], $84.4 million, is enough to give – the cost of that to the ordinary Canadian taxpayer – we could pay every senior citizen in this country on the [Old Age] supplement an extra $70 at Christmas rather than pay for those Liberal appointments.'[32] In subsequent campaign appearances, Mulroney insisted the federal Liberals were wasteful and lacking in compassion except vis-à-vis each other. After all, John Turner's initial action as prime minister 'was not to help the unemployed or the elderly but to reward fellow Liberals.'[33]

Mulroney likely fashioned his compassionate rhetoric to counteract Canadian fears that American Republican politics would spill over the 49th parallel. Before winning his first majority government, Mulroney met President Reagan and set in place the foundation for what became a close personal as well as working relationship between the two men. Mulroney's admiration for the rhetorical flair and pro-business optimism of his American mentor was tempered, however, by a realistic grasp of just how far a Canadian Conservative could push his ties with a US Republican. For Mulroney, the dividing line between acceptable and out-of-bounds seemed to turn on the difference between prudent fiscal and vindictive social or moral discourse.

Brian Mulroney had practised labour law in Quebec and served as president of a Cleveland-based mining subsidiary, the Iron Ore Company of Canada, before becoming party leader. He was comfortable with the pro-market, anti–big government rhetoric of American conservatives, and used this language effectively in a series of speeches and rallies during the early 1980s. According to Mulroney, deregulation, privatization, and individual initiative were beneficial – indeed crucial – to economic growth; each had been ignored due to the bloated bureaucratic and confrontational ways of the Trudeau Liberals.[34] In the words of the new Conservative leader, 'the tragic process of swedenizing Canada must come to a halt.'[35]

Yet how much de-'swedenizing' of Canada could any prime minister carry out, given the extent to which provinces controlled employment, welfare, health, and education policy? As well, Brian Mulroney was anxious to avoid the intergovernmental conflicts of the Trudeau years. In his view, these spats had tied the country in knots, and isolated politicians in Quebec in particular from federal elites and from their counterparts in other provinces. It was 'time for reconciliation,' as Mulroney told his campaign audiences, time for federal leaders to start working cooperatively with the provinces.[36]

Mulroney's pro-business rhetoric plus his views on the need for flexible federalism meant he was prepared to adopt a very different policy tack than had his predecessors. First, Canadian Conservatives were ready to give market forces if not the upper hand, then at the very least far more clout than they had enjoyed under the Liberals. Second, the Tories were dead set against antagonizing the provinces, especially the more decentralist ones such as Quebec and Alberta. These priorities could be read as an open-door invitation to sub-national leaders in Canada to try various social experiments, including workfare programs. In his own policy talk, Brian Mulroney remained careful not to play around with welfare hot buttons that could spook moderate voters. He imposed no such constraints, however, on other politicians who wanted to press those buttons. Instead, by emphasizing the need to unleash market forces, eliminate the federal deficit, de-'swedenize' Canada, and respect the provinces, Mulroney offered a great deal of leeway for others to fill in the blanks.

Mulroney-Era Policies

During their nine years in government, leading federal Conservatives continued to speak in fairly cautious terms about social policy reform, at the same time as their budgetary decisions moved the Canadian welfare state in a far more selective, decentralized, and residual direction. This shift hardly occurred in a smooth or coherent manner, nor was it visible or transparent for all to see. Instead, the process was more stealth-like, involving a series of complex lurches in the direction of fiscal restraint, occasional retreats from that path, and then more lurches forward.[37] Fundamental changes beginning in 1986 partially de-indexed both transfers to the provinces to pay for health and education, as well as payments to mothers under universal family allowances. These decisions meant the Tories could whittle away at social programs (by removing full inflation protection from them, for example) without risking the outcry that might have followed from their flat-out dismantling.[38]

Over time, Conservatives managed to define their key social policy challenge as making programs more fiscally sound and effective, so as 'to help those who need it most.'[39] Their announced intentions were to reduce the federal deficit and to reconfigure welfare and unemployment schemes in a manner that made more Canadians self-sufficient.[40] In the process, universal family allowances disappeared and, as in the US under Ronald Reagan, the unemployment insurance system was vastly scaled back while tax changes were tailored to benefit upper-income groups.[41]

The more punitive side of federal Conservative thinking on social policy reform also became clearer after 1984. One outspoken member of the Ontario caucus, Barbara Greene, was appointed chair of the House of Commons subcommittee on poverty. In this capacity, Greene pressed her subcommittee to focus its attention on redefining the poverty line so that fewer Canadians would fall below it.[42] Kim Campbell, a British Columbia MP who briefly replaced Brian Mulroney as party leader and prime minister, lashed out against critics who condemned the Tories' decision to reduce the deficit through cuts to social spending. In Campbell's words, 'Our Government does not view Canadians as victims and does not see it as the role of government to perpetuate weakness and dependency.'[43]

In 1985, the Mulroney government signed the joint Agreement on Enhancement of Employment Opportunities for Social Assistance Recipients (SAR) with the provinces. This deal offered provinces an opportunity under the Canadian Jobs Strategy to develop a variety of pilot programs – including work-for-welfare schemes that penalized non-participants – with full federal cooperation and generous federal funding. The agreement was Canada's own version of AFDC waivers in the United States, since provincial premiers (like American state governors) were able as of 1985 to experiment with different ways of addressing the 'employability' of welfare recipients.

Lost in the commotion surrounding Mulroney's more high-profile policy forays, notably continental free trade and two unsuccessful constitutional accords, the SAR agreement's stated goal was 'to promote the self-sufficiency of social assistance recipients and to reduce their dependence upon federal and provincial income support programs by enhancing their employability through the application of appropriate employment and training measures.'[44] The federal minister of health and welfare insisted the program would offer 'vastly increased opportunities for self-sufficiency. There is no coercion, simply increased opportunity.'[45] This reassuring language meant, in effect, that the Mulroney government wanted to get more Canadians off the welfare rolls, where half the costs were paid by the federal government under the terms of CAP, and into jobs.

Relative to past practices in many Canadian provinces, changes introduced after 1985 tended to push social assistance policy in more of a work-readiness rather than income-support direction. Focused on reducing spending, tightening eligibility rules, ferreting out fraudulent users, and imposing penalties on welfare recipients who were defined as eligible for workfare but who refused to participate in such programs (these definitions varied from province to province), Canadian strategies appeared punitive to be sure. At the same time, provincial regulations gradually changed definitions of employability in such a way as to lower the age of the youngest child, and hence assigned more lone mothers to the category of 'employable.'

Over time, more and more women faced provincial sanctions including benefit cuts if they did not meet workfare requirements. By 1993, the Alberta government required single parents of children aged six months or older to search for work.[46] In Quebec, benefit levels for welfare recipients who were considered able to work were highest for those who participated in a workfare program, and lowest for 'employables' who refused to join a program.[47] Although these policies were criticized by many progressives as stringent and coercive, they arguably did not constitute mandatory or compulsory workfare, since benefit sanctions did not entirely wipe out cash payments to individuals.

The degree to which provinces experimented with 'employability enhancement' programs varied widely. Some poorer provinces, including New Brunswick, were anxious to strike a deal with the federal government that could reduce not only public and private sector labour costs, but also welfare expenditures. According to one account, more than 85 per cent of the training, wage supplement, and course costs for six years under the New Brunswick Works program were covered by the federal government.[48] New Brunswick and British Columbia also experimented with a self-sufficiency program, designed to provide significant earnings supplements to single mothers leaving social assistance for full-time employment, while Quebec and Alberta used the SAR framework to try to increase work readiness and cut what they viewed as welfare dependency during the 1980s.[49]

If one province was decidedly out of step with this scenario, it was Ontario. As Canada's long-standing centre of economic and political gravity, Ontario was governed after 1985 by a succession of left-of-centre Liberal and New Democratic party (NDP) governments. The perspective of Ontario decision-makers on welfare issues in this period was captured in the 1988 report of the Social Assistance Review Committee (SARC), which recommended higher, fully indexed welfare rates so people living on social benefits would no longer have to survive below the poverty line.[50] In response, Liberal and NDP provincial governments raised welfare payments and oversaw growing social assistance caseloads, as the impact of recessionary times and economic restructuring in the wake of continental free trade took their toll.

Federal Tories interpreted Ontario decisions to increase benefits in a context of growing unemployment and unstable tax flows – and in the framework of a cost-sharing agreement under CAP that saw the federal government pay half of provincial social assistance costs – as a direct challenge to their fiscal agenda. The Mulroney government retaliated by limiting the growth in social transfers to the three wealthiest provinces (Ontario, Alberta, and British Columbia) to no more than 5 per cent per year. Even though about one-half of Canada's poorest people lived in these provinces in 1990, the federal government maintained all three could afford to assume more of the costs of welfare assistance.[51] The so-called cap on CAP cost the Ontario treasury an estimated $10 billion over five years; by 1995, the federal government's share of social assistance costs in Ontario had fallen from roughly 50 per cent to less than 30 per cent.[52]

The cap on CAP combined with more experience in office took the shine off the Ontario NDP's critique of punitive, pro-workfare attitudes. As a graduate student, Bob Rae had viewed Beatrice and Sidney Webb's dichotomy between the deserving and undeserving poor as too locked in with the prissy mindset of 'the Victorian governess.'[53] By 1993, Premier Rae had embarked on a voyage in the opposite direction; as he told one audience, 'simply paying people to sit at home is not smart.'[54] Welfare recipients, according to the leader of Ontario's NDP government, needed to share the pain of the fight against government deficits. Rae's NDP cabinet established an intensive system for investigating welfare fraud and, according to one leaked document, considered benefit sanctions against recipients who failed to participate in counselling, training, or work activities.[55]

The NDP government of British Columbia responded to the Tories' cap on CAP by imposing a three-month residency requirement for new welfare claimants, and by litigating against the cap in the courts. Like most other efforts to pursue social rights for Canadians by using the judiciary, however, this case was not successful.[56] Mike Harcourt, British Columbia's NDP premier, also appointed a new social services minister to crack down on what Harcourt called 'welfare cheats and deadbeats ... We want to catch those varmints.'[57] His suggestion that people who fraudulently collected social benefits needed to be trapped and caught like rodents indicated the extent to which punitive rhetoric and policies had seeped across the Canadian political spectrum by 1993.

At a constitutional level, the Ontario government introduced a draft social union document in 1992 that included provisions for 'social services and welfare based on need, so as to ensure that all Canadians have access to a minimum level of housing, food and other basic necessities.'[58] This proposal was eventually watered down in the legal text of the failed Charlottetown Accord, in which Canadians were only assured of 'adequate' services and benefits, plus 'reasonable access' to necessities.[59] Moreover, as critics of the constitutional deal were quick to note, the Charlottetown agreement protected governments from having to provide court-ordered shelter or food by stating that the terms of the social union 'should not be justiciable.'[60]

In the field of child care, the federal Conservatives proposed a $4 billion investment over seven years to assist the provinces, a sum that would create approximately 200,000 new child-care spaces across Canada.[61] While critics on the right (including the anti-feminist organization known as R.E.A.L. Women) condemned the Conservatives for their willingness to subsidize child care by persons other than mothers, progressives charged the Tories with relying too much on the tax system and the provinces.[62] Mulroney withdrew most of his government's child-care proposals on the eve of the 1988 federal election.

Overall, federal social spending as a share of GDP during the Mulroney years fell from 10.5 to 8.5 per cent.[63] A significantly broadened definition of what constituted an employable single mother took hold, as provinces introduced more carrots, sticks, and harsh rhetoric to push 'employable' women into paid work. From this perspective, the Mulroney government effectively prepared the groundwork both for more far-reaching fiscal austerity measures by the next federal government, and for more conservative social policy experimentation involving low-income mothers by future provincial regimes.

Restoring 'Victorian Virtues'

After becoming leader of the British Conservative party in 1975, Margaret Thatcher worked to develop an issue platform that showcased her core belief in individual freedom. Thatcher's opposition to what she viewed as the heavy-handed interventionism and pro–trade union bias of the Labour government then in power provided a crucial foil for her defence of 'the liberty of the people under the law.'[64] Individual initiative would be reignited by changing social values and altering government programs in such a way as to reinstil 'the "Victorian virtues."'[65] The latter became Thatcher's favourite code phrase to celebrate achieving individuals who took care of themselves and their families – people whose personal initiative would help return Britain to its glory days.

Like Ronald Reagan, Margaret Thatcher stood out as a moralistic, populist opponent of single mother households. Keith Joseph, who served in the cabinet of Conservative prime minister Edward Heath, played a crucial role in shaping her outlook. In a widely quoted 1974 speech, Joseph condemned 'the permissiveness of our time,' and targeted single mothers who 'are producing problem children, the future unmarried mothers, delinquents, denizens of our borstals, subnormal educational establishments, prisons, hostels for drifters.'[66] His discussion went on to lament the decline of 'our human stock' caused by the rabbit-like fecundity of uneducated teenage mothers 'in social classes four and five.'[67]

In contrast to the anti–family planning outlook of US Republicans, however, Keith Joseph endorsed contraception as a useful way to reduce lower-class birth rates.[68] Moreover, British Conservatives were far more concerned than their Republican counterparts about the threat to the family that would be posed if mothers of young children were forced into paid work. At the same 1977 Conservative party conference where Thatcher declared 'We are the party of the family,' the shadow social services minister warned against placing too much pressure on young mothers. According to Patrick Jenkin, an overly strong push in the direction of paid employment 'devalues motherhood itself.'[69] British Tories had additional reasons for resisting harsh, pro-workfare policies modelled on American experiments. As Thatcher reflected in her own memoirs, enforcing paid employment in return for social benefits 'can be both expensive and frustrated in practice by bureaucratic obstruction.'[70]

Thatcher believed other avenues were more amenable to change, and targeted council (local authority) apartments that she said offered an incentive for young girls to get pregnant and leave their parents' homes. Thatcher insisted her government would curtail what she termed 'queue-jumping by single parents' to gain public housing.[71] On questions of work and social benefits, Thatcher's thinking paralleled North American conservative arguments on the need for low taxes, minimal regulation of labour markets, and reduced government spending as a way to 'recreate a predominantly free-enterprise economy and to encourage a capital-owning society.'[72]

In their 1979 campaign manifesto, British Conservatives committed themselves to five tasks that, in Thatcher's words, would contain state power and 'work *with the grain* of human nature, helping people to help themselves – and others. This is the way to restore that self-reliance and self-confidence which are the basis of personal responsibility and national success.'[73] The phrase 'personal responsibility' would prove pivotal both for conservatives and subsequent Third Way politicians, since it captured in short-hand format the argument that the state should do less while individuals should contribute more toward building a prosperous, high-growth economy.

Two of the five tasks identified in the Tory manifesto spoke directly to questions of work and welfare. One proposed to 'restore incentives so that hard work pays, success is rewarded and genuine new jobs are created in an expanding economy.'[74] Again foreshadowing Third Way language, this commitment was linked to Conservative criticisms of the crippling effects of unwieldy labour laws and high taxes that blocked economic growth. A second challenge responded to Thatcher's concern over the disintegration of traditional values. It pledged to 'support family life,' including by 'concentrating welfare services on the effective support of the old, the sick, the disabled and those who are in real need.'[75] The phrase 'real need' resonated both with Ronald Reagan's talk of 'the truly needy' and with Brian Mulroney's notion of 'those who need it most.'

For Margaret Thatcher, lone mothers – especially teenage mothers – who relied on social benefits were not only wasting public monies, but also perpetuating what she described in her memoirs as 'a cycle of criminality.'[76] Just as Reagan maintained that the framers of the American New Deal had understood the limits of welfare state expansion, so too Thatcher argued that the Beveridge Report had long ago warned against idleness and stifled initiative and of the dangerous consequences that could follow from them.[77] Thatcher relied heavily on American welfare state critics including Charles Murray in railing against the particular damage done by poorly socialized members of a dependent underclass. In her words, 'Not only in such circumstances do children grow up without the guidance of a father: there are no involved, responsible men around to protect those who are vulnerable, exercise informal social control or provide examples of responsible fatherhood. Graffiti, drug trafficking, vandalism and youth gangs are the result and the police find it impossible to cope.'[78]

Thatcher's recipe for greater individual self-sufficiency and less crime was clear. Under a Conservative government, access to public housing would no longer provide implicit encouragement for teenage girls to get pregnant. Workplace regulations would no longer block the creation of jobs for low-skilled workers. Most important, generous social benefits and high rates of personal income tax would end so that subsidized idleness could not operate as a convenient alternative to hard work.

British Conservative Policies

Since they held fused executive and legislative powers for about eighteen years, British Conservatives were able to put into effect much of what they promised in opposition. The broad goal of creating a more enterprising culture of self-sufficient individuals who were less dependent on the state was revealed in many different ways. Overall, tighter benefit rules, lower benefit levels, and increased emphasis on private market solutions (especially in the housing and employment fields) became hallmarks of Tory social policy between 1979 and 1997.

As in the United States and Canada, much of this change occurred through complex budgetary and regulatory decisions that were hard for average members of the public to follow. For example, unemployment benefits were reduced and eligibility rules narrowed at least fifteen times during the Thatcher years, when rates of unemployment rose sharply.[79] Universal family allowances were initially de-indexed and then frozen, so the value of government payments dramatically declined. The cumulative effect of such changes was to push more potential claimants away from the unemployment rolls toward other benefits, and to make universal programs a less and less significant part of the social policy mix.

At the same time, Thatcher-era actions succeeded in making it more and more difficult to collect what remained of the increasingly selective, means-tested benefits that could be termed 'welfare.' Beginning in 1983, greater resources were devoted to the fight against benefits fraud. In 1986, the Restart scheme for long-term unemployed people was initiated; those who missed their mandatory interviews or who turned down 'available work' risked losing benefits for as long as thirteen weeks.[80] Supplementary payments that had been available to welfare recipients as grants were changed to loans under the terms of the 1986 Social Security Act.[81]

Conservatives were convinced that private-sector solutions to 'welfare dependency' were close at hand. Consistent with Thatcher's views about the relationship between teenage motherhood and access to public housing, the Tories authorized a steep rise in council housing rents.[82] During the same period, government tax regulations were altered in order to encourage more people to purchase public flats under the Right to Buy program. According to critics, higher council rents paid by the poor effectively financed tax concessions (including mortgage relief) offered to middle- and upper-income groups; to these observers, it was no surprise that many council tenants who could not afford to purchase their properties were low-income single mothers. For Margaret Thatcher, however, the declining supply and quality of council flats meant fewer teenage girls would be tempted to get pregnant.[83]

British Conservatives also worked to inculcate a notion of private parental rather than collective societal or state responsibility for children. As Thatcher announced in July 1990, 'Parenthood is for life.'[84] A campaign beginning that year closely resembled efforts during the same period in the United States. British benefits administrators began to deduct child maintenance payments directly from absent fathers' wages. In turn, these payments reimbursed the state for benefits paid to mothers who had custody of their children, and who collected Income Support benefits.[85] Margaret Thatcher thus explained the Child Support Act (CSA), passed in 1991, as a direct 'attempt to enforce decent levels of provision for an abandoned family.'[86]

Although many feminist and anti-poverty campaigners agreed with Thatcher that more men should pay child support, they vigorously opposed both the portrayal of single mother households as deviant and incomplete and the government's means of implementing its objectives. As of 1993, the newly created Child Support Agency required single mothers on Income Support to name each child's father so he could be compelled to pay maintenance. Mothers who did not prove that they or their child would be at risk due to such disclosure faced a 20 per cent cut in benefits for up to eighteen months.[87]

Critics claimed the CSA was not only regressive and punitive but also dangerous, because it compelled every lone mother to establish the risk of harm or distress that could result from naming the father and empowering the agency to collect payments from him. In particular, the legislation was seen as encouraging women and their children to have contact with and become financially re-dependent on men who had been violent in the past. Moreover, observers charged that many orders compelling men to provide maintenance were completely unrelated to their ability to pay. Interests that questioned how the Child Support Act would ever work in practice subsequently described its operations as a 'fiasco.' One account concluded that implementing the CSA entailed 'huge delays and backlogs, inaccurate assessments, and incompetent or nonexistent enforcement [which] resulted in confusion, distress, and a general loss of confidence in the agency' responsible for making the legislation work.[88]

At the 1993 Conservative party conference, Thatcher's successor John Major issued his 'back to basics' rallying cry; it merged traditionalist rhetoric about the family with an anti-crime, pro–rule of law focus.[89] Major's speech, especially the phrase 'back to basics,' became a favourite target of ridicule once horror stories about both the operations of the Child Support Agency and the less than conventional family lives of some Tory politicians made the headlines. Nevertheless, the Major government continued to pursue core Thatcherite ideas about labour markets. In 1993, the Trade Union Reform and Employment Rights Act (TURERA) effectively eliminated minimum wage regulations (under Wages Councils) along with other workplace rules. About four-fifths of the low-income workers covered by Wages Councils were women.[90] Thatcher endorsed such action on the grounds that inflexible labour laws destroyed jobs, especially for less skilled workers.[91] Conservatives applauded both TURERA and the child-care tax allowance brought in during the same year to encourage (rather than force) mothers on benefits to pursue paid work.[92] This allowance, along with a small pilot scheme that provided nursery school vouchers to employed parents, were among the only policy actions on child care taken during the Thatcher and Major years.

Provisions of the CSA that came into effect in 1993 contained an additional incentive for women to work rather than collect benefits. Employed mothers who qualified for Family Credit (the name assigned in 1988 to an older program created in 1970 to assist low-income households with children) were permitted to keep a portion of the maintenance payments received from ex-partners and faced no cut in benefits, whereas mothers on benefits who received maintenance awards but did not work for pay obtained no such 'disregard.' For British Conservatives, payments collected via the CSA were explicitly designed to foster parental responsibility, reduce benefit costs, and *not* serve as a disincentive to paid work.[93]

During its last year in office, the Major government overhauled existing unemployment insurance schemes to create the Jobseekers Allowance. Tory cabinet ministers insisted 'the old system was too lax' because it benefited foreigners, single mother 'crooks,' and the 'undeserving poor.'[94] Under the terms of the new allowance, benefits paid to people under the age of twenty-five were reduced, the maximum duration of benefits was cut, claimants were forced to accept work that 'they can reasonably be expected to do,' and monitoring of efforts to find work was scheduled to commence.[95] These changes coincided with a widely publicized crackdown against benefits fraud in 1996. The goal of both initiatives was to lower social spending and reinvigorate the 'enterprise culture' values about work that rested at the heart of Thatcherite thinking.

All told, decisions during the Thatcher and Major years moved British social policy in increasingly punitive, selective, and residual directions. Wrapped in powerful moralistic rhetoric, these actions helped to identify single mother households as abnormal social structures that were hotbeds of crime, benefits fraud, and calculated 'queue-jumping' for public housing. Although Tory elites were loath to introduce mandatory workfare schemes comparable to those in use in the United States, they were prepared to use various work incentives and benefit penalties to not only lower spending, but also encourage paid employment.

Their best efforts, however, proved somewhat fruitless, since British social spending remained stubbornly stuck in the roughly one-quarter of GDP range through the 1990s.[96] In short, the Tories contained the growth of the welfare state but hardly managed to abolish it.[97] The proportion of births outside marriage more than doubled between 1979 and 1992, while the percentage of lone parent families increased at nearly the same rate.[98] Even more serious from the perspective of Conservative social policy were data that showed declining levels of paid employment among single parents, along with a growing reliance among this group on government benefits.[99] Clearly, Tory rhetoric and action on 'family policy' failed to reverse many of the patterns they set out to challenge.

Conclusions

One intriguing feature of conservative social policy in the United States, Canada, and Great Britain was the extent to which national leaders of different countries pursued strikingly similar objectives. Clearly, Ronald Reagan, Brian Mulroney, Margaret Thatcher, and their respective party successors all preferred free market solutions to interventionist meddling by the state. All defined social programs as a heavy weight on the public purse, which in their view had become an unaffordable burden in an age of high government deficits and debts. Each wanted to lower social spending – especially spending on people who were not, in their view, truly needy.

Particularly in North America, conservative critics of the welfare state sought to challenge traditional assumptions that poor single mothers were unemployable and hence 'deserving' of public benefits until all their children had finished school or, for that matter, entered school. In some US jurisdictions, welfare reformers defined lone mothers as able-bodied and employable from the time their infants reached twelve weeks of age. Right-of-centre politicians wanted to encourage more of a work ethic or what Thatcher called an 'enterprise culture'; at the very least, they strongly endorsed benefit penalties plus employment incentives to get that point across. The conservative message about the need to reward economic achievement was also communicated by tax changes benefiting upper-income at the expense of lower-income citizens.

Anglo-American conservatives contrasted their goal of fostering achieving, enterprising individuals in an open marketplace with what they saw as the lamentable 'dependency' or lack of self-sufficiency of welfare claimants. Particularly in the cases of Reagan and Thatcher, leaders advanced a definition of the problem of social assistance that highlighted either individual character flaws among recipients or else misguided statist thinking in government programs. In no case did their diagnosis ever address structural or material problems in the labour market, including the availability of secure jobs, patterns of sex segregation in paid work, unequal pay, or the like. The obstacles posed by limited educational opportunities, discrimination at work, and the lack of high-quality, affordable child-care programs in these countries were generally ignored as well.

Nor did conservative elites devote much attention to the need to reward unpaid nurturing work done by mothers, especially poor mothers, despite the fact that this rationale had provided the underpinning for early welfare programs in all three countries. Although Reagan, Mulroney, Thatcher, and their successors celebrated the good deeds performed by volunteers, and encouraged more people to engage in volunteer work, they invested virtually none of their rhetorical firepower in a defence of the unpaid social contributions of disadvantaged women.

It was around hot button questions of family, work, and benefits that profound differences divided these three leaders. Overall, in the United States and Britain, the language about what was a proper family was much more directive, emphatic, and exclusionary than it was at the national level in Canada. American elites condemned 'welfare queens,' for example, while their British counterparts attacked what they called 'pretending families.'[100] By way of comparison, the language of federal decision-makers in Canada remained relatively nuanced and muted through the Mulroney years. Canadian Tories clearly wanted to cut social spending and 'enhance employability' among welfare mothers, but they chose to use a less polarizing approach that advocated better targeting of government programs and, far more than in the other two countries, a willingness to discuss child-care issues. Yet at least one Canadian provincial leader compensated for the reticence of federal elites in his own outburst against fraudulent welfare claimants.

In all three countries, public attention to child-care issues increased over time, but the willingness of leaders to devote substantial state resources did not.[101] For example, Margaret Thatcher and John Major both said they wanted to move forward on nursery education, but did not act because of fears about higher spending.[102] Anglo-American conservatives tended to prefer private (including family-, neighbourhood-, or employer-based) rather than state provision of child care. Each offered various incentives for mothers on benefits to work, including through the use of child-care supplements and tax allowances. Large-scale spending programs that would have provided universal and, according to progressives, higher quality services were generally avoided.

Other differences emerge in comparing ideas about reproductive issues. Although reforms to Canadian abortion law were proposed during the Mulroney years, they were not linked directly to discussions of welfare policy. This contrasted with the situation in the United States, where conservative politicians like Ronald Reagan wanted to reduce teenage pregnancies, but certainly not by providing open access to family planning or abortion services. On the other side of the spectrum, some socially conservative Tories in Britain were vocal libertarians who wanted the state out of the business of providing welfare benefits and out of the practice of regulating reproductive practices. If more open access to contraception and abortion reduced the uptake of social benefits, as Keith Joseph and others believed was the case, then all the more reason for a free market to prevail on reproductive issues.[103]

Finally, Anglo-American conservatives differed in their views about how much work compulsion was necessary to reorient the values of single mothers on social assistance. Some Canadian provinces imposed benefit penalties on recipients who did not pursue paid work or training programs; they were not punished by the federal government for doing so. By the Major years, British regulations under the Jobseekers Allowance scheme docked claimants who did not attend interviews or participate in work programs. Yet in neither of these cases was the movement toward mandatory work obligations anywhere near the point reached in the United States during the Reagan/Bush years. Fed up with incentives, American conservatives pressed a compulsory jobs theme that seemed rigid, paternalistic, and unforgiving from a Canadian or British perspective.

Arguably the most lasting legacy shared by all three conservative regimes was their firm imprint of hypocrisy. Although the rhetoric and actions of leaders varied, they all emphasized some version of private, individualized self-sufficiency to reduce fiscal burdens on the state and to reinvigorate families and individuals. Yet changes under their watch in the fields of employment, social services, government benefits, and housing policy arguably placed a great deal of additional stress on individuals and families.[104] Moreover, conservative rhetoric about the need for more targeting or selectivity so that spending was directed toward the most needy was betrayed by decisions to cut precisely those benefits and programs that served the most vulnerable low-income citizens. Overall, the ability of conservative elites to fudge the details of a state-free personal independence was nothing short of remarkable. What remained to be seen was how their successors would begin to grapple with the profound social tensions unleashed by their discourse and actions.

CHAPTER THREE

Promises, Promises

In their efforts to push aside conservative leaders and assume top executive office, Third Way politicians presented an intriguing combination of abstract ideas and concrete proposals. The campaign rhetoric of Bill Clinton, Jean Chrétien, and Tony Blair highlighted the importance of restoring faith in some notion of the common good, which had been eroded and endangered in their view by Republican presidents and Conservative prime ministers. Third Way talk about restoring more community-based values, however, often focused on a nostalgic revival of traditional norms in which ambition, hard work, and commitment to the nuclear family paid off. In the jargon of British New Labour elites, 'post-conservatism' would offer achieving individuals an enhanced sense of social inclusion.

At the level of policy proposals, Third Way leaders in North America and Britain offered a welfare state platform that sought to reassure middle-class voters in an age of social and economic insecurity. Better schools, improved access to health care, plus more job training and apprenticeship programs figured prominently in the 1992 Clinton platform, the 1993 Canadian Liberal Red Book, and the 1997 New Labour manifesto. In each of these documents, the core message on social assistance was one of enforced conformity to the standards of a middle-class work ethic: welfare programs would be redesigned as active pathways to personal self-sufficiency, so that paid employment or job training assumed centre stage.

Among the most memorable messages of the 1992 Clinton campaign was 'ending welfare as we know it.' As a popular short-hand expression, this phrase pressed hard on hot button concerns about fraud, wasteful spending, and disincentives to work associated with the existing Aid to Families with Dependent Children (AFDC) program. Clinton's promise to move means-tested benefit recipients, primarily single mothers on AFDC, into paid employment relied heavily on academic research by David Ellwood and others. These experts prepared the fine details behind Clinton's promise to 'make work pay,' particularly its emphasis on expanding tax credits for low-income workers and changing the culture of welfare so that it became a time-limited springboard toward economic independence.

In Canada, the Chrétien Liberals drew a direct link between coping with economic change, modernizing the welfare state, and improving child care provision. Red Book discussions of 'investing in people' emphasized the need to improve Canada's education, apprenticeship, and work training programs, and to transform passive income support systems into active projects that fostered 'full economic participation.'[1] Liberals understood, however, that most lone parents could not simply walk out the door as autonomous breadwinners. They proposed a national child-care program as one measure to 'help break the chain of dependence.'[2] If provincial cooperation could be secured and if economic growth reached 3 per cent a year, the federal Liberals promised 150,000 new child-care spaces during their first term in power.

In the run-up to the 1997 election, New Labour in Britain proposed a compulsory welfare-to-work scheme for unemployed youth that included educational upgrading, job counselling, and an end to benefit payments in the absence of work or training. This program, known as the New Deal, would be financed by a windfall profits tax on privatized utility companies. It was envisioned that the New Deal might be extended to lone parents on a voluntary basis.[3] When combined with a national minimum wage as well as enhanced nursery-school and after-school programs, all endorsed by New Labour, the New Deal was seen as a way to 'not simply abolish the hand-out,' but instead to 'replace it with a hand-up which enables each individual to find serious work with a prospect of stable employment.'[4]

Overall, Third Way proposals began with a fundamental assumption that the welfare state was a flawed, if not failed, social project. Any effort to improve its operations would entail investing either in fields of middle-class priority, including health and education, or in areas where middle-class norms about individual ambition and hard work could be brought to bear, notably welfare-to-work initiatives. Third Way leaders were unwilling to get bogged down in the finer details of this transformation, including in debates over mandatory versus voluntary workfare. Instead, as political pragmatists, they presented a range of general proposals to overhaul social assistance schemes. These ideas varied across the three cases, from time-limited welfare and enriched work supplements in the United States, to more workfare experimentation plus a national child-care program in Canada, to a national minimum wage plus the New Deal jobs and training scheme in Britain. The common normative thread linking all of these ideas was clear: once all able-bodied adults worked for pay, the need for wasteful welfare expenditures and any notion of rights-based entitlement to them could be eliminated as a matter of course.

In relative terms, these approaches to social assistance reform seemed more reasonable and compassionate than those advanced by conservative political elites. Particularly in comparison with the rhetoric of Reagan- and Thatcher-era proposals, Third Way ideas sounded like balanced, level-headed routes toward moving welfare recipients from what was described as marginalized social dependency toward inclusion in the dynamic mainstream of Anglo-American labour markets. Yet, on closer inspection, these same prescriptions likely contained serious problems of their own. For example, would meaningful supports for paid employment (including child care programs) actually be set in place by Third Way leaders, given the political and fiscal costs associated with them? During economically insecure times, even for well-educated, middle-class citizens, how likely were ex–welfare recipients to locate stable, full-year employment that offered a decent chance of market-based self-sufficiency? How would eventual downturns in the North American and British economies be addressed once social assistance schemes had been transformed into job support or work preparedness regimes?

At least as important as these nuts and bolts issues were questions about the citizenship consequences of Third Way proposals. The ideas about welfare reform presented by US Democrats, Canadian Liberals, and British New Labourites in 1992 and following accepted at their core an incomplete or compromised version of social citizenship – one that established paid work readiness and labour force engagement as basic conditions of human belonging. People who were unable or unwilling to meet the conditions imposed by an employment-based definition of social inclusion risked being consigned to the category of non-contributors and hence partial or impaired citizens.

The prospects for a truncated form of social citizenship were probably most ominous in the United States. Leading members of Bill Clinton's domestic policy brain trust proposed a time-limited program of welfare to work, under which cash benefits would be denied after a specified period of temporary, transitional social assistance had expired. Clearly, once government responsibility was withdrawn under the ticking clock rule, many lone mothers would face the dubious choice of either unpaid, full-time caring for their children without any entitlement to social assistance or else paid employment at the bottom of an insecure labour market on top of caring responsibilities, or perhaps obligatory marriage to escape (likely temporarily) the first two options. To a cynical observer, it looked as if US Democrats had fashioned their own punitive angle on welfare reform, in this case time limits, but dressed it carefully to fit in a larger bundle of less threatening proposals about supports for working parents.

The Clinton Plan

The 1992 Democratic campaign platform, titled *Putting People First*, responded directly to widespread concerns over the future of America. After the recessionary bumps of the Reagan/Bush years, middle-class voters were worried and anxious. Federal debt and deficit levels were high, permanent work was hard to find, and health care security even for employed people seemed more and more tenuous. The sturdy myth that those who worked hard and played by the rules could, in their own lives, realize the American Dream appeared to be in danger. Above all, incumbent president George Bush seemed far more absorbed by distant forays including the Persian Gulf War than by domestic concerns over the country's prospects.

Under the leadership of a pragmatic small-state governor, Democrats in 1992 were well positioned to capitalize on the angst of the times. Presidential candidate Bill Clinton had built his career in Arkansas, a poor but intensely proud southern state, as a self-made politician of the flexible middle. Lacking the New England patrician trappings of George Bush, Clinton got by on a powerful combination of nerve, charm, intelligence, and intense personal ambition. Much like Ronald Reagan, Bill Clinton had built his national profile around a campaign as state governor to reform welfare policy. Given his modest family background, Clinton could relate to Americans' frustration with what seemed to be a dream gone astray. Hard work did not necessarily translate into access to health care, or education for one's children, or even secure work tomorrow. By way of contrast, collecting welfare benefits appeared to offer all kinds of perverse guarantees, including for government-insured health care under the Medicaid program as well as future benefits ad infinitum. As a 'New' or moderate Democrat who had taken a leading role in the centrist Democratic Leadership Council, Clinton was convinced he had a formula for regaining the support of middle-class voters.

Putting People First presented an optimistic plan for rewarding work in such a way that welfare would no longer be necessary. First, the platform pledged health insurance for every American. Candidate Clinton maintained that reforms to health care would extend coverage to millions of uninsured Americans (including many low-income working people) and, at the same time, allow significant cuts to the federal deficit. Second, Democrats promised in 1992 to 'end welfare as we know it,' largely by moving means-tested AFDC recipients into paid work.[5] This would be accomplished by 'making work pay,' a phrase that entailed widening health care coverage, raising and indexing the minimum wage, extending low-income pay supplements under the Earned Income Tax Credit, and expanding apprenticeship, technical training, and college loan programs geared toward offering greater opportunities for better jobs to more Americans.

The phrase 'ending welfare as we know it' was consistent with Bill Clinton's political rhetoric in Arkansas since the mid-1970s. It spoke to the notion of social policies offering 'a hand up, not a hand out,' meaning government would assist disadvantaged individuals to share in the opportunities available to middle-class Americans, if they fulfilled the requisite responsibilities.[6] As Clinton's own rhetoric maintained, 'welfare should be a second chance, not a way of life.'[7] Not meeting these requirements meant the hand up would be history within two years. In the memorable phrase 'two years and out,' Democrats in 1992 insisted they had a workable plan to make welfare a temporary, transitional stopover on the path to self-sufficient paid employment; their proposal imposed a 24-month time limit on cash benefits in exchange for guaranteed jobs at the end of that period.[8]

Taken as a group, the key social policy proposals of *Putting People First* could be read as a popularized and condensed version of the ideas of prominent US academics. Robert Reich, who had first met Clinton when they were Rhodes scholars, argued in a series of books that enriched education and training programs offered the best way for nations to remain economically competitive in an emerging globalized system. Reich's emphasis on a human investment agenda for the 1990s, together with that of MIT economist Lester Thurow, was reflected in sections of *Putting People First* that talked about the shrinking value of American paycheques for workers in the lower tier of the labour force, and the need to put public money into the development of a productive, highly trained, and technologically adept workforce.[9] In the words of the 1992 platform, 'Our national economic strategy puts people first by investing more than $50 billion each year for the next four years to put America back to work ... These investments will create millions of high-wage jobs ... They will also help move people from welfare to work and provide lifetime learning.'[10]

The language of *Putting People First* reassured Americans that Democrats had a coherent strategy for addressing unpopular welfare programs, one that was both consistent with prevailing values and, at the same time, less extreme than some Republican proposals. According to the 1992 campaign platform, welfare reform occurs 'not by punishing the poor or preaching to them, but by empowering Americans to take care of their children and improve their lives.'[11] Bill Clinton's pithy recipe for individual empowerment was obvious. In his words, 'Work is the best social program this country has ever devised.'[12]

Two of Reich's Harvard University colleagues, David Ellwood and Mary Jo Bane, played a crucial role in fleshing out the welfare reform directions of the 1992 platform. Ellwood's 1988 text, *Poor Support: Poverty in the American Family*, agreed with conservative welfare state diagnoses (including by Charles Murray) of a fundamental clash between the dependency-inducing norms of AFDC and the personal self-sufficiency values of the broader society. Ellwood rejected prevailing reform proposals as misguided. In his view, 'The aim must not be to make welfare function better. The objective should be to replace welfare with something that takes much better account of the problems faced by the poor – a system that ensures that everyone who exercises reasonable responsibility can make it without welfare.'[13]

Ellwood's 1988 suggestions included a national system of child support payments collected via payroll deductions, with government-assured supplements in place when payments from the absent parent (usually the father) fell below a prescribed minimum. According to his analysis, assured child support combined with a higher minimum wage would boost the income that single mothers could expect to derive from half-time employment. Lone mothers raising children on their own, in Ellwood's view, could not be expected to work for pay on more than a half-time basis.[14]

Another way in which Ellwood, Reich, and others believed work could be made more attractive than welfare was through the use of tax credits to supplement the income of low-wage households. The Earned Income Tax Credit, according to *Poor Support*, needed to be expanded so that it functioned as more than simply a buffer against the payment of payroll taxes at the lower end of the wage scale.[15] In his 1988 book, Ellwood proposed a doubling of the EITC so that working poor households would de facto receive a 30 per cent wage boost, delivered without stigma via the tax code rather than the welfare system.[16] He also endorsed an expansion of existing child-care tax credits that primarily benefited middle-class households, so that they were refundable and extended to low-income families as well.[17]

The most contentious aspect of the Ellwood prescription that found its way into *Putting People First* involved time limits on social assistance. Initially advanced in a 1986 Urban Institute study by Irwin Garfinkel and Sara McLanahan, this idea assumed middle-class Americans would endorse an overhauled income assistance regime that provided poor people with *transitional* support toward self-sufficiency.[18] As Ellwood framed his 1988 version of temporary assistance,

> People who are not working because of temporary difficulties, such as the loss of a job or a recent change in their family's circumstances, ought to be offered short-term transitional assistance that includes training and services that are designed to help them become self-supporting, coupled with short-term cash support ... Long-term income support beyond the supplemental support measures ought to come in the form of jobs – not in the form of cash welfare for an indefinite duration.[19]

This proposal was grounded in a fundamental American notion of fair play, meaning people who worked for pay and cared for their families deserved to be rewarded with some modicum of economic security. If private sector jobs did not exist, according to Ellwood, then 'the government ensures that last-resort jobs are available for people who have used up their transitional assistance.'[20]

This same core argument about time-limited social assistance and government provision of community service or last-resort jobs was elaborated upon further in a 1994 text, titled *Welfare Realities*, co-authored by Mary Jo Bane and David Ellwood. The book opened with a sustained critique of the culture of welfare bureaucracies in the

United States. It portrayed the prevailing casework model of social assistance as obsessed with establishing client eligibility and verifying compliance with existing program rules – which, in many cases, defined paid employment as a violation of welfare regulations. By way of contrast, Bane and Ellwood insisted that innovative welfare reform would reject any 'dependency trap' regimentation of both clients and bureaucrats, and would embrace the goal of personal self-sufficiency via paid employment.[21]

Bane and Ellwood's details of how to make a self-sufficiency model work, and hence eliminate welfare as we knew it, grew in part from their frustration with the limits of the 1988 Family Support Act. In their view, this Republican-era effort failed for two main reasons: first, the FSA was layered on top of the existing rule-driven climate of welfare eligibility and compliance; and second, it was implemented during a period when many states could not afford to offer the education, job training, and other services mandated by the legislation. Serious welfare reform, according to Bane and Ellwood, would cost serious money, since there were major expenses associated with educational upgrading, job training, health care reform, and child-support assurance programs, not to mention the costs of an enriched Earned Income Tax Credit and government provision of last-resort jobs.

In *Welfare Realities*, Bane and Ellwood professed an agnostic position on the question of mandatory versus voluntary welfare-to-work programs. Their bottom line remained the same as Ellwood had laid out earlier in *Poor Support*; that is, stable, high-quality, work-oriented programs should be established to replace what welfare had allegedly become, namely a long-term, passive income support regime. In their words,

> [I]f we had an effective child support enforcement and insurance system, if we ensured that people got medical protection, if we made work pay, there would be far less need for welfare. Single parents could realistically support themselves at the poverty line if they were willing to work half time, even at a job paying little more than the minimum wage ... If people can realistically support themselves, then the notion of a time-limited, transitional assistance program for both single-parent and two-parent families makes sense. A rich set of training and support services ought to be included as part of the benefits. But the cash benefit program would be of limited duration.[22]

How long transitional assistance might last, according to *Welfare Realities*, would depend on the age of the youngest child in each household. Bane and Ellwood proposed a time limit of eighteen to thirty-six months, and emphasized that this ceiling should not be extended because of the birth of a new baby.[23]

The time limits proposal offered people who exhausted their cash benefits an opportunity to qualify for more of them by working for an unspecified period of time. As well, Bane and Ellwood suggested that some support services, 'certainly child care and some training,' might continue after transitional cash benefits ran out.[24] Moreover, they believed the US government would need to step in to 'provide full- or part-time jobs for those who exhaust transitional support, so that people can, in fact, support themselves.'[25] Finally, they admitted that the country 'will need some system for exempting and protecting people who truly cannot work,' including the disabled.[26] This particular challenge, according to Bane and Ellwood, could be addressed 'on a case-by-case basis' and would not interfere with the larger purpose of turning welfare into a work-based self-sufficiency program.[27]

If members of the 1992 Clinton campaign team had any inkling as to the costs of a transitional assistance scheme à la Bane and Ellwood, then they were loath to discuss them. Robert Reich's post-election account reveals that Ellwood estimated 'a stripped-down' version of his plan would cost 'at least $2 billion a year *over* current welfare expenditures.'[28] Yet for the duration of the 1992 presidential contest, these figures remained under tight wraps. The focus of attention became reducing federal spending, offering employed Americans a chance to believe in tomorrow, and, to quote Bill Clinton's high-flown rhetoric, campaigning 'to save the very soul of our nation.'[29]

How much compromise would a new Clinton administration be prepared to entertain on welfare reform? Close observation of the 1992 campaign period suggested that considerable policy elasticity existed inside the presidential entourage. Over time, welfare reform thinking in the Democratic Leadership Council and its affiliated think tank, the Progressive Policy Institute, moved remarkably close to Republican positions. As law and public policy specialist Joel Handler noted in his survey of welfare reform dynamics, Institute publications during the early 1990s echoed conservative claims that 'welfare is undermining the American values of "work, family, individual responsibility, and self-sufficiency."'[30] Furthermore, Institute experts tended by 1993 to agree with Republican critics of increased spending on job training and basic education, arguing that these programs 'are "extravagant," not cost effective, and not proven to work.'[31] From a US New Democratic perspective, limited public funds were best directed toward low-cost, fast-track job searches that could produce quick work placements.

Above all, the partisan atmosphere of the 1992 presidential campaign seemed dark and foreboding. Independent candidate Ross Perot, presenting an economic plan calling for $416 billion in federal spending cuts, won nearly 20 per cent of the popular vote. The Republican platform of that year reflected the strong influence of social conservative interests who wanted to outlaw abortion, reinforce traditional forms of family organization, and, in the words of New Right campaigner Pat Buchanan, win the 'culture wars' against the political centre and left.[32] Beginning on election night, leading Republicans claimed to speak for the combined Bush/Perot majority; that evening, Senate Minorty Leader Bob Dole warned Clinton that 'it's not going to be all a bed of roses.'[33] Within a few months, the Republican Whip in the House of Representatives, Newt Gingrich, announced his goal was 'cooperation without compromise. Our role in the minority is ... to offer intelligent criticism of their dumb ideas.'[34]

In short, Democrats won back the White House in 1992, but they did so with only 43 per cent of the popular vote. Moreover, the new presidential leadership of the party seemed willing to imitate and extend – rather than challenge – key aspects of the Republican approach to welfare reform.

Canadian Liberal Proposals

Packaged inside a bright red cover with a maple leaf image on the front, the 1993 Liberal party campaign platform was formally titled *Creating Opportunity: The Liberal Plan for Canada*. Better known as the Red Book, this document promised to reinvigorate the federal social policy presence following nine years of Conservative government; it emphasized job creation, a strengthened public health care system, additional child-care funding, and, echoing the 1992 Clinton plan, 'investing in people.'[35] Liberals promised to respond to both the economic 'disarray' of the country, in their words, as well as to social problems including child poverty and the threat of a two-tiered health system.[36] Like the Clinton Democrats, the Chrétien Liberals integrated some of the ideas of Robert Reich and Lester Thurow in their pledge to stimulate industrial growth by investing in research and development, and by providing better training and apprenticeship opportunities for young people.[37]

In the Red Book sections on social policy, Liberals stressed their party's contributions to welfare state development during the postwar years. The platform distinguished between Liberal commitments to 'fundamental fairness and decency,' achieved through a pooling of social resources, and what it described as a systematic weakening under Conservative governments of 'the social support network that took generations to build.'[38] *Creating Opportunity* underlined the willingness of a new Liberal government to defend the social policy priorities of middle-class Canadians, notably by preserving high-quality, universal health care and working with the provinces and the private sector to improve education at all levels.

Overall, Liberals argued, Canadians who had endured nine years of Conservative government faced a crisis of confidence over the country's future. Debt and deficit levels were higher on a per capita basis than in the United States, while the depths of economic recession during the early 1990s were arguably more severe north of the 49th parallel. Liberals thus viewed their central priorities in 1993 as, on track one, fostering economic growth and reducing unemployment and, on track two, cutting the federal deficit.[39]

As the federal party leader, Jean Chrétien was a pragmatic populist, a scrappy veteran of the flexible middle. In his best-selling memoirs *Straight from the Heart*, published in 1985, Chrétien wrote with great enthusiasm about the fruits of private sector investment in his home town of Shawinigan, Quebec and, with equal fervour, about the good things government had done to help diversify the area's pulp and paper economy.[40] While he lamented the 'idle hands and lost pride' caused by a social safety net that 'undermines incentive and is abused,' Chrétien was not prepared to see the state fold up its tent entirely.[41] As he observed in 1985, 'the nature of work has changed,' and this shift would ultimately require even more public investment in education and job training.[42]

Jean Chrétien's avoidance of what he viewed as dogmatic or ideological positions equipped him well to straddle difficult issues during the 1993 campaign. After absorbing the pro–human investment message delivered by US economist Lester Thurow at a 1991 Liberal policy conference, Chrétien declared, 'Globalization is not right-wing or left-wing. It is simply a fact of life.'[43] This emphasis on what Liberals claimed was a realistic response to the country's predicament followed as well from domestic pressures. Queen's University economist Thomas Courchene was among the most influential academic voices calling for serious cuts to federal social spending in order to reduce the deficit.[44] Supported by an array of powerful business groups, this line of argument insisted government programs should be small, carefully targeted, and focused on getting more Canadians into paid work. From the perspective of Courchene and others, expensive, expansive, passive income support schemes needed to be supplanted by low-cost, selective, and employment-based approaches.

Liberals claimed they were better able than their Tory predecessors to manage economic change, reduce the deficit, and switch to a self-sufficiency model of welfare policy – all without destroying Canada's social fabric. The Red Book committed the new government to renegotiating fiscal arrangements with the provinces as well as free trade agreements with the United States and Mexico in such a way as to 'assist individuals and firms to deal with the restructuring that is occurring as a result of trade liberalization.'[45] In short, Canadian Liberals in 1993 did not oppose the processes of globalization and restructuring; rather, they claimed the ability to cope more effectively than other parties with international economic pressures. The Red Book, as well as Chrétien's campaign speeches, emphasized the need to make more Canadians self-sufficient during a period of rapid technological change. Apprenticeship schemes, a Canadian Youth Service Corps, and, above all, a national child care proposal were introduced as concrete routes toward creating a high-value, productive, and competitive work force.

Much like their US Democratic counterparts in 1992, Canadian Liberals in 1993 tended to avoid specifics. The broad objectives of welfare reform according to the Red Book were as follows:

> It is our goal to help people on social assistance who are able to work, to move from dependence to full participation in the economic and social life of Canada. The current passive support programs, which offer income to people in need but no plan for achieving self-sufficiency, are not enough. New Brunswick and British Columbia, together with the federal government, have established pilot programs of active income support, to offer people on social assistance the opportunity for employment-related

> counselling, training or education, and work experience ... Canadians want to earn their own livings. Some are prevented from doing so by the limitations in current programs that create disincentives to full economic participation. Active income support methods are the way of the future.[46]

Readers were left to assume that a Liberal government would try to extend incentive-based workfare projects to all the provinces.

Above all, the Red Book section on child care stated that a federal Liberal government would add '50,000 new quality child care spaces' per year for up to three years, if it obtained provincial cooperation and if economic growth were to reach 3 per cent annually in each preceding year.[47] According to the document, 'Many single mothers today are dependent on welfare because, even though they want to earn a living, they cannot find good child care for their children. As a result, they are mired in a life of poverty, welfare, food banks, and inadequate housing ... Measures that help to break the chain of dependence are good economic policy.'[48] The pledge to bring in a national child-care program was costed out in the Red Book as $120 million per year for each block of 50,000 additional spaces.[49]

Workfare rather than child care turned out to be a very contentious subject of debate during Chrétien's 1993 campaign tour. At an appearance in Stephenville, Newfoundland, the Liberal leader announced that he was thinking about introducing mandatory workfare, given the high costs to the federal government of welfare and unemployment insurance benefits. This remark touched off a torrent of commentary, primarily positive from people like New Brunswick premier Frank McKenna, a Liberal whose provincial workfare program had been lauded in the Red Book. According to McKenna, Chrétien 'deserves credit for having the guts to stand up as a national leader and say people should move from welfare into the workforce ... This is Liberalism for the 90s and I'd like to be there with him.'[50]

By way of contrast, leaders of the National Anti-Poverty Organization (NAPO) were harshly critical of Chrétien's campaign musings, particularly his later attempts to clarify the initial remarks. The Liberal chief elaborated on his ideas as follows: 'People on welfare or unemployment insurance don't contribute to society. But when they are able to go out and work, they not only contribute to society, they also get a salary and they pay taxes instead of drawing benefits.'[51] As the controversy over compulsory work programs continued, both Chrétien and McKenna maintained that debates over mandatory workfare were irrelevant, since so many Canadians were flooding into existing incentive-based programs that offered 'the dignity of work.'[52] To observers in NAPO, however, the very suggestion that Canadians might need coercive workfare programs to get them off government benefits was insulting and misguided. According to the group's executive director, Lynne Toupin, 'The politicians are operating under the myth that these people do not want to work and that is absolutely false ... We are all for job-creation but let's ensure they are good jobs that restore dignity to families.'[53]

Lurking in the background behind this controversy were a number of important political dynamics. First, Liberals in Atlantic Canada faced serious competition from the left-of-centre New Democrats, who accused Chrétien of being harsh and punitive in his treatment of poor people.[54] Second, in neighbouring Quebec, the demise of the federal Conservatives opened up space for a pro-sovereignty party in 1993. The threat to the Liberals posed by the nascent Bloc Québécois meant that Jean Chrétien had to tread cautiously in areas of provincial jurisdiction, including social assistance policy.

A third challenge followed from middle-of-the-road concerns in Quebec and English Canada over what was rumoured to be a secret Conservative plan to overhaul federal social spending. Fears about how the Tories under their new leader, Kim Campbell, would fulfil a promise to eliminate the federal deficit in five years focused on the contents of a carefully shielded document on welfare state reforms.[55] The ability of the Liberals to capitalize on these concerns, as well as on the general implosion of the Conservatives during the 1993 campaign, rested in large part on avoiding the same images – that is, Jean Chrétien could ill afford to be cast as a bumbling carrier of equally sinister ideas about the future of federal social policy.

Finally, Liberals arguably faced their most significant challenge from Reform party interests in Western Canada. Building on yet another shattered pillar of the Mulroney era, Reform brought together regional grievances against central Canadian domination of the federal system, together with strong doses of fiscal as well as social conservatism. As the most prominent protest voice in Western Canada, Reform leader Preston Manning argued in 1993 for a reduced federal presence in many areas, including health care, unemployment insurance, seniors' pensions, and multiculturalism. His campaign statements targeted approximately $19 billion in federal spending cuts, and claimed the federal deficit could be eliminated within three years without tax increases.[56]

Parallel with Republican directions in the United States, the Reform party pursued a socially conservative agenda that was anti-abortion, in favour of traditional 'family values,' and highly critical of feminist and other pro–welfare state interests.[57] Moreover, Reform maintained that Quebec had received unduly generous treatment by previous federal governments.[58] On questions of social policy, Reform was consistently opposed to universal programs; the party maintained that very narrow, selective targeting was the only way to ensure that public money was efficiently spent. Preston Manning heartily approved, therefore, of Jean Chrétien's 1993 campaign musings. He indicated to reporters that poor and unemployed Canadians 'should be required to perform community service or take job-training or retraining' in order to collect social benefits.[59]

Like the Clinton Democrats, the Chrétien Liberals thus faced a serious challenge from political interests that endorsed federal social policy retrenchment. Both Reform and the Bloc Québécois endorsed a minimal welfare state role for the federal government, a perspective that challenged the historic predilections of the Liberals. The electoral strength of these new parties in 1993 meant that Jean Chrétien won a compromised majority based on only 41 per cent of the popular vote. As one post-election commentator noted, 'Canadians have not overwhelmingly embraced the Liberals in this election campaign. The Liberals' success is due more to the collapse of the NDP vote and the damage the Reform Party and the Bloc Québécois have done to the Conservatives than to a clamouring to return to what Liberal Leader Jean Chrétien described ... as the good old days.'[60] The combined vote share for Reform and the Conservatives reached 35 per cent, a figure that massively overshadowed the 7 per cent won by the NDP.[61]

How the Liberals would govern with a divided five-party parliament, including an official opposition drawn from the ranks of separatist forces in Quebec, remained to be seen. What was clear in 1993 was Jean Chrétien's consummate political pragmatism. The Liberal leader seemed at times to veer to the left, notably with Red Book promises about child-care expansion, and at other times to the right, in his musings about mandatory workfare. On social policy, the terrain he consistently returned to was a flexible and oftentimes vague middle ground that celebrated the pursuit of self-sufficiency in an ambitious new Canada.

The New Labour Blueprint

After 1979, the British Labour party spent nearly two decades in political opposition – ample time to develop a platform for governing. The party's left-wing campaign manifesto of 1983 marked the starting point for a gradual but pronounced shift toward pragmatic centrism. By the time Tony Blair became leader in 1994, Labour had lost four consecutive national elections, yet it had moved a considerable distance down a moderating path under his two immediate predecessors, Neil Kinnock and John Smith.

Many changes that enabled Blair to wield tight control over the party were set in place in 1983, when Kinnock appointed a professionalized communications staff and introduced a more centralized decision-making process to limit the clout of left factional as well as affiliated trade union interests. The process of making Labour more appealing to masses of middle-class voters was given a further boost during Smith's brief tenure as leader, when he named an independent Commission on Social Justice (CSJ) 'to develop a practical vision of economic and social reform for the 21st century.'[62]

On the fiftieth anniversary of the Beveridge Report that mapped out the British welfare state, the commission was asked to study how a modern Labour party could address the challenges facing that state. A succession of Conservative governments under Margaret Thatcher and John Major had rendered illegitimate traditional Labour demands for higher taxes to finance increased public spending. Yet 'fanatics of the free market economy,' as Social Justice commissioners referred to the Conservatives, were themselves on the hook as problems of homelessness, sub-standard education, and a general social malaise came to be attributed to long years of right-wing government.[63] Within this climate of unease, the CSJ was asked to provide Labour with a policy blueprint.

In its 1994 report titled *Social Justice: Strategies for National Renewal,* the commission presented a moderate vision that merged the values of social justice with a commitment to economic success. It underlined three overarching goals for the new century: first, creating what was termed 'an intelligent welfare state' based on the reality of insecure work in a competitive global economy; second, improving access to learning programs for all ages, since (following the ideas of Robert Reich) 'education and skills are the route to opportunity, employability and security' in a neo-liberal era; and third, promoting responsible families and communities that recognized the paid as well as unpaid work of mothers in particular.[64]

Parallel with Bill Clinton's rhetoric during the same period, *Social Justice* maintained that 'the welfare state must enable people to achieve self-improvement and self-support. It must offer a hand-up, not just a hand-out.'[65] To change 'the welfare state from a safety net in times of trouble to a springboard for economic opportunity,' the document proposed remedies very similar to those offered by Liberals in Canada.[66] The CSJ suggested extending child-care availability so that mothers with school-age children could 'be available for at least part-time work if they want to claim benefit.'[67] Increasing the paid work engagement of single mothers was viewed as a high priority by commissioners because 'only one in two lone mothers is in employment; indeed, the UK is the only country in the European Union where lone mothers are *less* likely to be in employment than women with a partner.'[68]

The CSJ's strategy for moving single mothers into paid work entailed changing labour market and education policies. The commission recommended a national minimum wage, 'minimum legal rights at work,' and 'universal pre-school education for 3- and 4-year-olds, coupled with new investment in childcare.'[69] Each of these policies was viewed as essential to making paid work more attractive to more adults. As well, *Social Justice* proposed overhauling the benefits system so that income support schemes would be geared toward offering greater opportunities to work and to 'promote personal independence.'[70] For example, the commission suggested merging benefits and unemployment agencies into a single Re-employment Service; its mandate would be to get more people working, including by helping lone parents with child-care arrangements.[71] The CSJ also endorsed higher government wage supplements and universal Child Benefit payments in order to make low-income work more appealing.[72] To ease the transition to paid jobs, the 1994 report proposed looser earnings exemptions for people on means-tested Income Support, which contradicted the British Conservative policy of 'high tax on low pay.'[73]

The commission diverged from prevailing North American directions in its pronouncements on means-testing, the value of caring, and the nature of families. *Social Justice* opposed making benefits more narrowly targeted, or directed 'only to the people who "really need them,"' on the grounds that the use or uptake of selective benefits was low because many members of the target group did not know about them.[74] As well, means-testing was seen as complex, exclusionary, and costly to administer; it discouraged people from saving money (because of restrictive asset tests to qualify for benefits), was full of disincentives to work, and, above all, created a narrow benefits regime that was fundamentally irrelevant to middle-class voters.[75] Instead, the 1994 report endorsed an expansion of social insurance schemes and reduced reliance on means-tested benefits.

One of the signature CSJ proposals called for a Participation Income, designed to pay basic support to anyone who was working for pay as well as 'those unable to work because of sickness, injury or disability, those unemployed but available for work, those in approved education or training, and those caring for young, elderly or disabled dependants.'[76] By requiring an active contribution to society, whether through paid work or caring, the CSJ architects of a Participation Income hoped to blunt criticisms of the 'something for nothing' element of nonparticipatory guaranteed income schemes.[77]

As well, *Social Justice* explicitly argued against prevailing Anglo-American notions that children were the primary responsibility of their individual parents, and that single mother households were by definition a problem. In the words of the 1994 document:

> [I]n a society where people's worth seems increasingly to be measured by how much money they can earn, the unpaid work of parents – especially mothers – is regarded as little more than an impediment to their earning power. If we really want to create a better society, we must value children and the families that nurture them far more highly than we do now ... Children are not a private pleasure or a personal burden; they are 100 per cent of the nation's future.[78]

According to the CSJ, the challenges facing children and families in the UK could not be resolved through 'lazy stereotyping of some families' or 'the offensive moral authoritarianism' of Tory leaders.[79] Policies that would ensure children's needs were met, 'empower women,' and get men to share more of the responsibilities of parenthood were viewed as constructive avenues for action. As the commissioners concluded, 'Instead of allowing ourselves to be obsessed with family structures, we need to concentrate on family *functioning*.'[80]

The core trio of themes within *Social Justice* – a reformed welfare state, a renewed focus on education, and an emphasis on responsible individuals and communities – fit well with Tony Blair's personal outlook. As a successful lawyer and MP who grew up in northern

England and Scotland, Blair was strongly committed to repositioning Labour as a balanced centrist formation. Once he became leader in 1994, Blair pursued an intensive process of 'party modernization,' meaning a shift toward less radical policy positions and more centralized elite control. He pressed the party to adopt some CSJ perspectives, including its emphasis on addressing globalization (rather than struggling against it) via reforms to the education, employment, and benefits systems.

To the extent that Blair's statements offered a philosophic vision for New Labour, they revealed an antipathy toward countercultural values of the 1960s, as well as a strong belief that individual opportunities would be enhanced within 'a new concept of citizenship in which rights and responsibilities go together.'[81] He believed personal ambition and duty were compatible; indeed, Blair rejected what he viewed as the indifference of the left – likely including the CSJ – to family breakdown, crime, and 'poor parenting.'[82] One early statement as party leader suggested that his personal beliefs were far more traditional than those of commission members. As Blair told one BBC interviewer, 'If what you are saying to me is do I believe that it is best that kids are brought up in a normal, stable family, the answer is yes, I do believe that.'[83] Blair later tried to nuance these comments, including in a newspaper article where he claimed to 'resent the way the Tories have stigmatised single-parent families ... We want fewer politicians spouting about "family values" and more politicians who value families – whatever their circumstances.'[84]

Yet it remained clear that Tony Blair's core New Labour vision was constructed to allay the fears of middle-class voters. He spoke at length about extending ethical Christian values to build a society in which all responsible individuals could become stakeholders, and give back to their communities as part of the duties owed to that collective unit. As explained by Frank Field, a Labour MP and former anti-poverty campaigner, stakeholding provided the basis for a welfare and pensions system grounded in notions of inclusion and responsibility, rather than marginalization and 'dependence.'[85] This theme of mutual responsibility posed a direct challenge to older Labour emphases on rights, whether those of unionized employees or benefits claimants. As well, Blair's version of the stakeholding society was insistently work-oriented, and remained far less concerned than was the CSJ with questions about women's unpaid caring or other barriers to paid employment.

Above all, Blairite discourse was far to the right of Labour's historic positions on issues of welfare and workfare. By maintaining that personal responsibility was the key to a successful New Britain, Blair endorsed the idea of a 'second-generation welfare' that operated as 'a springboard to success and not a safety net to cushion failure.'[86] In his view, the latter too often 'trapped' people in 'a life on benefits,' thus creating an 'underclass ... excluded from society's mainstream.'[87] Blair also condemned the costs of keeping lone parents on benefits, an expense that he claimed had 'risen by 250 per cent under the Conservatives.'[88]

Blair also stepped onto the contentious terrain of workfare. He argued that since most people on benefits wanted 'independence, dignity, self-improvement, a chance to earn and get on,' it was the job of the welfare system 'to lift people off benefits into work.'[89] This transformation, according to New Labour, likely required a stronger dose of compulsion than had been proposed by the Commission on Social Justice. In one 1996 party document, for example, compulsory workfare programs in the state of California were cited as examples of the 'world's best practice.'[90]

Blair's shadow cabinet floated a number of trial balloons on the shift from a rights-based benefits regime to a responsibility-oriented workfare system. During the fall of 1995, for example, shadow chancellor Gordon Brown announced plans for a welfare-to-work scheme for unemployed youth. Under Brown's plan, people who refused jobs or training options would suffer a 40 per cent benefits cut.[91] Despite intense internal debate over the penalty idea, including among senior ranks of the shadow cabinet, neither Brown nor Blair backed down from the idea. In fact, Labour's New Deal on welfare-to-work, unveiled before the 1997 election campaign, contained a 40 per cent benefits sanction for unemployed youth.[92] Participation in the program would be compulsory for young people between the ages of eighteen and twenty-four, who had been out of work for at least six months.

Labour also proposed a voluntary New Deal scheme for lone parents whose youngest child was at least four years old. Single mothers would be offered a personal interview with a career adviser to discuss training, jobs, and child-care opportunities; because the program was initially designed as a voluntary one, no benefits penalty would follow at that time from failure to participate. In addition, Labour committed itself before the 1997 elections to universal child care for four-year-olds, and said it would try harder to collect child maintenance payments from non-custodial or absent parents (mostly fathers). According to Tony Blair, parental responsibility rested at the heart of the stakeholding bargain. In his words, 'a society without responsibility is the enemy of the society built on merit and hard work.'[93]

New Labour's first official campaign platform, titled *New Labour: Because Britain Deserves Better*, proved to be modest. It lowered expectations of dramatic change by promising to retain Conservative spending estimates for two years and not raise income tax rates.[94] Labour proposed a windfall profits tax on privatized utilities that would finance the New Deal training and placement program. Official party statements referred to the need for a national minimum wage, improved standards of public health care and education provision, constitutional change including a devolution of power to Scotland and Wales, and lowered spending on social benefits through a shift from welfare to paid employment. In general, New Labour's positions during the 1997 election campaign remained general rather than specific, and tended to echo proposals already offered in the previous parliamentary term.[95]

How a Blair government might reach these goals was far from clear. The promise to retain Conservative spending estimates, for example, meant New Labour would face a veritable time bomb during its first year in office. Tory estimates contained a reduction in lone parent rates of social benefits to the rate for couples, a move that abolished the single parent premium for new claimants. This proposal was vigorously criticized, particularly by Labour party women and anti-poverty campaigners, as part of a punitive and mean-spirited attack on lone mothers. New Labour's ability to meet this policy challenge would be put to the test in short order.

In broader terms, it was unclear whether a Blairite Third Way could provide the ideational glue necessary to keep Labour together. Leading party modernizers were outspoken critics of what they saw as a pessimistic and outdated Old Labour reliance on economic redistribution and social 'levelling.' Instead, Blairites wanted to provide enhanced chances for individual success; they spoke of ensuring greater equality of opportunity via education and training, for example, rather than increased equality of results via steep tax rates at the high end. The terms social inclusion, mutual responsibility, and stakeholding were elevated above traditional words such as poverty, marginalization, and inequality. This shift raised serious doubts among progressive observers, who questioned whether New Labour offered much more than a reconstituted liberalism for the 1990s. To critics on the left, Blair's talk of 'a hand up, not a hand out' sounded eerily close to the rhetoric of US Democrats, as did his elevation of personal responsibility and duty above notions of rights and social citizenship.[96]

Conclusions

At first glance, the social policy campaign promises of Bill Clinton, Jean Chrétien, and Tony Blair seemed to differ markedly. Clinton was the only candidate of the three to propose an explicitly time-limited social assistance system, for example, while Blair was alone in his ability (as opposition party leader in a unitary state) to promote a voluntary national welfare-to-work scheme for lone mothers. Yet the broad lines of their campaign platforms were arguably more similar than divergent. Moreover, to the extent that their proposals differed, these distinctions were primarily the result of disparate policy traditions in each country that created the benchmark against which change could be measured.

At the level of ideas, Clinton, Chrétien, and Blair all advanced a view that individuals, no matter how modest their origins, could succeed in an opportunity-filled society as long as they were dutiful, responsible, and ambitious. In this respect, all three leaders fashioned a path to power to the right of the historically centre-left positions of their own parties. Clinton, Chrétien, and Blair embraced notions of individual ambition, maintained that the state's key job was enhancing opportunities for individual self-sufficiency, and emphasized the importance of personal duty and responsibility – elements drawn from traditional liberal and conservative doctrines. Like new conservatives, these leaders tended to look negatively on interest group and social movement mobilization, seeing collective action of that variety as inherently less legitimate than the actions of achieving individuals.

Clinton, Chrétien, and Blair also dismissed what they portrayed as the extreme anti-societal notions of their conservative predecessors – by insisting that they were more compassionate, more balanced and less dog-eat-dog social Darwinist than Reagan, Mulroney, or certainly Thatcher. Third Way leaders claimed they drew on the best in liberal, conservative, and social democratic traditions, merging these strengths while rejecting the excesses of either unfettered individualism or unwieldy statism. As Clinton argued with respect to the United States in his 1996 text *Between Hope and History*, 'America is about *both* individual liberty and community obligation.'[97]

The rhetoric of 'post-conservative' elites was in this respect less polarizing than that of their conservative counterparts. Instead of pursuing the same hot button language as Ronald Reagan and George Bush had used in the United States, and Margaret Thatcher and John Major had employed in Great Britain, Bill Clinton and Tony Blair spoke in more muted terms about the challenge of welfare reform. Each attacked what was described as a benefits-dependent underclass that needed normative realignment – but avoided more loaded phrases employed by their predecessors about 'welfare queens' or 'Victorian virtues.' At a discursive level, then, it seemed as if Third Way leaders might adopt a less vengeful and divisive approach to social assistance issues, given their shared emphasis on renewed social cohesion in the wake of corrosive conservative precedents.

Despite varied policy histories in the United States, Canada, and Great Britain, therefore, the paths laid out by Third Way leaders were strikingly parallel in several respects. First, each sought to make the ability to collect social benefits increasingly contingent and conditional, primarily on paid work. Remunerative employment or some form of preparation for it via education, job training, or career counselling was defined by Clinton, Chrétien, and Blair as the main grounds on which legitimate claims to public support could be based. This common theme established a notion of 'work-tested' and, to varying degrees, 'education-tested' social benefits as one crucial component of Third Way welfare reform.

Parallel with work-testing was a second common thread about 'making work pay.' Supporters of this concept recognized that in Anglo-American systems, low benefits were in many cases more attractive than low pay. Moving single mothers from income support programs toward paid employment was particularly challenging, since as residual, meagre, and means-tested as welfare benefits might have been, they at least came with some promise of security plus ancillary benefits. These fringe benefits varied across jurisdictions, but often included such crucial supports as hospital care in the United States, dental and pharmaceutical provisions in Canada, or access to housing and emergency social funds in Britain.

Third Way leaders offered a variety of responses to the dilemma of how to 'work-test' benefits and, at the same time, control social spending. Clearly, the solution for elites who wanted to avoid the negative 'tax-and-spend' images that had plagued their parties in the past was *not* to create masses of public jobs via community works schemes. Far more attractive options rested in operating within the existing labour market to raise or, in the British case, create the minimum wage; provide incentives, subsidies, or tax-based credits to supplement that wage; or extend the welfare system so that low-income households could enjoy some of the benefits that had previously accrued only to social assistance claimants. Each of these proposals involved an expert, technical approach to the problem of welfare 'dependency.' Each promoted an essentially taxified or fiscalized response to the challenge of welfare reform, and shifted the question of how lone mother families would survive from the remit of social service bureaucracies to the more rarified world of finance departments.

Finally, Third Way thinking about welfare policy was noteworthy for its emphasis on ideas of economic or market-tested citizenship. Rather than defending an expansive notion of social citizenship in which the state offered whatever supports were necessary for all citizens to engage at a basic level in each society, Third Way discourse proposed an increasingly tenuous, eroded, or compromised notion of human belonging.[98] In the United States, Democratic talk during the 1992 presidential campaign about 'two years and out' presupposed that basic income support could be a time-limited, transitory offer rather than a permanent, rights-based entitlement. In fact, the proposal resembled North American television promotions for music albums or car wash gadgets, where viewers were instructed to 'hurry, because this offer ends at midnight tonight.'

In Canada and Britain, Third Way campaign promises broke in less visible, but nevertheless significant ways with older social citizenship norms. The Liberal Red Book insisted that individual self-sufficiency was the sole aim of public spending on welfare, and endorsed labour market enhancement projects in New Brunswick and elsewhere that imposed sanctions on people who refused to participate. Similarly, New Labour proposals in Britain for a New Deal for unemployed youth contained a built-in benefits penalty for those who did not choose one of the four available options.

Overall, these core directions in Third Way welfare reform promises reflected a sustained emphasis on individualistic concepts of personal responsibility. In contrast to an inter-war and post-war notion of collective and especially state responsibility for disadvantaged people, the perspective advanced by Bill Clinton, Jean Chrétien, and Tony Blair was one that underlined the responsibility of individuals to take care of themselves and those around them. People could no longer expect to be dependent on state transfers, except if they were actively seeking work or actively making themselves more work-ready. According to Third Way leaders, people from modest social origins could succeed despite the odds. They just needed, in the words of Clinton and Blair, 'a hand up, not a hand out.' The role of the state from this perspective was to act as a facilitator, above all for dutiful, moral action on the part of responsible individuals who took up the opportunities available to them in an ambitious, achieving society.

CHAPTER FOUR

'Post-Conservative' Developments

The promise of Third Way public policy, encapsulated in Anthony Giddens's commitment to rejecting market fundamentalism in favour of a renewed focus on social inclusion, needs to be juxtaposed against performance in office. Two full terms of the Clinton administration, two consecutive Canadian Liberal majority governments and one New Labour majority term provide the empirical grounding for this comparative assessment of 'post-conservative' welfare reform.

Our core conclusions can be summarized as follows. In the United States and Canada, decisions of the Clinton and Chrétien eras replaced shared-cost federal social programs with block grants (or fixed, lump-sum payments), cut spending on cash benefits, awarded greater control over social policy to sub-national governments, and stripped what remained of a national entitlement to income support based on need. This record eclipsed in a regressive way not only Republican and Conservative precedents in this field, but also Democratic and Liberal campaign promises.

In the United States, provisions of the Personal Responsibility and Work Opportunity Reconciliation Act (PRWORA) ended the AFDC program, imposed time limits and work requirements for benefits, insisted all welfare mothers disclose the paternity of their children, and offered financial bonuses to states that reduced non-marital births but kept abortion rates from rising. The Canada Health and Social Transfer eliminated what had been an open-ended cost sharing deal for provincial and territorial social assistance and social service programs, but included none of the socially invasive regulations about paternity or illegitimacy contained in US reforms of the same period. Since the Transfer did not prohibit the introduction of such provisions by provinces, some sub-national conservative governments (including in wealthy jurisdictions such as Ontario) moved directly into the breach that opened up in 1996.

In Britain, the Blair government instituted a voluntary job counselling, training, and placement program for single parents, during the same term as it carried out a Tory promise to scrap lone parent premiums for social benefits. Overall, New Labour's directions in office were more consistent with Third Way expectations than were those of Democratic and Liberal political executives in the US and Canada. Yet Tony Blair's campaign talk about rebuilding frayed fabrics and promoting social inclusion gave way over time to far less tolerant language. For example, Prime Minister Blair spoke in 1998 of ending 'the something-for-nothing welfare state,'[1] while New Labour's first minister for social security, Harriet Harman, insisted that 'life is about work, not just about claiming benefits.'[2] Given the consistent emphasis of Blair and his colleagues on notions of personal duty and responsibility, these statements suggested that during a second term in office, Labour might adopt the more punitive directions of North American welfare reform initiatives.

Three common threads linked 'post-conservative' social policy records in the United States, Canada, and Great Britain. First, beleaguered social citizenship norms in each of these countries came under sustained siege during the mid-1990s and following. The idea of a fulsome right to social engagement, available to all regardless of sex, economic status, race, family status, or other factors was clearly endangered by the highly invasive terms of PRWORA, signed in the summer of 1996 by President Clinton. Decisions in Canada to eliminate most federal guidelines for social programs (except in the field of health care) as of 1996 opened the way for provinces to adopt elements of US welfare reform policy, including socially conservative, 'pro-family' regulations along with compulsory work for welfare. Changes to the social assistance appeals process in North America directly undermined any assumption of a latent right to benefits.[3] In all three countries, means-tested income support schemes became increasingly temporary, transitional, and conditional, and contained more visible penalties as time passed.

Second, Third Way leaders tended to prioritize pro-market, paid-work-is-all-that-matters principles. Blair introduced and Clinton enriched a system of tax-based employment incentives – what we term work-tested benefits – that differed from traditional social spending programs. The expansion of the Earned Income Tax Credit under the Clinton administration, the creation of a National Child Benefit in Canada during the Chrétien years, and the introduction of a Working Families Tax Credit by New Labour in Britain all reflected growing reliance on complex fiscal manoeuvres to 'fix' social problems.

Third, by operating in the arcane domain of economists and tax specialists rather than the more accessible world of social workers and anti-poverty activists, these provisions tended to move questions about human needs from the remit of social service and labour departments to the taxified purview of finance or treasury departments. A technical discourse about income credits or work incentives thus overshadowed older concerns about food, shelter, basic income, and labour market regulation, as a fiscalized and work-tested outlook came to dominate Anglo-American social policy debates.

In short, we maintain, a crucial part of the Third Way record rested in its promotion of not only a tenuous and compromised form of social citizenship, but also a work-tested, increasingly fiscalized view of welfare policy. At the level of explanation, these patterns can be linked to a pragmatic recognition by Clinton, Chrétien, and Blair that it was easier to run with than oppose the prevailing moralistic climate of opinion on welfare reform. Hiding new social expenditures in tax credits for employed adults provided a convenient alternative to higher-visibility and often unpopular spending programs that rested outside the tax regime. Moreover, particularly in the United States and Canada, fiscal and decentralist pressures from an energized political right meant that the 1990s were 'post-conservative' in name only. Both Bill Clinton and Jean Chrétien appropriated conservative language and arguments in their efforts to claim credit for lowering welfare spending and, at the same time, increasing the flexibility available to sub-national governments in federal systems. Given that US states and Canadian provinces could and did reach independent decisions about welfare programs, it was not surprising that North American social policy assumed an increasingly variegated and decentralized character through the Third Way years.

Clinton-Era Welfare Reform

Despite the prominence given to 'ending welfare as we know it' in the 1992 Democratic campaign platform, White House proposals on this subject were slow to get off the drawing board. Lengthy delays with the 1993 economic plan resulted in part from a growing sense inside the new administration that the fiscal situation of the federal government rendered unworkable much of the *Putting People First* agenda. As detailed by Bob Woodward of the *Washington Post*, the Clinton inner circle was badly fractured once deficit hawks in top White House staff and cabinet positions (including Treasury Secretary Lloyd Bentsen and Federal Reserve Board chairman Alan Greenspan) pushed aside supporters of an 'investing in people' agenda (including Labor Secretary Robert Reich).[4] As Reich described in his account of the lengthy battles surrounding the 1993 budget, deficit hawks in Congress and the administration pressed for and won a $500 billion deficit reduction over five years that effectively meant 'the investment agenda is stone-dead.'[5]

Clinton's comprehensive health care reform proposal of 1993–4, described as an ambitious plan for 'inclusive managed competition,' became bogged down in conflicts with congressional Republicans. After months of bitter wrangling, the president's plan never reached a vote on Capitol Hill.[6] Studies of this particular policy failure suggest that House Republicans under the leadership of Newt Gingrich consciously chose to deny Clinton a victory on health care as a way of winning back control of Congress later that year. Gingrich's strategy relied on cultivating fear among middle-class Americans that the Clinton plan would jeopardize their existing health insurance arrangements.[7]

Given the administration's early problems with economic and health care policy, it is not surprising that the 1994 Clinton welfare plan, known as the Work and Responsibility Act (WRA), had an uneven start. Democratic experts on Capitol Hill, including Senator Daniel Patrick Moynihan of New York, disputed the White House decision to delay welfare debates in order to address health care first.[8] Not only was the president weakened by the health care loss, but also his welfare plan arrived in Congress after more than twenty other bills on the subject had already been introduced.[9] In short, the administration ventured into a veritable policy minefield in June 1994.[10]

Clinton's Work and Responsibility Act reflected the influence of David Ellwood and Mary Jo Bane as senior administration officials; the plan set out a two-year time limit for cash benefits beginning at age eighteen, after which recipients would have to find either private sector work or else accept government-provided community service jobs.[11] Child care was provided for the offspring of welfare recipients, if the latter enrolled in education or work programs, and could be extended after parents left the AFDC rolls. AFDC recipients who did not attend school or job training programs, or did not look for work, would lose their benefits.

In order to make paid employment more attractive, Clinton's bill raised the earnings and savings disregards for people who combined work and benefits. Under its phase-in provisions, about 10 per cent of AFDC households would enter government or government-subsidized jobs within six years of the bill's passage. Although the WRA did not include a child support assurance scheme, it established a national system to raise support collection rates and penalize fathers who failed to pay maintenance (by withholding drivers' licences, for example).

Several elements of the WRA echoed social conservative ideas that had over time penetrated the Democratic party. First, the plan required welfare applicants to identify the father of each child and compelled mothers to help locate those fathers. Second, the WRA permitted states to impose a child exclusion rule or 'family cap,' defined as a ceiling on benefits to households so that payments would not increase for children conceived or born while their mothers were on AFDC. Third, the WRA required teenage mothers on benefits to live with an adult rather than on their own.

In budgetary terms, the WRA was projected to cost about $9.5 billion over five years; this money would be recouped by narrowing the eligibility rules for existing programs.[12] Under the Clinton plan, non-citizens would be denied AFDC, disability insurance, and Food Stamps benefits, and denied access to low-income pay supplements under the Earned Income Tax Credit.[13] As well, people who were disabled owing to drug or alcohol use would be disqualified from receiving social benefits.

Although many elements of the Clinton plan (including changes to eligibility rules to pay for the scheme) were repugnant to progressive social policy campaigners, these same provisions were castigated as overly soft or weak by Republican leaders. For example, conservative politicians criticized what they saw as loopholes in the legislation that allowed welfare recipients to work part-time rather than full-time. During the summer of 1994, the same partisan intransigence that had characterized health care debates surfaced once again, and this time Republicans blocked the WRA as part of their successful campaign to win back control of both houses of Congress in midterm elections.

Once they held a majority of seats on Capitol Hill, Republicans began the process of translating the broad proposals contained in their

1994 election platform, the Contract with America, into social policy. The Contract promised to 'reduce government dependency, attack illegitimacy, require welfare recipients to work, and cut welfare spending.'[14] In early 1995, Republicans in the House of Representatives drafted a bill that not only ended AFDC as a national shared-cost program, but also eliminated any entitlement or rights-based eligibility to benefits on the grounds of need. In place of AFDC, they proposed a system of block transfers to the states that imposed minimal federal standards, and denied cash payments to unmarried teenage parents.[15] Senate Republicans viewed the latter provision as too harsh, but retained the fundamentally decentralist, budget-cutting rationale that rested behind proposals coming from the lower house.

Complex negotiations ensued among congressional and White House players between the fall 1994 elections and the eventual passage of the Personal Responsibility and Work Opportunity Reconciliation Act (PRWORA) in the summer of 1996. Much of this haggling centred around the president's insistence, in his own words, on a 'welfare reform agreement that is tough on work and responsibility, but not tough on children and on parents who are responsible and want to work.'[16] Clinton believed that some floor needed to be placed under state-level spending, so that welfare and training programs did not disappear completely. As well, he endorsed a continuation of Medicaid and Food Stamps as entitlement-based programs, unlike Republicans, who planned to transform both schemes into block grants.

Ultimately, the emphasis of *Putting People First* on mandated work requirements, time-limited benefits, and extended job training programs was trumped by the even more punitive and restrictive terms of the Contract with America. Despite strong opposition among some Democrats, including a few members of his own cabinet, Clinton signed PRWORA – which stood as a largely Republican welfare reform initiative. More drastic than earlier legislation of the Reagan/Bush years (including the 1988 Family Support Act), the 1996 bill aimed to cut federal expenditures by about $55 billion over six years by ending any legally enforceable right of individuals to collect social assistance, defining time-based benefit limits, and further off-loading program responsibility to state governments. PRWORA eliminated existing AFDC and JOBS programs, and replaced them with Temporary Assistance for Needy Families (TANF) block grants to states, under which sub-national governments 'have the broad flexibility to determine eligibility, method of assistance, and benefit levels.'[17] The legislation imposed 'hard time limits,' meaning adults could receive welfare benefits to a lifetime maximum of five years, but less if states so decide. States had six years as of 1996 to ensure that half of their welfare recipients were in work activities, meaning 50 per cent of all single parents on welfare were expected to work thirty hours per week by 2002.[18]

By repealing older federal entitlement provisions, PRWORA undermined the ability of potential welfare recipients to appeal any state-level denial of benefits. Due process protections that had evolved through sixty years of case law development in the United States were essentially swept into the history books by a legislative text that only obligated states to set forth 'objective criteria' for eligibility and 'opportunities ... to be heard in a State administrative or appeal process.'[19] The content of the criteria to be applied in determining eligibility and, more importantly, the bases on which denials of benefits or services could be appealed were left open to the discretion of dozens of subnational units. Neither judges nor litigants could rely any longer on a national entitlement as the foundation for discussion; this shift suggested to one expert commentator that 'a piecemeal system of rights and protections, or lack thereof, will gradually develop.'[20]

Of particular interest to feminist analysts were the components of PRWORA that dealt with paternity and out-of-marriage births. Under the terms of the legislation, all welfare mothers were compelled to disclose the paternity of their children. Teenage mothers had to live with their parents or other adults, and participate in education or training programs, to be eligible for assistance. Moreover, states that successfully reduced out-of-wedlock births without increasing abortion rates became eligible for extra federal funds under the terms of an 'illegitimacy bonus.' States were offered the chance to impose child exclusion rules or 'family caps.' Overall, the 1996 legislation eliminated any legally enforceable right of individuals to obtain social assistance and introduced provisions that, in the words of political scientist Gwendolyn Mink, 'pressure poor single mothers to surrender their civil rights as a condition of economic assistance.'[21]

Leaders of several American women's organizations were harshly critical of PRWORA, and strongly opposed President Clinton's decision to sign it. National Organization for Women (NOW) president Patricia Ireland participated in a hunger strike against the bill as well as a three-week vigil near the White House to try to pressure Clinton to veto it. Ireland summarized her objections as follows: '[W]ith a stroke of his pen, Bill Clinton dismantled the New Deal and replaced it with a

Raw Deal for poor women and children.'[22] Former NOW president Eleanor Smeal maintained that ending AFDC 'eliminates the safety net for women and children and forces women into a jobless workforce without making any provisions for job creation.'[23] A prominent group of women writers and academics, known as the Women's Committee of One Hundred, organized during this same period to fight PRWORA and develop alternatives to it.[24]

At a practical level, feminists questioned several core assumptions behind the 1996 reforms: first, that large numbers of women on welfare who had limited skills, little education, literacy problems, small and in some cases disabled children, plus a history of traumatic life experiences (including violent abuse) could easily find and keep paid work; second, that the paid work they found would provide adequate household income; third, that existing child-care arrangements were of sufficient quality and quantity to warrant forcing single mothers into paid employment, with the attendant loss of a parent's presence at home; and finally, that the various sanctions available to states under PRWORA constituted acceptable strategies for changing human behaviour.

In particular, NOW contended that the offer of federal 'illegitimacy bonuses' as high as $25 million to states that reduced non-marital births without increasing abortion rates would likely lead to more unsafe, illegal abortions. Similarly, the group opposed withdrawing 25 per cent or more of benefits paid to women who refused to identify each child's father. According to NOW, survivors of incest or other forms of violence could not reasonably be expected to want contact with the father, and should not face financial sanctions if they refused to do so.[25]

Given these criticisms, why did President Clinton sign PRWORA? A strategic calculus argument suggests his move was contingent on the ability to claim credit for reducing social spending and 'fixing' welfare by rewarding work, and also avoid blame by shifting already devolved program responsibility to state governments. Clinton's pragmatic approach to winning power and retaining it meant he was prepared to adopt the moralistic language of social policy conservatives, tone it down slightly for middle-of-the-road consumption, and then claim that he had responded to public demands to 'end welfare as we know it.'[26] Within this calculus, the concerns of progressive campaigners about punitive sanctions against women and perverse incentives for state governments were rendered irrelevant.

Yet consistent with feminist claims about the unequal consequences of seemingly gender-neutral laws, eliminating AFDC as a federal entitlement program and replacing it with a more residual, decentralized, and socially invasive regime placed much of the human burden of welfare reform in the 1990s on impoverished single-mother households, more than half of them with minority backgrounds.[27] As Frances Fox Piven, a distinguished social scientist who was active in the Women's Committee of One Hundred, remarked in 1996, welfare reform was an effective issue for Clinton and others once it 'became an argument about why poor women were to blame for so much that was wrong with America.'[28]

Insiders suggested that Clinton decided to sign PRWORA after pollster Dick Morris convinced him that vetoing it would bring defeat in the fall 1996 election.[29] The president's public statements tried to fudge matters by maintaining that the legislation passed by Congress had 'serious flaws,' but was 'a real step forward for our country, our values, and for people who are on welfare.'[30] This perspective was at odds with the position of Clinton's appointee as secretary of health and human services, Donna Shalala, and other cabinet members who had lost earlier debates over the 1993 budget, including Robert Reich.[31] Senior officials in Shalala's department who were charged with implementing the 'ending welfare as we know it' pledge, including assistant secretaries David Ellwood, Mary Jo Bane, and Peter Edelman, resigned to protest Clinton's decision to make a deal with the Republicans.

In a harshly worded account titled 'The Worst Thing Bill Clinton Has Done,' Edelman went public with his criticisms, once the president had secured re-election. In Edelman's view, the welfare system 'contributed to chronic dependency among large numbers of people' and needed to be fixed, 'but the bill that President Clinton signed is not welfare reform. It does not promote work effectively, and it will hurt millions of poor children by the time it is fully implemented.'[32] Edelman maintained that Republicans had used Clinton's rhetoric on time limits and 'ending welfare' in order to ensnare him in their own web, which featured a five-year lifetime limit on cash benefits, no federal eligibility standards, and the elimination of any national entitlement to cash assistance.

PRWORA critics who quit the administration frequently cited a 1995 study commissioned by the Department of Health and Human Services. It showed that, if implemented, the leading welfare reform bill drafted by Senate Republicans would leave an additional one million

American children in poverty.[33] This number was subsequently revised upward because of additional spending cuts to Food Stamps, disability benefits, Medicaid, and child nutrition programs in the 1996 bill.[34] Ex–insiders portrayed PRWORA as a mean-spirited bill that annihilated much of the federal welfare state via severe spending cuts and jurisdictional decentralization.

In Peter Edelman's words, 'The bill closes its eyes to all the facts and complexities of the real world and essentially says to recipients, Find a job. That has a nice bumper-sticker ring to it. But as a one-size-fits-all recipe it is totally unrealistic.'[35] Parallel with problems that had emerged under the 1988 Family Support Act, critics argued, PRWORA's budget for training and child-care costs would fall short by billions of dollars. Compared with earlier periods, states would be more free after 1996 to shift around federal block monies and their own funds, and could turn over welfare programs to other units such as counties or church and private sector organizations.

In his account, David Ellwood alleged that administration opponents had twisted beyond recognition the very phrases he had helped to craft for the 1992 presidential campaign.[36] Expressions like 'ending welfare as we know it' or 'two years and you're off' meant to the Clinton team that AFDC would be replaced by a better system of guaranteed jobs at the end of two years on cash benefits. According to Ellwood, specialists inside the administration could not find the funds to pay for firm job guarantees, nor could they hold off competing demands from economic conservatives for less spending, reduced government regulation, and more decentralization, and from social conservatives for tight new rules to promote traditional 'family values.' Any coalition among these unwieldy elements was destined to produce legislation that was short on funds, long on state-level control, and riddled with rigid, ideologically driven rules. The utter unworkability of reform proposals coming out of both houses of Congress after the 1994 elections, according to Ellwood, suggested that the Republicans' 'real goal is to end federal spending on welfare entirely ... [T]his is the first step on that slippery slope.'[37]

Critics who left the Clinton administration also intimated that an even more ominous future faced poor American women. Both Mary Jo Bane and Peter Edelman, who published separate reflections in early 1997, argued that directing such a large share of public training monies to 'current or past welfare recipients – almost all of whom are women – is likely to be self-defeating.'[38] As Edelman argued, 'By allocating to long-term welfare recipients such a large share of the limited resources available for jobs and training, we may be draining funds and attention from others who deserve to be a higher priority. Inner-city young men come to mind.'[39] This outlook set the stage for a potentially debilitating struggle for pieces of a shrunken pie between poor, often minority women versus poor, often minority men, all in the context of one of the world's richest societies.

Two actions of the first Clinton term that coincided with campaign promises involved increases to the national minimum wage (effective in 1996 and following) as well as the Earned Income Tax Credit (EITC).[40] The latter targeted adults working for pay who might otherwise find social assistance to be more attractive than employment. Although the 1993 rise in the EITC paralleled the position contained in *Putting People First*, the increase was less than three-fourths of that requested by President Clinton. One assessment of congressional manoeuvres surrounding the EITC concluded that even though Republican pressures to reduce federal spending limited the money available for many initiatives, the congruence between an enriched EITC and middle-class pressures to reward work over welfare ensured some increase in the tax credit.[41]

The growth of the EITC during the Clinton years demonstrated the increasingly taxified or fiscalized character of US social policy. Budget changes in 1993 injected more than $20 billion over five years into tax credits to supplement low-income families in which at least one parent was working for pay.[42] By 1996, US federal spending on this low-income credit reached nearly $25 billion, or roughly twice the level of federal spending on the old AFDC program.[43] The EITC only applied, however, to workers who filed a tax return. One account estimated that as many as two million eligible low-wage earners in the US failed to receive refunds because they did not file a return.[44]

Optimists hoped the second Clinton term might prove distinct from the first, since Republican efforts to win back the presidency in 1996 and strengthen their control on Capitol Hill in 1998 were both unsuccessful. Yet Clinton's vulnerability to right-wing critics seemed to grow over time, as evidenced by Republican efforts to impeach him in the Monica Lewinsky scandal. From a feminist perspective, the president's behaviour with a young White House intern, and his sustained refusal to admit what had occurred even to his own family, revealed a very tenuous understanding of one of his favourite themes, personal responsibility.

Clinton's second administration continued in much the same vein as the first, building a work-oriented social policy regime that operated in large part via the tax system. The White House championed tax credits for employers who hired long-term welfare recipients, for example, and endorsed Food Stamps benefits for people on social assistance who were seeking paid work. As promised in his 1996 re-election bid, Clinton reinstated government benefits for legal immigrants who had been denied them under the terms of PRWORA.

In summary, the 'post-conservative' social policy record in the United States offered little for progressives to celebrate. Increases to the minimum wage and the Earned Income Tax Credit, combined with improvements in child-care funding plus child support enforcement that were folded into the PRWORA legislation, could not counter the very negative weight of ending the national cash benefit entitlement, imposing time-limited benefits, decentralizing control, and imposing more rigid, socially conservative regimentation in the lives of poor women. The constraints on appeals processes that were predicted to follow from a lack of due process language in the text of the 1996 legislation compounded a sense of impending doom.

These developments pointed toward the narrowing of social citizenship as one key legacy of the Clinton era. As well, US welfare policies became increasingly work-oriented, even work-obsessed, after 1993, while older federal social spending programs like AFDC were supplanted by tax-based initiatives including the EITC. This combination of eroded social citizenship norms, a more taxified or fiscalized approach to welfare policy, and an overwhelming focus on paid employment as the *sine qua non* of useful human activity stood as crucial policy hallmarks of Third Way reform in the United States.

The Chrétien Government Record

Like the Clinton Democrats, the Chrétien Liberals veered sharply to the right during their first term in office, as concerns over deficit reduction grabbed the spotlight in discussions of social policy. This shift away from the priorities of the 1993 Red Book was difficult to discern, since the initial signals revealed in the October 1994 federal green paper, *Improving Social Security in Canada*, suggested a moderate emphasis on modernizing programs 'for the 21st century.'[45] Only two of the approximately ninety pages of the green paper document, however, were devoted to child care, a key plank in the 1993 Liberal platform.[46]

During this same period, the House of Commons Standing Committee on Human Resources Development held public hearings in dozens of cities and towns, and asked tens of thousands of Canadians to fill out workbooks offering their suggestions for change.[47] The committee's January 1995 report presented some views that were consistent with those of the Red Book, along with others that reflected Reform party and Bloc Québécois (BQ) preferences for a limited federal welfare state presence.

At the same time, the federal Department of Finance was locked in virtual crisis mode over what it saw as back-to-the-wall fiscal pressures. If the proverbial 'freight train' that eventually doomed White House welfare reform ideas originated among Republicans on Capitol Hill, then the analogous vehicle in Canada originated among Finance and leading federal opposition interests, notably the BQ and Reform.[48] Ultimately, the massive changes that followed from the February 1995 federal budget bore closer resemblance to Finance and opposition positions than to the Red Book document.

As federal minister of finance, Paul Martin maintained that unless Canada's debt and deficit were brought under control, the country risked a huge loss of economic confidence – including lower international bond ratings. His ability to make this case was assisted by the fact that neither the federal government green paper nor the House of Commons review had generated a coherent, fiscally sound proposal for policy change. Simply put, the demands for more jurisdictional decentralization emanating from the BQ and Reform parties, together with an unrelenting emphasis by Reform and business groups on lower taxes and balanced budgets, could not mesh with the Red Book's focus on strengthening the federal role in new or improved social programs.[49]

Into the vacuum stepped Paul Martin, a formidable cabinet presence who had placed second behind Jean Chrétien in the 1990 Liberal leadership race. As a successful entrepreneur and scion of a prominent Liberal family, Martin had built a loyal following both inside and outside the party. Moreover, as an astute parliamentarian from the Montreal area, he understood the need for the federal government – on the eve of the 1995 Quebec referendum – to demonstrate flexibility and openness toward decentralist arguments. Martin used each source of leverage to maximum effect, as Finance went about redefining the contours of the Canadian welfare state.

Unveiled in 1995 and effective as of 1996–7, the Canada Health and Social Transfer (CHST) replaced the older Canada Assistance Plan

(CAP) and Established Programs Financing regimes with a less regulated system of block transfers to the provinces, reduced funding for those transfers, and combined social assistance with health and education monies. The CHST involved major reductions in federal controls over how provinces spent money – with virtually no conditions attached, for example, to how much sub-national governments devoted to health versus post-secondary education versus social assistance.

More than $7 billion were slated to be cut from federal grants to the provinces during the Transfer's first two years of operation.[50] This constituted about a 40 per cent reduction in federal social transfers to the provinces.[51] The switch from an open-ended cost sharing framework between the federal and provincial governments under the 1966 Canada Assistance Plan to the close-ended block transfer scheme under the CHST beginning in 1996 demonstrated to many observers that deficit reduction had become the top priority of the federal cabinet. According to one account, introducing the CHST allowed the finance department in Canada to 'impose its own unilateral fiscal fix on the country's social programs.'[52]

The social welfare implications of ending CAP and replacing it with the CHST were far from trivial. As political scientist Susan Phillips observed at the time, merging all social transfers into a single block grant

> directly pits the aspirations of middle-class Canadians, keen on assuring affordable, quality health care and postsecondary education for their children, against the interests of lower income Canadians who might need support from social assistance. In a zero sum game played with significantly fewer resources, this will exacerbate class tensions in a way that has been uncharacteristic of this country. Ultimately, the CHST is likely to force a redefinition of ourselves as a political community and contribute to making Canada not only a leaner, but a meaner nation.[53]

Analysts were especially concerned about the loss of CAP principles or guidelines that had been in place since 1966. Under the CHST, provinces and territories were no longer obliged to offer social assistance and services to all people in economic need, nor would mandatory appeals processes exist for those denied support, nor were work requirements prohibited as a condition for receiving assistance.[54] The only CAP principles that remained in force as of 1996 concerned mobility rights, meaning the right to apply for social benefits regardless of province of origin. As well, the popular public health care standards that had been in place under the Canada Health Act continued under the terms of the Transfer. In short, sub-national governments could, as part of their own policy reforms, determine their own welfare eligibility criteria, require mandatory participation in workfare programs, and impose very narrow terms of recourse or appeal for people denied benefits.

Like Bill Clinton's decision to sign PRWORA, Jean Chrétien's decision to pursue the CHST reflected an ingenious and highly pragmatic strategy of claiming credit and avoiding blame.[55] Creating the CHST enabled federal Liberals to argue that they were taking seriously the need to control spending, reduce the deficit, and encourage policy flexibility in a diverse federation. Like the Clinton Democrats, the Chrétien Liberals could claim that their actions responded to public concerns about overly generous social assistance programs.[56] Moreover, Canadian federal politicians managed to escape responsibility for the damage caused by these changes by using the complex terms of federal/provincial fiscal relations as a cover.

This view needs to be refined, however, in light of feminist arguments about unequal consequences. The CHST eliminated what had been an open-ended federal cost-sharing arrangement under CAP to pay half of eligible provincial and territorial social assistance and social service expenditures. Roughly 70 per cent of single parents in Canada, most of them women, received some form of social assistance in the 1990s. As well, social service funding under CAP included subsidies for low-income child care and shelters for battered women.[57] The reduction in funds going to the provinces under the CHST, together with an end to older CAP principles that persons in need had the right to income and to an appeal of welfare decisions, revealed a clear fiscal and jurisdictional retreat by the federal government from an area of critical importance to poor women.[58]

Chrétien-era social policy decisions also held important labour market implications. The bulk of Canadian welfare state workers in the education, health care, and social service fields were female, and they were more likely than women in the US to be unionized public sector employees.[59] Canadian women, therefore, faced specific risks under the CHST both as welfare state clients and workers, even though the terms of the Transfer contained none of the socially invasive regulations about paternity, illegitimacy, and teenage motherhood found in American reforms of the same period.

Within months of the 1995 federal budget, a vigorously right-wing Conservative party won power in Ontario, Canada's most populous province. Under the leadership of Premier Mike Harris, the Ontario Tories slashed welfare payments by more than 20 per cent directly after taking office.[60] Next, they introduced what political scientist Leah Vosko termed 'Canada's first mandatory welfare-to-work program.'[61] The 1997 Ontario Works Act eliminated older provisions for the differential treatment vis-à-vis employment of single mothers, poor adults without children, and disabled people.[62] According to official documents, Ontario Works set out to 'establish a program that recognizes individual responsibility and promotes self-reliance through employment' by offering 'temporary financial assistance to those most in need while they satisfy obligations to become and stay employed.'[63] The Ontario legislation explicitly allowed cash assistance to be contingent on education, job training, or work participation by recipients, and permitted authorities to refuse assistance to people who failed to comply with those conditions; a related bill prohibited the unionization of people in workfare programs.[64]

The 1997 law also made it more cumbersome and difficult to appeal a denial of benefits, in part by introducing rigid rules on the timing of notices to appeal. Other Ontario Conservative decisions reduced spending on legal aid programs, and raised the intensity and visibility of anti-fraud campaigns. For example, the provincial government created a telephone hotline to solicit welfare fraud information from members of the public, and made people convicted of welfare fraud ineligible for benefits for the rest of their lives.[65] Harris-era legislation offered private sector firms the opportunity to operate job training, work placement, and other workfare-related programs, and awarded broad discretionary powers over the determination of eligibility criteria, asset limitations, assistance levels, rules affecting appeals, and penalties for failure to comply with the legislation to the provincial cabinet. As a result, important social policy decisions would no longer necessarily be implemented by public bureaucrats, nor would they be subject to debate in the provincial legislature, legislative committees, or public hearings.

The specific terms of Harris-era regulations governing single mothers paralleled US welfare reform directions in Wisconsin and elsewhere. Ontario Conservatives abolished provisions dating from 1987 that allowed benefits recipients to live with a member of the opposite sex for three years without financial penalty. As of 1995, cohabitation arrangements were assumed to equal 'spouse-in-the-house' relationships, and benefits could be denied as a result. This decision meant that as many as ten thousand potential welfare recipients in Ontario, overwhelmingly women, were deemed ineligible for benefits, resulting in a savings to the provincial government of about $45 million per year.[66] Single mothers of children aged three years and older were compelled to select one of the following options or else face sanctions: (a) enter a skills training program, (b) sign up with a private sector broker who would be paid to match the person with a job, or (c) perform community service work for up to seventeen hours a week.[67] Given that the Harris government reduced spending on subsidized child-care spaces during the same period, many mothers with young children found it hard to meet these conditions.

As well, the Ontario Works Act imposed an 'obligation to pursue resources' on all welfare claimants, meaning people on benefits had to make 'reasonable efforts to obtain compensation or realize a financial resource or income that the person may be entitled to or eligible for.'[68] Critics worried that this clause could be used to require social assistance applicants to prove that they had tried and failed to obtain maintenance support from ex-partners.[69] Overall, a crucial goal of the Ontario provisions was to reduce government spending by shifting support payments away from the state, especially toward fathers; this change moved the burden that followed from identifying and pursuing non-custodial fathers onto the shoulders of mothers and children.

Much of the social assistance delivery machinery in Ontario rested in the hands of local governments, the same municipalities that saw their size, authority, and policy responsibilities vastly altered during the Harris years. Six local government units that made up the core of Canada's largest city, Toronto, were forcibly amalgamated by the Ontario Conservatives in 1998. Once cities including Toronto began to resist the Harris agenda on mandatory workfare, in part because of pressure from their own unionized public service employees, the Tories decided to make fiscal transfers to cities and towns contingent on compliance with the terms of Ontario Works.[70]

Other federal government actions in this period held equally important consequences. The changeover from CAP to the CHST was accompanied by the introduction of a National Child Benefit, under which universal family allowances (ended during the Mulroney years) were replaced by a new benefit payable primarily to low-income employed parents through the tax system. As of the year 2000, the National Child

Benefit was not passed on to parents on welfare in eight of the ten Canadian provinces. The two provinces where it was initially transferred to parents on welfare, New Brunswick and Newfoundland, contained only about 5 per cent of the national population. Supporters maintained the National Child Benefit was a worthy, targeted program for assisting low-income families.[71] Critics portrayed it as little more than 'a work-incentive program' that reinforced the efforts of wealthy and populous Canadian provinces like Ontario to emulate US-style workfare programs.[72]

Even fervent admirers admitted the National Child Benefit was at best a small first step toward reforming social policy in Canada. With a projected cost of $1.7 billion in 2000, it was expected to assist about 12 per cent of low income, single parent families.[73] As welfare expert Margaret Little argued, focusing government attention on 'worthy' workers eligible for new, narrowly targeted programs like the National Child Benefit 'further impoverished unemployable single mothers in relation to the working poor. Through the child tax benefit, single mothers were financially penalized if they were not involved in paid work.'[74]

In the field of child care, Red Book promises to create 50,000 new spaces annually to a total of 150,000 if economic growth reached 3 per cent a year were not fulfilled.[75] Liberals claimed that a combination of lower growth and provincial disinterest caused them to abandon the proposal, although other factors appeared to be at least as significant.[76] In particular, the strength of decentralist and, in the case of the Reform party, anti-deficit voices in the House of Commons after 1993 probably played a crucial role in decisions *not* to follow through on the child care promise and to pursue the CHST.

A similar explanation can be applied to the Liberals' willingness to vacate the social housing field. In 1995 and following, the federal government divested itself of virtually all administrative responsibilities in the area, and left the field open for private sector developers and sub-national governments if they were so inclined. Only two provincial governments, in Quebec and British Columbia, remained active in the social housing field after the federal exit. As one observer noted, the federal withdrawal meant the 'Liberal government has, for the most part, allowed housing issues to be decoupled from social policy debates.'[77]

Powerful BQ and Reform party voices were also reflected in the area of labour market policy. Red Book promises to enhance training and apprenticeship opportunities – as part of a better targeted Unemployment Insurance system – seemed to be upstaged by the same anti-deficit and pro-devolution pressures that shaped the creation of the CHST. Reductions of $8 billion in UI funding, a restructuring under what became known as Employment Insurance, and shifts toward greater provincial control in this area were notable directions in Liberal decision-making after 1993.[78] One of the only labour market actions during the Chrétien years that was consistent with party promises involved a 1996 raise in the federal minimum wage, which applied to federal government employees and workers in federally regulated industries.[79]

Overall, the Chrétien government's first term record entailed reduced spending, less federal control over programs, and, in the words of social policy specialists James Rice and Michael Prince, a further 'lowering of the safety net and a weakening of certain bonds of nationhood and citizenship' that had begun during the Mulroney years.[80] The ability of the federal Liberals to escape blame for the impact of these changes was eased by a fiscal and institutional setting that allowed the presumed benefits of deficit reduction and decentralized policy control to take precedence. The fall-out from policy retrenchment for less affluent interests, including lone mother households on social assistance or part-time women workers seeking to collect maternity benefits under a revised unemployment scheme, was overshadowed by the Liberals' presumed success in eliminating the federal deficit, coupled with their compelling rhetoric about the benefits of flexible federalism.

During their second majority government, the Chrétien Liberals faced ongoing fiscal and decentralist pressures, including threats of another Quebec referendum. One response to these circumstances was the lofty document known as the Social Union Framework Agreement of 1999, a non-constitutional deal that committed the federal government to consult with the provinces before introducing new spending initiatives or programs. This agreement, however, included no provisions for interest group or public consultations.[81]

Liberal social policy largely continued along its first-term path of cost containment and decentralized provision. To the extent that some negative effects of the CHST were redressed, this compensatory action occurred primarily in areas of middle-class priority such as health care and post-secondary education. In short, a strong argument could be made that through his second term, Jean Chrétien (like Bill Clinton) continued to operate, in the words of one critic, as 'the master of left-wing talk and right-wing action.'[82]

In the years following 1993, Chrétien government decisions in the field of social policy were arguably regressive on a number of levels. With respect to notions of social citizenship, ending the Canada Assistance Plan extinguished guidelines in place since 1966 to the effect that persons in need had the right to income support, and the right to appeal denial of that support through a provincially established appeals process. Although CAP had 'prohibited the provinces from requiring social assistance applicants to accept employment *as a condition of receiving assistance*,'[83] the CHST contained no such provision. Provinces and territories were free as of 1996 to experiment with social welfare policies in a context that was devoid of many older provisions, including national entitlements to benefits and services, guaranteed access to an appeals process, and a prohibition against mandatory or 'hard' workfare that linked cash support directly to compliance with job requirements.

By borrowing elements of the W-2 regime from the state of Wisconsin, Ontario Conservatives set a new benchmark for the use in Canada of work-tested social benefits. Under the terms of the Ontario Works Act introduced by the Harris government, lone parents could be denied cash assistance if they failed to comply with the terms of a three-tiered workfare system. Moreover, single mothers who applied for benefits in Ontario risked facing many of the same socially conservative strictures as those enforced in the United States, including mandatory paternity establishment.

Liberal actions at the federal level also helped to create an increasingly taxified and work-tested social policy regime. With the finance department and decentralist opposition parties in lead positions, debates over what constituted a meaningful social citizenship regime, or how single mothers could combine paid work with unpaid caring or nurturing responsibilities, became less and less relevant. Instead, discussions about the future of Ottawa's role in social policy became overwhelmingly fiscal and jurisdictional: How much would it cost to retain shared-cost programs, and how much could be saved by introducing block grants? Which activities could be off-loaded to the provinces to pacify nationalist interests in Quebec and regional interests in Western Canada? Had policy devolution gone too far, if a majority of provinces could transform the means-tested National Child Benefit into a work-tested program?

From the perspective of progressive campaigners, fiscalized approaches to welfare reform during the Chrétien years produced a disappointing policy legacy. In the aftermath of the decentralist and cost-cutting CHST, the National Child Benefit emerged as a taxified and, in most provinces, work-tested program that revealed just how eroded social citizenship had become during the Third Way years in Canada.

New Labour in Power

After winning a majority government in May 1997, Britain's New Labour leaders followed the broad lines of their pre-election social policy blueprint. The long years in opposition had left ample time to create a middle-of-the-road agenda with firmly costed promises. Moreover, compared with US Republicans and Canadian Conservatives, who spoke at length about debt and deficit pressures but did relatively little to address them while they held top executive positions, British Conservatives kept a tighter lid on public spending and bequeathed fewer fiscal surprises to their successors.

This background helps to explain fundamental differences between decisions by the Blair government, on the one hand, and those of the Clinton administration and Chrétien government, on the other. Although New Labour endorsed increased autonomy for Scotland and Wales, and greater authority for local governments throughout Britain, at no time did party modernizers propose a decentralized social policy system comparable to North American federal arrangements. Moreover, unlike both Bill Clinton and Jean Chrétien, Tony Blair was committed to spending more rather than less money on his welfare reform project. This fiscal infusion identified New Labour's trajectory as distinctive from the cost-cutting and off-loading (to states or provinces) orientation of its North American counterparts.

Tony Blair's first major address as prime minister took place at a run-down public housing estate in southeast London, where he set forth plans

> to tackle what we know exists – an underclass of people cut off from society's mainstream, without any sense of shared purpose ... Thirty per cent of people live in a household dependent on a means-tested benefit, which discourages work and encourages people to hide any money that is earned. The task of reshaping welfare to reward hard work is daunting. But we must make absolutely clear that our challenge is to help all those people who are not working with the jobs, the training and the support that they need.[84]

He reiterated the 1997 party manifesto promise to move 250,000 youth aged eighteen to twenty-four from benefits into work via the New Deal program. Youth who had not worked for at least six months and were claiming Jobseekers Allowance unemployment benefits would be offered a 'gateway period' of up to four months for job counselling and advice. They would then select one of four options: subsidized private sector work for up to six months, up to twelve months of full-time education or training in an approved program, voluntary sector work for six months, or environmental task force work for six months.[85] As an incentive to take on New Deal youth, employers were offered a £60 per week wage subsidy plus training allowances for up to six months. Wages or allowances paid to New Deal participants had to at least equal what they would have received on benefits.[86]

New Labour politicians repeated their policy mantra over and over again: 'There is no fifth option.'[87] This expression meant that eighteen- to twenty-four-year-olds who refused to participate in the national New Deal beginning in April 1998 would be denied benefits. The sanctions were initially defined as 100 per cent of benefits for two weeks in the absence of 'good cause,' and 40 per cent of benefits after that point. Youth who refused to participate in the New Deal on a second round would lose full benefits for one month.[88] These sanctions became tougher in the fall of 1999, when maximum penalties increased to a full loss of benefits for six months.

Blair later announced a voluntary welfare-to-work scheme beginning in October 1998 for lone parents on Income Support whose youngest child was five years of age or older. Each lone parent would be invited to meet with a personal adviser who could assist with information on training, part- or full-time jobs, child care arrangements, and in-work benefits. Under the terms of the New Deal for lone parents, Income Support payments would continue during the first two weeks that participants held paid employment. In order to improve access to child care, Chancellor Gordon Brown announced that 50,000 youth would be trained as child care assistants, while funds from the national lottery would be devoted to after-school clubs.[89] A third New Deal program was announced for long-term unemployed people over age twenty-five who had been claiming Jobseekers Allowance for more than two years. Employers who offered jobs to these individuals could claim a £75 per week wage subsidy.[90]

The various New Deals for youth, lone parents, and the long-term unemployed were funded by an anticipated £5.2 billion tax on the windfall or excess profits of utility companies that had been privatized during the Conservative years. At least half of this amount (£$2.6 to £3.5 billion) was targeted at the youth program. By way of contrast, £350 to £450 million was targeted for the age 25 plus group, even though estimates indicated that hundreds of thousands of long-term unemployed people qualified for it during the first year of operation.[91] Only £200 million was dedicated to the voluntary New Deal for approximately 500,000 single mothers of children age five and up. Of this amount, £50 million was committed to child-care costs and the training of child-care workers.[92] Taken as a group, New Deal programs were intended to reinforce in a concrete way New Labour's view that 'rights and responsibilities must go hand in hand, without [the option] of life on full benefit.'[93]

Since New Deal programs offered a variety of training and job options, limited benefit sanctions, and an entirely voluntary approach to lone parents, they attracted relatively muted criticism from progressive campaigners. British trade unions, for example, endorsed New Labour's decisions to impose minimum wage regulations for subsidized New Deal jobs, and to stipulate that firms not lay off regular employees in order to create vacancies for subsidized New Deal workers. Unions objected, however, to New Labour's failure to classify most voluntary sector and environmental task force participants as employees; in their view, this omission meant the latter could be paid less than non–New Deal workers in comparable jobs.[94]

Echoing the ideas of American experts including Mary Jo Bane and David Ellwood, New Deal strategies sought to change the focus of British unemployment and social service bureaucracies from claimant eligibility issues to one-on-one mentoring. Private consultations with personal advisers to establish interests, goals, and a workable job plan were designed to make the New Deal gateway period a crucial stage in building not only résumés and interviewing skills, but also confidence. In media accounts, lone parents who entered the voluntary New Deal stream often cited the program's contributions toward raising their own self-esteem and that of their children. From this perspective, the program was presented as offering lone parents a valuable opportunity to escape isolation at home, often via part-time work during children's school hours.[95]

Official data on various New Deals in action, however, indicated they were considerably less successful than had been anticipated. During its first two years of operation, the New Deal for unemployed youth offered training or work experience to about 80,000 members of the target group.[96] This figure fell short of the Blair government's promise to move 250,000 youth into jobs in four years, which translated into about 125,000 over two years. In the first nine months of the voluntary New Deal for lone parents, about 80,000 adults attended an initial interview, of whom about one-quarter found jobs as a result. The initial data on single parents suggested an overall success rate of less than 10 per cent, since the total number of parents invited to an interview vastly outnumbered those who found jobs.[97]

Observers from across the political spectrum questioned government claims that a 40 per cent drop in youth unemployment occurred during the first two years of the compulsory program, and 70 per cent during the first three years. In their view, economic growth independent of massive public investment in the youth New Deal could have produced the same results. At the point when Gordon Brown initially proposed the idea from the opposition benches, more than 250,000 youth had been unemployed for over six months. New Labour launched the program when only about 100,000 were expected to be in that category.[98] As well, critics claimed, few New Deal placements were offered by top British employers, and few were located in districts with high youth unemployment rates.[99] Even the private sector chair of the New Deal task force admitted that most jobs were offered in three sectors commonly associated with low pay and limited mobility: hospitality, catering, and retail sales.[100]

Official data also showed that many eligible youth chose training over immediate job placement. In some cases, under-25s recruited to subsidized New Deal employment only remained on the job for a short period of time before leaving to pursue a subsidized New Deal training opportunity. Employers were less than delighted, and costs to the public purse were high.[101] Moreover, not all New Deal participants experienced the same national program, since wide variations existed in the quality of staff in local employment offices. Some were highly motivated models of best practice, while others appeared to be mired in an older approach that elevated rule enforcement above all else.[102]

In the same period as it created the New Deal programs, New Labour announced with great fanfare the establishment of a Social Exclusion Unit. This initiative followed from Tony Blair's emphasis on the need to build in Britain a society with greater opportunities, 'where everyone has a stake,' and where 'ambition is matched by compassion, success by social justice, and rewards by responsibility.'[103] Blair's notion of a stakeholder economy was grounded in his view of a wealth-creating (rather than the Old Labour emphasis on a wealth-distributing) system 'in which opportunity is extended, merit rewarded and no group of individuals locked out.'[104] Excluded people, defined by the New Labour elite as those without paid employment who often lived in 'workless households,' formed the target population for the new unit.

Progressive campaigners identified an obvious contradiction between this talk about social exclusion and Blair's decision in the fall of 1997 to reduce the lone parent rate of social benefits for new claimants to the rate for couples, and thus abolish the single parent premium. Announced by the secretary of state for social security, Harriet Harman, this controversial action was congruent with budget estimates inherited from the Conservatives but was inconsistent with what feminist and anti-poverty interests expected from a Labour government. Opponents of the cut estimated it would affect about one million lone parents and their two million children, for a 'trivial' savings of about £60 million per year.[105] The depth of internal discontent over Blair's decision became clear as a major backbench revolt and junior ministerial resignations were registered on the government side in the House of Commons. As a loyal partisan, Harriet Harman valiantly defended the cut to lone parent benefits, even though many people close to her suspected she personally disagreed with it. Within about six months, in July 1998, Harman was removed from Blair's cabinet.[106]

The cut to lone parent benefits served as a lightning rod for left critics of Blairite policy, who argued that the New Labour project was exclusionary in its assumption that people could only be part of society if they were working for pay. As evidence, they cited Harman's memorable 1997 comment to the effect that 'life is about work, not just about claiming benefits.'[107] Subsequent decisions by the New Labour government to cut disability benefits reinforced critics' claims that Blairite modernizers endorsed a narrow, punitive, and work-obsessed approach to social policy reform, even if it remained carefully hidden much of the time. An aide to former party leader Neil Kinnock, for example, alleged that members of the Blair cabinet were 'privately claiming the [lone parents] benefit cut is a piece of social engineering designed to discourage the rise in single parents, something no Minister has yet been prepared to say in public.'[108] When pressed to justify the benefits cuts, Harman and others insisted they would help lone parents be less of a burden on the state. At the same time, New Labour elites claimed these cuts were more than compensated for by the infusion of new monies into the New Deal for lone parents.

Concerns about New Labour's directions in power surfaced as well in debates over the 1999 Welfare Reform and Pensions Act. This legislation introduced changes to pensions and widowed parents' benefits, and established a 'single work-focused gateway' to streamline job placements for unemployed young people. Prime Minister Blair described the broad purpose of the bill in terms of individuals' 'responsibility to accept work, train themselves for jobs, be flexible in the jobs they take and avoid dependency where they can. It marks an end to the something for nothing welfare state. The days of an automatic right to benefit will go. It's tough, but the right thing to do.'[109] Provisions imposing a means test and tighter eligibility rules for new disability benefit claimants were especially contentious. The 1999 bill became a target of sustained protest by a series of previously compliant campaigning groups, including the Child Poverty Action Group.[110] When it reached the floor of the House of Commons, more than 80 Labour MPs, including a handful of newly elected women members, refused to support the legislation.[111]

The negative fallout from debates over benefits changes pushed Tony Blair's government in several unanticipated directions. In the March 1998 budget, New Labour raised Child Benefit levels and, in the framework of its new Working Families Tax Credit (WFTC), offered an expanded child-care tax credit for low-income employed parents. As Chancellor, Gordon Brown announced his commitment to emulating the success of the US Earned Income Tax Credit. Unlike the older Family Credit system established by the British Conservatives, the WFTC would operate as a pay subsidy that rose as earned income increased, reaching a gradual phase-out point that was high enough to encourage work over benefits.[112] Yet unlike the EITC, the WFTC would be delivered via the pay packet rather than the tax system, meaning it imposed a direct administrative burden on low-wage employers. Campaigning groups worried that employers might resist paying the credit; as well, they suspected workers might either be reluctant to ask for it or else unaware that they qualified to collect a credit. Moreover, because the WFTC was usually paid directly to wage earners, feminist groups argued that many women and children who lived in households with a male breadwinner would not benefit from it at all.[113]

The 1999 and 2000 budgets raised Child Benefit levels once again, lowered personal income tax rates, and increased spending on health, education, and the elderly. According to New Labour's perspective, reducing income tax at the bottom end was crucial to 'making work pay,' since it offered another incentive alongside the national minimum wage for people to choose work over benefits. The Blair government also announced its intentions to raise the minimum wage gradually, enrich the WFTC, and extend the four options that had been available only to youth New Deal participants to older unemployed people as of April 2001.

At the same time, New Labour introduced important changes to the New Deal for lone parents. Beginning in April 2001, new and existing Income Support claimants would be compelled to attend a work-focused interview with an employment adviser if their youngest child was five years of age or older. After failing three chances to attend this interview, new applicants would be refused benefits, while existing ones would be penalized about £10 per week. All lone parents would also gain access to three 'new choices.' These included training with a £15 per week benefit bonus, paid work with a £20 per week earnings disregard under Income Support, or paid work with guaranteed wage floors of £155 per week for sixteen hours of part-time or £214 per week for full-time employment.[114] In announcing these changes, Gordon Brown stressed that even though the numbers of lone parents on Income Support had declined since Labour came to power, the percentage in paid work (under 45%) remained significantly below levels in the United States, France, and elsewhere. The chancellor maintained that the new choices available as of 2001 would 'remove old barriers to work' and offer 'help with back-to-work costs and with child care.'[115]

How could British social policy decisions after May 1997 be explained? One crucial factor behind both the New Deal and the decision to cut lone parent benefits rested in the profoundly pragmatic focus of Tony Blair and his New Labour colleagues. Intent on winning power after long years in opposition, Labour party modernizers left little to chance in the run-up to the 1997 elections. Great efforts were taken to ensure that New Labour presented a middle-of-the-road manifesto that contained none of the alleged 'tax and spend' excesses of its Old Labour antecedents. Once installed in government, the Blair team pressed a pro-work, anti-benefits, and pro–personal responsibility approach that was consistent with the individualistic climate of the times.

The relatively weak Conservative opposition facing Tony Blair during his first term, however, contrasted with the far more potent Republican and Reform ranks that confronted Bill Clinton and Jean Chrétien. If Blair was buffeted about on social policy after 1997, it was primarily by his own disgruntled backbenchers and by campaigning groups on the political left – who wondered, for example, why they had to endure nearly twenty years of Tory rule only to have New Labour cut lone parent benefits. In a curious way, the Blair government's pragmatism in office often became a search on the social policy side for innovations that would temper criticisms by progressives rather than conservatives, as was the case in North America. Decisions to enrich the universal Child Benefit or to provide a guaranteed income floor for low-wage workers (via the Working Families Tax Credit) showed New Labour was anxious to blunt criticisms coming from the political left.

From the perspective of women and public policy, this difference between the North American and British political contexts helps to explain why the New Deal was clearly distinguishable from PRWORA as well as the CHST. The New Deal for lone parents, while far less generous than its youth counterpart, provided a net infusion of funds into counselling, child care, and other services. It was far less coercive than both the youth New Deal and many welfare-to-work schemes for single mothers then operating in North America. In short, even though critical questions were raised about the rhetoric and actions of New Labour elites, their New Deal for lone parents diverged in fundamental ways from policies set in place during the 1990s in the United States and Canada.

In the field of labour market policy, the Blair government made significant improvements that had proven impossible during the Thatcher and Major years. Provisions introduced in 1998 and 1999 for a national minimum wage, improved rights of union recognition, and enhanced terms of parental leave and part-time work stood out as crucially important changes.[116] Establishing a national minimum wage, albeit at a rather low starting level of £3.60 per hour for adults, was integral to the welfare-to-work strategy. As in the United States, British Third Way leaders were convinced they had to 'make work pay' in order to encourage people on benefits to take up paid employment. Despite serious qualms about this strategy, many progressive interests saw post-1997 changes in labour market policy as useful, although limited, first steps in the direction of assisting workers – many of them women – in low wage jobs.

The challenges facing New Labour during its first term in office raised important questions about the future of the British welfare state. Would the UK move in the same direction as North American systems by downloading and privatizing more of its social policy apparatus? In the summer of 1997, Harriet Harman announced that three private firms would be allowed to '"shadow" different parts of the Benefits Agency with a view that, if they could demonstrate ways of providing a better standard of service, they might be given the contract to run the agency.'[117] Harman's junior colleague at Social Security, Frank Field, endorsed what he called greater 'local discretion,' meaning local social security departments could better determine how to allocate their budgets than bureaucrats in Whitehall. Field was not prepared, however, to support disparate local benefit rates.[118]

The Blair government also grappled with the question of more versus less means-testing of social benefits. Labour's 1997 campaign manifesto said universal child benefits would be retained, and a coalition of experts inside the party (including Frank Field) endorsed the use of more universal and social insurance approaches instead of wider means-testing. Field maintained that a 'poverty trap' was created by rigid, residualized schemes that discouraged work, thus pushing people who could not survive on benefits alone into a dependent, morally deficient, and oftentimes criminal underclass.[119]

By way of contrast, Tony Blair, Gordon Brown, and others seemed anxious to expand means-testing so that limited public resources could be spent on people who were, in the prime minister's words, in 'genuine need.'[120] Parallel with Canadian positions dating from the Mulroney years, British arguments for means-testing after 1997 claimed universal benefits were unacceptably expensive. Moreover, they worried that Frank Field's expansive social insurance ideas would require large start-up investments and ultimately leave many people without even the minimal coverage that existed under older means-tested schemes.[121] Unfortunately for New Labour, the internal conflict over means-testing entered the national spotlight at the same time as the lone parent benefit crisis. According to a December 1997 press report, senior officials in the Treasury wanted the new government to tax or means-test all benefits.[122]

Finally, Labour decision-makers faced the contentious question of compulsory versus voluntary workfare. If unemployed youth aged eighteen to twenty-four were forced by a threat of full withdrawal of benefits into one of the four New Deal streams, then why were lone mothers who were not in paid work and possibly of the same age exempt? Was the Blair cabinet prepared to treat the latter as caregivers, whether full- or part-time? If Labour carried through on its promise to offer public nursery-school spaces to all four-year-olds on a full-day basis, then what barriers stood in the way of embracing a more North American approach to lone parent 'self-sufficiency?' For British proponents of a moralistic approach to rehabilitating lone mothers, the answer to this last question was 'nothing at all.'[123] Progressive campaigners worried that single parents would be subject to mandatory workfare rules during a second Labour term, particularly if the numbers leaving benefits under more voluntary arrangements remained low.[124]

What general conclusions can be offered about the Blair government's decisions? First, some social policy changes bore a striking resemblance to actions in the United States dating back to the 1970s, in the sense of emphasizing incentives for people to get off welfare and work for pay. For example, New Labour efforts to introduce the Working Families Tax Credit instituted an important work-tested social benefit, although Labour's New Deal was education-tested in a way that was not permissible in many North American jurisdictions. Second, parallel with Third Way directions elsewhere, the Blair government pursued social policy initiatives using tax and labour market vehicles rather than traditional spending programs. Relevant examples of this preference included the creation of the Working Families Tax Credit, which in turn contained a child-care tax credit for low-income employed parents, as well as the national minimum wage.

Other elements of the New Labour approach revealed a distinctly British twist. During the Blair years, welfare-to-work rules explicitly permitted New Deal workers to be unionized and were introduced at the same time as national minimum wage regulations. These provisions, combined with a guarantee that New Deal participants would not displace regular employees, exceeded those in place in the US as well as some Canadian provinces, including Ontario. As well, the fact that the New Deal for lone parents was not initially compulsory meant that British notions of citizenship vis-à-vis single mothers had not been entirely commodified, or transformed from baseline supports for social engagement into primarily economic or labour market–contingent values. In the case of New Labour, therefore, there existed some official recognition that people could participate in and contribute to society other than through paid work.

Conclusions

It is important to step back from the empirical details at this point in order to pose some broader questions. First, were the decisions of Third Way leaders to work-test social benefits, taxify social policy, and circumscribe older, more expansive concepts of social citizenship likely to do much about what was once termed poverty? This line of enquiry overlooks a fundamental point: that is, once poverty was defined as a moral problem rather than as an economic or material condition, as was occurring over time in all three countries, whether people were poor in work versus poor on benefits mattered very significantly. To proponents of an unwavering pro-work, anti-'dependence,' and pro-'personal responsibility' approach, the pursuit of punitive solutions became not just morally defensible but also ethically essential. At their core, hot button claims insisted it was irrelevant whether people had enough to eat – they just needed the proper work ethic.

Second, how did public policy reach this point? A climate of ideas argument with respect to the erosion of social citizenship posits that Third Way politicians stressed an individualistic notion of personal responsibility that borrowed heavily from their more right-of-centre competitors. Responsible citizens in the jargon of the Third Way became defined as people who took care of themselves and those around them, meaning they were not dependent on state transfers. If they were allowed to be state-dependent for a temporary period of time, then it was only with the proviso that they were either actively seeking work or actively making themselves more work-ready.

According to Bill Clinton, Jean Chrétien, and Tony Blair, people from modest social backgrounds could succeed despite the odds, they just needed – in the words of Clinton and Blair – 'a hand up, not a hand out.' Using labour market, social policy, and taxation levers, the state pressed individuals to work, just as it used lower taxes and constrained social benefits to encourage businesses to locate in a given jurisdiction. The fact that in federal systems like those of the United States and Canada, the national government gradually ceded a great deal more authority to sub-national states and provinces during the Clinton and Chrétien years – especially in an area like social assistance policy where these sub-national units had long wielded considerable clout – meant that federal governments became primarily rhetorical facilitators of an increasingly moralistic agenda about personal responsibility.

What about people who were not 'responsible' in the jargon of the Third Way? Was this just another way of returning to older notions of the deserving versus the undeserving poor – with the virtuous widow epitomizing the deserving social assistance recipient, for example, and the unmarried teenage mother the undeserving one? It can be argued that regulating and categorizing the poor was hardly a novel idea, and that political leaders during the 1990s simply adopted different phrases for setting up the terms of the very old 'moral' debate about good versus evil.

Perhaps some new angles did shape Third Way debates. First of all, there emerged a fundamental tension between the emphasis of Clinton, Chrétien, and Blair on personal self-sufficiency, on the one hand, and their neo-communitarian focus on healthy societies, on the other.[125] It was difficult for these leaders to claim they cared about the fabric of the collectivity when they pushed ideas of personal responsibility and independence so hard that citizens heard very, very little about notions of interdependence – except in the context of the nuclear, and predominantly heterosexual, family unit. Given the profoundly anxious times in which they governed, surely there was something to be said for human interdependence on a larger scale.

Second, as our discussion in chapter 6 of the emergent duty state argues, Third Way welfare reform policies seemed to contain more than a hint of social authoritarianism. As Ralf Dahrendorf remarked in an article in *Foreign Affairs*, there was something unsettling about leaders who maintained that the state 'will no longer pay for things but will tell people what to do.'[126] Dahrendorf claimed that Clinton, Blair, and company tossed aside fundamental notions of human liberty in their pursuit of social cohesion – but one could go farther and ask if indeed social cohesion was any more central to the Third Way world view than was individual liberty. New Labour's own push on cohesion and social inclusion issues, after all, tended to overlook any basis for exclusion other than failure to pursue paid employment. Surely the unequal consequences of labour market engagement in all these countries for different genders, classes, and races stood as an integral element of any human liberty or social cohesion agenda.

Ralf Dahrendorf's questions about the Third Way were particularly important because they suggested a bridge between broad philosophical issues about social policy and specific nuts-and-bolts questions about welfare reform and its effects. In chapter 5, we examine the implications to date of Third Way changes in the United States, Canada, and Great Britain.

CHAPTER FIVE

Charting the Consequences

How can researchers assess the impact of public ideas and policies that remain very much in play at the time of writing? Some welfare reform analysts have focused on the measurable fallout from leaders' decisions. In the United States, for example, the elimination of Aid to Families with Dependent Children (AFDC) and its replacement by Temporary Assistance for Needy Families (TANF) in 1996 generated a great deal of interest in the more obvious, empirically straightforward consequences of policy change. American writers often addressed quantifiable issues such as caseload decline, rather than the larger question of how Bill Clinton's promise to 'end welfare as we know it' shifted the terms of welfare state development in that country.

Similarly, the dismantling of the Canada Assistance Plan and creation of the Canada Health and Social Transfer, both announced in 1995, led researchers to examine patterns of public spending on health, education, and welfare. Did social assistance caseloads decline? What federal compensatory action occurred after cuts to social programs became a focus of public debate? As in the United States, considerably less attention was directed toward more complex issues, including how Canadian reforms altered the broad contours of policy discussion.

In Great Britain, the very newness of New Deal programs rendered the study of consequences even more difficult. Once again, quantitative indicators became popular yardsticks for researchers, since central government departments that administered welfare-to-work schemes were anxious to disseminate their extensive data. Yet knowing how many lone mothers who attended interviews with personal advisers increased their hours of paid work, for example, hardly told the full story about welfare reform dynamics in the UK after 1997.

This chapter pushes beyond standard measures of social policy impact in order to pose a more critical question about 'post-conservative' consequences. Boldly stated, did Third Way patterns of policy talk and policy action in the United States, Canada, and Great Britain have much impact? In particular, how did 'post-conservative' leaders affect anti-poverty and feminist campaigning interests? Were progressive groups able to stake out their claims for a different kind of welfare reform?

Materials presented below suggest that the Clinton, Chrétien, and Blair years were indeed significant to pro–welfare state activists. Under Third Way political executives, feminist and anti-poverty groups often seemed as much on the defensive as they had been through the 1980s, struggling against a powerful climate of ideas that was 'post-conservative' in name only. In their efforts to contest a moralistic approach to welfare reform, progressive activists seemed disheartened, frustrated, and, at times, angry at their lack of influence over public discourse as well as social policy.

Each of the following sections opens with a brief summary of the measurable effects of benchmark social policy decisions during the Clinton, Chrétien, and Blair years. We then turn to the campaigning interest dimension in each country, using data gathered through in-depth interviews with anti-poverty and feminist activists and experts. Interviews in each country were conducted over several years so as to provide a cross-time perspective for each system. In the United States, a total of thirty-eight interviews about the consequences of Clinton-era welfare reform were conducted between 1994 and 1999.[1] In Canada, thirty-nine respondents were questioned about Chrétien-era developments between 1994 and 1999.[2] In Great Britain, a total of forty-five interviews were conducted about the Blair years between 1997 and 2000.[3]

Reform Implications in the United States

Proponents of the 1996 Personal Responsibility and Work Opportunity Reconciliation Act (PRWORA) trumpeted the contributions of this legislation toward 'ending welfare as we know it.' Press releases from the Clinton White House often pointed to very low rates of unemployment in the US, declining welfare case loads, and sustained job growth as evidence of PRWORA's success.[4] Yet a closer look at the same period suggested that the threat of time limits and increasingly rigid work requirements in the US likely pushed better-educated, better-skilled, and less 'difficult' social assistance recipients into paid employment, while leaving those with more limited resources to cope with shrinking benefits.[5] Did the paid work found by former welfare recipients in the United States provide a survivable wage? Was it likely to displace other women and men in better-paid, unionized public service jobs, thus accelerating a state-by-state 'race to the bottom' of social standards? How quickly and dramatically would an economic recession overturn the pattern of declining welfare caseloads? These questions remained open to speculation, and difficult to research, largely because 'most [US] states do not have the capacity to effectively trace ... families [who have left the welfare rolls], even to find out if they have remained employed.'[6]

At the same convention that nominated Al Gore as the Democratic party's unsuccessful presidential candidate, Bill Clinton celebrated his own domestic policy accomplishments. Clinton claimed that as of August 2000, there were 'more than 7.5 million people who have moved from welfare to work, and the welfare rolls in our administration have been cut in half.' In Clinton's words, ending the AFDC program meant that 'those who can work must work,' a goal that was advanced by expanding the Earned Income Tax Credit (EITC) to 'help 15 million families work their way into the middle class.'[7] Teenage pregnancies decreased after 1992 and, according to Bill Clinton, 'the American people achieved the longest economic expansion in our history.'[8]

Many of these same indicators were employed in scholarly assessments of welfare reform in the United States. Social assistance caseloads were among the most commonly cited measures, since they offered a straightforward comparison of the pre- versus post-PRWORA uptake of government benefits. As Kent Weaver, a Brookings Institution senior fellow, summarized the available data, 'Welfare rolls are unquestionably down dramatically. AFDC rolls peaked at 14,225,591 in 1994. By June 1999 there were just under 6.9 million TANF recipients, a decline of more than 51 percent since January 1994.'[9]

Accounts by Weaver and others, however, noted significant variations within these aggregate caseload data. First of all, welfare rolls declined far more significantly in some states than in others, and tended to drop more steeply among whites than among inner-city minority recipients.[10] Second, under enforced workfare schemes, caseload decline seemed relatively easy to effect among welfare recipients who had a reasonable chance of finding paid work during expansionary times. As political scientist Stephen Teles pointed out, it was highly unlikely that less fortunate recipients who 'faced some combination of very low intelligence, poor to nonexistent schooling, a history of physical and mental abuse, significant psychological problems, little if any social network, drug and alcohol addiction,' or other problems could be placed successfully in private sector jobs – even in a heated US economy.[11]

Third, studies of the quality of paid employment found by ex-welfare recipients reported that 'moving from welfare to work is not necessarily synonymous with a rise in economic well-being.'[12] Research from across the United States indicated that eliminating the AFDC program made growing numbers of single mother households increasingly reliant on insecure, low-wage employment. More job-seekers than jobs existed in this segment of the labour market, even during the expansionary times of the late 1990s, and many of the positions that were available 'typically provide low pay, few benefits, limited hours, and are particularly susceptible to economic fluctuations.'[13]

According to one account by law and public policy expert Joel Handler, PRWORA's 'work-first' philosophy, which placed immediate paid work ahead of training and education, was unlikely to lift ex–welfare recipients above the poverty line. Households headed by a single mother could usually rely at best on one adult earner's wages, which were typically depressed by women's lower rates of pay relative to those of men. Estimates of annual child-care costs in 1996, the year AFDC was eliminated, averaged around $3000, thus reducing further the income after expenses of single parent households.[14] Discrimination against workers from minority backgrounds, notably African-American women living in inner city neighbourhoods, further depressed income levels, so that roughly four in ten ex–welfare recipients in paid work remained officially poor – even during economic boom times.[15]

Fourth, researchers examined take-up rates for other means-tested benefits that had been mandated under the terms of AFDC, but not under TANF. Over-time studies revealed drops in participation in the Medicaid health insurance scheme as well as the Food Stamps system that were so large as to 'exceed those that could be attributed to the economic recovery.'[16] Students of intergovernmental fiscal relations in the United States suggested that the switch from shared-cost arrangements under AFDC to block grants under TANF encouraged states to tighten Medicaid eligibility in order to save themselves money.[17] Other accounts maintained that under work-first welfare reform schemes, US states could prevent adults and children who were eligible for government health coverage from ever enrolling in the first place. Once the automatic link between welfare and Medicaid that had existed before 1996 was severed, some states built effective diversion schemes that made it hard to apply or reapply for Medicaid.[18]

Finally, researchers evaluated the impact of the Clinton-era expansion of the Earned Income Tax Credit. This infusion of funds meant that by 1996, the US federal government spent nearly twice as much on the work-tested, tax-based EITC as had been spent on the means-tested, cash benefits regime called AFDC.[19] Clearly, one very significant by-product of ending a national entitlement to social assistance during the Clinton years was the enrichment of tax-based earnings supplements via the EITC.

The latter were obviously vulnerable, however, to the same limitations that affected low-wage employment in general. That is, the EITC could 'make work pay' better, but no once-a-year tax credit would reverse the job insecurity, pay discrimination, or health insurance problems that faced workers at the bottom of the labour market. Moreover, the fact that collecting the EITC required filing a tax return meant that many people who were eligible for the credit never received it. One measure of this obstacle was revealed in data on the city of Chicago, where the Democratic mayor stated that nearly $100 million per year in potential EITC payments remained unclaimed. According to Richard Daley, this pattern resulted partly from the failure of many wage earners to file a return, and partly from the absence of an EITC item in the most common tax form used by low-income people.[20]

Obviously, this broad pattern of developments was not entirely attributable to the PRWORA legislation of 1996. A long history of virtually automatic federal government waivers to states to experiment with various ideas (including mandatory workfare) dated back to the Reagan years, and tended not only to reduce caseloads but also to increase reliance on low-wage work.[21] Given that AFDC cash benefit levels had no inflationary protection for decades before they ended, it was not surprising that take-up rates fell precipitously once the US entered a period of sustained growth and low unemployment. Moreover, the absence of universal public health care provisions led US states to use the Medicaid program in all kinds of discretionary ways long before Bill Clinton's election in 1992. For example, states began during the 1980s to direct federal Medicaid funds toward people who were not on welfare.[22] As well, the EITC with all its flaws was first introduced in 1975, and expanded in a series of steps (including in 1986 and 1990) before Bill Clinton ever entered the White House.[23]

Taken as a group, these patterns suggested that low-income households in the United States were crucially vulnerable for some time, but they were arguably *more* vulnerable to economic downturns after 1996 than before. Instead of a counter-cyclical program like the cost-shared AFDC, which expanded during hard times, the TANF regime was a pro-cyclical, block grant scheme that could not respond in the same way to the effects of an economic recession.[24] As well, TANF operated as a highly decentralized program that offered even greater room for cross-state (as well as within-state) variation than had AFDC – which was itself a very devolved program. After 1996, for example, twenty-three of the fifty US states opted to impose a child exclusion rule (known as the family cap) that denied additional cash benefits to families with new babies. To show how serious they were about enforcing paid employment, more than thirty states eased asset limits and earnings disregards as a means of encouraging more adults to work.[25] In short, the devolution of control inherent in TANF offered more opportunities and incentives for states to create their own social policy regimes.

As important as these empirical patterns are, they obscure an equally significant dimension of the welfare reform story. How lasting was the impact of hot button rhetoric from the Reagan years and following? Were progressive interests likely to exert much influence over the future of TANF when it came up for congressional review in 2002? When questioned in interviews, American activists and experts seemed far from optimistic about their ability to get out from under the shadow of the Reagan/Bush years; many saw themselves as quite isolated and marginalized despite the promise of 'post-conservative' times.

Respondents interviewed in 1994 spoke of an ongoing backlash against poor women, especially those from racial minority backgrounds. Activists described 'a turning against public life,' and an 'anti-public discourse' that treated 'welfare mothers as the personification of evil, of dependency ... Here the welfare evil woman is a black woman who is a single mother.' One campaigner termed this context 'a poisoned public atmosphere,' in which poor women from minority backgrounds were targeted as the main source of declining social values. Another claimed that women of colour were singled out by a harsh rhetoric that 'depicted them as promiscuous and lacking discipline. It's been very hard to debunk these myths.'

Given that many feminist and anti-poverty interests favoured sustained government investment in education, job training, health insurance, and child-care programs, these activists were unable to defend AFDC as an ideal social program. Yet even before Democrats lost control of both houses of Congress in 1994, many interviewees had reached two crucial conclusions: First, they acknowledged that Bill Clinton also held highly punitive views, including about 'irresponsible' teenage mothers; and second, that because Clinton's own views on welfare were quite conservative and decentralist, he might agree to just about any reform proposal. One respondent, speaking in March 1994, argued that the president's background as a small-state governor meant he 'believes in flexible policy-making. He wants to provide governors with as broad a flexibility as he wishes existed when he was a governor. He will allow for things he doesn't agree with in order to give that flexibility.'

The ominous sense conveyed by this statement was compounded by an even deeper feeling of dread that set in after the 1994 mid-term elections. In March 1995, a veteran activist confessed that 'this new Congress has scared us. It's depressing. Until we lost on health care, we thought we were on the brink of real accomplishment. We're kind of in a dark tunnel now. We are on the defensive, trying to argue against dismantling things that we know are flawed [AFDC], but we need something instead of nothing. We are defending deficient programs, which is a real irony.' Respondents in this period worried that the rapid, virtually breakneck speed of Republican legislative activity left no time for opponents of the Contract with America to organize themselves.

At the level of ideas, hot button rhetoric that targeted low-income Americans became especially fashionable once Republicans assumed leadership positions in both houses of Congress. According to one observer, the 1994 mid-term elections helped to resuscitate an older 'emphasis on the frontier mentality. If you make it, it's all due to your own merit. If not, it's your own fault ... The flip side of "greed is good" is that the disadvantaged are getting what they deserve. The language distinction between deserving and undeserving poor came back with a vengeance.' Groups opposed to regressive welfare proposals found themselves stuck between a rock and a hard place. On one side, well-reasoned, point-by-point rebuttals of repugnant ideas attracted neither public nor media interest. On the other side, vigorous condemnations of 'welfare as we know it' – whether by Bill Clinton or congressional Republicans – meant the AFDC program was hardly defensible.[26]

Campaigners argued that, over time, the Clinton administration became committed to satisfying both conservatives on Capitol Hill and power-hungry state governors. As one commented in March 1995, 'States and counties do the worst job of solving things. They are the most corrupt. They *don't* solve problems, yet here we are going headlong into granting them more control.' Another claimed Republicans in Congress were using decentralist arguments about flexible federalism to cover up their mean-spirited plans to abolish social assistance entirely: 'These guys don't give a sh– if it's better to run programs at the local level. It's baloney. They don't want programs at any level ... They really just want to cut the money.'

Respondents claimed conservatives were playing a race card on welfare reform in order to ensure that no credible progressive coalition got off the ground. In their view, linking racist imagery with moralistic rhetoric was compelling in insecure times, and effectively blocked competing interpretations of the same social reality. According to one interviewee,

> the welfare reform piece is a Contract *on* America for black people, and also for women ... The clock has really been turned back for us as black women. People want to play the race game, but they don't want to acknowledge how it divides the haves and the have-nots. Black women are always seen as lazy, with lots of children, trying to beat the system, but how can you beat the system on $200 a month with 2.2 kids and living in squalor?

Like many other activists, this respondent endorsed federal job training programs and better health insurance provisions, rather than punitive welfare policies. Yet it was hard to make that case given the emphasis on quick-fix, moralistic solutions, or what one observer called a 'stampede towards fast action' in Congress.

Explaining the limits of the Contract with America was far from easy. Technical terms including block grant and illegitimacy bonus had to be defined in recognizable ways so that potential coalition partners could begin to understand the policies under consideration. Republican legislators had built hugely effective right-wing support networks, including the Christian Coalition, that vastly eclipsed in speed, funding, and intensity any competitors on the centre or left of the spectrum.

As one women's organization leader who tried to mobilize an equivalent grass-roots network commented in late 1996:

> The damage done in 1994 is something we can't recover from, certainly not in a single election. Remember that of the 73 Republicans first elected in 1994, more than 50 were endorsed by the Christian Coalition. About 125 members of Congress had straight Christian Coalition voting records. In 1996, we contacted a million women in key congressional districts using fax and email. We did phone banks and used our toll-free telephone number as well. We are continuing the campaign and have kept our campaign staff to ensure that the far right isn't the only network out there.

These efforts, and others like them, probably assisted Democrats in the 1996 presidential and congressional elections, but they came too late to stop PRWORA.

In some cases, campaigners who opposed White House and Republican proposals found themselves facing a wall of silence as much as a wall of opposition. Activists reported that when they asked to meet with administration officials, they were usually granted access, meaning a polite audience, but no influence. One campaigner who managed to meet with senior White House appointees on four occasions about welfare reform admitted that 'they didn't listen to us.' Another critic of PRWORA claimed it was naive to expect much from these sessions:

> Women's groups and anti-poverty groups tended to do things a day late and a dollar short. That's why they were so excited when they got to meet with Leon Panetta when he was White House chief of staff. Unfortunately, they forgot that they would probably have no effect. It was their assumption that if they told Panetta and Clinton their side of the welfare story, then the administration would change the policy. Clinton *did* know the consequences and the details. Clinton does his homework and he knows the details. This is the level people are at.

Campaigners tended to agree that what one called the sustained 'demonization of poor minority women' on welfare meant that very few white, middle-class voters who mattered to politicians could be mobilized against PRWORA.

Moreover, public protests that did occur were rarely considered newsworthy. According to one observer, many critical 'contacts for the media had either been shut down or defunded since the last round of welfare debates in the Reagan/Bush years. Large social policy coalitions that relied on federal money were out of action. This meant crucial networks and sources of expertise had been destroyed and, as a result, the opposition to PRWORA was often rendered invisible.' Groups that remained alive found it hard to publicize either their arguments or their actions. During the summer of 1996, for example, a hunger strike staged by the National Organization for Women near the White House was barely covered in the media. One campaigner explained this wall of silence as follows:

> The amount of money the right has invested in polishing and publishing its ideas has been amazing. Journalists may be liberal, but station executives are not. The meaning of liberal has now been changed to something like 'not a fundamentalist.' Print journalism is quite conservative, and TV journalism is conservative because it is driven by crime. What is a liberal on TV? No one is to the left like Pat Buchanan is to the right ... Big corporations own the networks and the papers. Why would they offer free publicity to critics of welfare reform?

According to this activist and many others, it was next to impossible to get the larger story of what was wrong with PRWORA into the mainstream media.

Feminist and anti-poverty campaigners were pessimistic about the prospects for improvement during a second Clinton term. Some cited the resignations of Labor Secretary Robert Reich as well as academic welfare reform experts (in the Department of Health and Human Services) as evidence that the administration would lurch farther to the right over time. The virtual disappearance after 1994 of a moderate, centrist presence in the Republican party suggested that creating a bipartisan approach to social policy would entail working with extremely conservative federal legislators and state governors. Obviously, this was not a promising prospect for critics of PRWORA. As one commented in early 1997, 'that weirdo end of the Republican party still has people terrified.'

Feminist groups faced an additional challenge during the same period as TANF went into effect. The rise of a conservative 'family values' mobilization among American men, notably via the Promise Keepers and Million Man March organizations, meant that the campaign for fathers' rights was literally hitting the streets. Arguments that the lives of poor American women and children would be vastly improved by the presence of a male head of household attracted considerable support on the centre and left of the political spectrum, as experts in leading foundations and think tanks talked about the revaluation of African-American men.

Feminist campaigners wondered why those same foundations and think tanks had long ignored the devaluation of women, especially poor African-American women. At a practical level, one observer argued, 'there is nothing wrong with this initiative for black men. But why, in a country this rich, can't we help both poor men *and* poor women?' Another maintained that the fathers' rights initiative, running the gamut from right to left, presented a crucial obstacle for all American women:

> We have this dads' rights movement with the idea of putting men into low income jobs and then telling low income women to stay home. I can't figure out how it is supposed to work. A guy with two kids by two different women is supposed to marry which one? The critics of 'dependency' castigate poor women who need public assistance, but they celebrate dependence on men. This is all very perplexing to me, but one message is clear. Patriarchy is it. Men are in charge. That's the story.

Although progressives differed in their assessments of the challenge posed by fathers' rights efforts, most believed that organized feminism would be hard-pressed to battle on yet another front.

Given these circumstances, what could campaigners do? Some focused on changing PRWORA provisions that cut Food Stamps for 250,000 legal immigrants to the United States. By mid-1998, after nearly two years of pressing for this change, the Food Stamps recision was reversed by President Clinton. Others pursued state-level lobbying to try to blunt the sharpest edges of welfare reform. For example, activists who worried that the illegitimacy ratio provisions of PRWORA might lead to even more restrictive abortion laws focused their efforts on mounting a strong pro-choice lobby in state legislatures. Campaigners who wanted to ensure low-income citizens' access to Medicaid health insurance and Food Stamps programs worked to increase awareness of these benefits across the country. Campaigners who believed more education could improve the job prospects of women on benefits pressured states to use a flexible definition of work in their TANF regulations; by equating vocational training with employment, they argued, states could offer poor mothers a better chance of finding decent work when their cash benefits ran out. Organizations concerned about the children of low-income working parents lobbied states to create generous rules for child-care supplements, which in turn increased the number of families that were eligible for federal funds.

Rather than lobbying and organizing against the punitive directions of American welfare reform, other groups decided to focus on evaluating post-1996 changes. The decentralist push behind TANF meant that there would eventually be fifty different welfare systems in the United States, all financed to some degree by federal block grants, but lacking any national–level entitlement or income guarantee. Efforts to improve provisions using a state-by-state strategy meant groups had to know how PRWORA was being implemented across the country, which in turn necessitated intensive research.

The decision to study the consequences of welfare reform, however, may have sent campaigning groups down a highly ineffectual path. In large part, private sector firms that had long been involved in operating and evaluating social programs across the United States established the terms under which most research was conducted. As one expert commented in 1999, 'technocratic evaluations using highly quantified measures have become the norm in this area. Consultants usually employ an anti-welfare, pro-work rhetoric in their reports. They apply what amounts to a narrow accounting methodology in talking about labour market flows and stock. Simply put, the language of program evaluation is extremely de-humanized.' It was open to question whether more critical researchers could challenge the prevailing discourse about welfare reform and its consequences and, from that base, help organize for the next round of policy debates in 2002.

Overall, each of these post-1996 approaches was fraught with danger. They risked spreading the scarce, depleted resources of demoralized campaigning interests over fifty state jurisdictions (not to mention their sub-state units), thus watering down further the minimal progressive presence in the US capital. As one interviewee commented in late 1998, 'Women's groups and welfare rights groups largely withered on the vine. The rhetoric of the other side could rule the day.'

In the waning days of the Clinton presidency, anti-poverty and feminist campaigners seemed to be back at square one. Many dreamed of a robust federal welfare state, but instead were working piece by piece to study and build basic social policy provisions at the state level. It was difficult to imagine a more disheartening situation for activists in 'post-conservative' times.

The Impact of Change in Canada

In campaigning for a third consecutive majority government, Jean Chrétien defended his Third Way approach to governing Canada. In his words,

> The Liberal program is moderate and balanced. It contains important tax cuts for low- and middle-income Canadians, as well as reductions of the debt. We are talking about investments in health care and the environment, in innovation and research to prepare Canadians for the new economy. We have to be sure the national government remains strong and speaks for all Canadians all across the country to create opportunities for all.[27]

Although questions were raised about the 'moderate and balanced' nature of the Liberal record, as well as the prime minister's commitment to a strong federal government, Chrétien managed to win yet another term in office.[28]

Debates over Third Way leadership in Canada were bound up in disparate measures of success. Reduced unemployment levels, higher rates of economic growth, lower federal deficits and debts, and rising consumer confidence suggested Canada had surged ahead after 1993. More and more people were working for pay over time and, in Canada's industrial heartland of Ontario, welfare caseloads fell more than 60 per cent between 1995 and 2000.[29]

The flip side of this same picture revealed an increasingly uneven distribution of the fruits of economic expansion and fiscal restraint. Under the terms of the Canada Health and Social Transfer (CHST), announced in 1995, federal payments to sub-national governments were slated to decline by more than one-third, creating a squeeze that placed social assistance and social service spending in head-on competition with health and education programs.[30] The relatively affluent, middle-class constituencies that cared intensely about public health and education standards in Canada vastly overshadowed in clout and resources the far less influential interests concerned with social assistance rates or low-income child-care programs. This imbalance helps to explain Liberal decisions to restore more than $20 billion in health care funding just before the fall 2000 federal elections, and to create a $2.5 billion Millennium Scholarship Fund to assist Canadian students in post-secondary education programs.[31]

As of 1996, Canadians were left without a counter-cyclical national safety net for cash assistance, since block grants under the CHST contained fixed ceilings for federal transfers that did not vary with economic conditions. Unlike the situation in the health and education fields, no major federal compensatory action occurred to soften the impact of funding cuts for welfare and social services.[32] In quantitative terms, data showed that Canadian provinces as a group spent less per person on social assistance after 1995 than before, with Ontario and Alberta leading the way on cuts to welfare rates and tightened eligibility rules.[33] As well, the gap in after-tax income between the rich and poor in Canada widened after the federal Liberals came to power in 1993, largely because of spending reductions in the areas of social assistance and unemployment insurance.[34]

In particular, data from the National Council of Welfare showed an increase after 1995 in the already high percentage of young, single-mother-led families living in poverty. This rate rose from 83 per cent in 1995 to more than 91 per cent in subsequent years.[35] Various measures of child poverty in Canada also showed higher absolute numbers and higher relative percentages over time. Once again, the most common explanation was reduced federal transfers and reduced federal controls on provincial action under the CHST, along with tough federal cuts to unemployment insurance and significant provincial cuts to social assistance programs.[36]

The more complex dimensions of the declining caseloads story also began to emerge. In Ontario, Canada's most populous province, ending the CAP provision that prohibited work requirements as a condition for receiving cash assistance left the door open for a Conservative government to introduce mandatory workfare. As cash assistance payments were reduced and new rules were introduced to limit eligibility for those benefits in a context of economic growth, it was hardly surprising that welfare caseloads fell steeply. Yet the chronological coincidence between lower caseloads and mandatory workfare in Ontario masqued the fact that only a 'tiny' fraction, or roughly '2–5 per cent of welfare recipients were actually on workfare assignments.'[37]

During this same period, the Chrétien government failed to develop a national child-care program. Rather than adding 150,000 licensed child-care spaces, as Liberals had promised in their 1993 Red Book, they oversaw a decline in the availability of regulated care. Seven years after the first Chrétien government took office, approved spaces existed for less than 10 per cent of Canadian children under the age of twelve, roughly the same level as in 1990.[38] This pattern was particularly pronounced outside Quebec and British Columbia, two jurisdictions that offered relatively generous provincial subsidies to licensed facilities in order to create their own child-care schemes.[39] As a major federally financed report on child-care access concluded in 2000, '[E]arly childhood care and education services in most of Canada have been developed so incoherently that although each province and territory has a tangle of programs, only a minority of children and families has access to services that provide the reliable care parents need or the early childhood education services that are of demonstrated benefit.'[40]

The effects of tighter social assistance eligibility rules and compulsory workfare programs were most pronounced in provinces with minimal public child-care provisions. Under a series of Conservative governments in Alberta, the prevailing definition of who was an employable adult became increasingly stringent, so that by 1993 only lone mothers with children under the age of six months were exempt from paid work requirements.[41] In Ontario, the Conservative government elected in 1995 narrowed the work exemption for lone mothers to those with children under the age of three years, and reduced licensed child-care subsidies by nearly 20 per cent.[42] These changes to employability rules, coupled with limited efforts in provinces outside Quebec and British Columbia to ensure reliable, regulated, and affordable child-care programs, meant that single parents risked being pushed off cash benefits at the same time as they faced a highly uncertain future in paid work.

During the early Chrétien years, anti-poverty and feminist campaigners seemed relieved that the federal Conservatives had, after nine years in power, been reduced to a very small opposition rump in the House of Commons. Many viewed Brian Mulroney's misleading public assurances that social programs were a 'sacred trust' as a reason for dwindling public faith in both politicians and the possibility of positive government. One described the ceiling imposed after 1990 on Canada Assistance Plan transfers to Ontario, Alberta, and British Columbia as 'an incredible blow,' since it eroded the quality of social programs in better-off provinces that set the benchmark for the rest of the country. Another highlighted Tory efforts to isolate what were called 'special interests,' and saw the Conservatives as responsible for making Canada 'more divided, more racist, less tolerant, where people were far less concerned about looking after one another.'

By late 1994, respondents were at least as worried about the Liberals' policy directions. Their sense of foreboding was revealed in comments including the following: 'Paul Martin may make the Tories look mild as deficit cutters.' 'If people think Mulroney made cuts, just wait until Chrétien is done with us.' 'The attacks on social programs under the Conservatives were not nearly as stiff as we are going to see in the Chrétien/Martin years.' 'I think the new Liberal government is very centre-right. I don't think it's very concerned with women. It's not done much that's different from what Mulroney did. Other people believe the Liberals will protect social programs, but I'm not sure they will.'

A number of activists feared the Liberals would place a high priority on fighting the deficit, but would employ more compassionate rhetoric and a thicker veneer of consultation than had the Conservatives. In the words of one interviewee, the Liberals 'use our language of single mothers and poverty, but they offer no solutions. The advocacy groups are ignored by a Liberal government that is sleek and cunning.' Campaigners tended to viewed their influence as weak and waning, in part because they were being 'consulted to death' by a federal government that had no intention of following their advice. According to activists, the Liberals invited progressive social policy groups to present briefs to parliamentary committees, speak before various task forces, and meet with cabinet ministers and senior civil servants. The time frames were often extremely tight, especially for organizations with limited resources, but failure to participate meant that diverse perspectives were not represented. Moreover, groups reliant on public funding faced cuts to their federal subsidies in the next round of budget announcements if they veered too far to the critical side.

Feminist and anti-poverty activists based outside Quebec tended to portray social policy devolution and its proponents in negative terms. Provinces and municipalities were viewed as unlikely sites for progressive welfare reform, although federal cuts to social transfers hardly helped the situation. In the words of one campaigner, 'People don't blame the federal government when they see homelessness or begging on the street – they blame it on their province. Hence the feds escape responsibility for lots of the problems their policies cause.'

Training the spotlight on Ottawa's role in social policy decline was far from easy. According to one participant, a hunger strike by anti-poverty, feminist, and student organizations to protest the elimination of the Canada Assistance Plan 'got virtually no media coverage whatsoever.' Efforts by the same interests to challenge the creation of the

CHST using the United Nations Covenant on Economic, Social, and Cultural Rights resulted in 'a stinging rebuke of Canada's human-rights record,' but little else.[43] Another respondent maintained that in order to raise questions about the directions of welfare state development in Canada, 'we need to be more savvy and strategic. But who can do that with the barriers posed by a right-wing press?' A third noted that when media reports about the CHST did appear, they followed closely the lines of Department of Finance press releases. Published accounts thus stressed the ostensibly responsive and flexible nature of the Transfer, while ignoring its other implications.

Had they been able to capture public attention, activists insisted, they would have laid out the 'nightmare' consequences of Liberal decisions. These included the CHST, described by one campaigner as 'our version of Clinton's PRWORA – it abolished the entitlement and cut the funds six months before Clinton did.' Interviewees identified the gutting of older national guidelines and cost-sharing arrangements that had created a floor under social policy as the most negative aspect of the Transfer. Many also opposed changes to unemployment insurance and social housing programs, where the Liberals were seen as stripping the foundations of the federal welfare state via what one respondent termed 'dismemberment.' Campaigners tended to portray the National Child Benefit as a weak, means-tested supplement that was unavailable to most families on social assistance. Finally, the Social Union Framework Agreement (SUFA) of 1999 was portrayed as a closed-door deal that had been drafted without input from citizens. Its high talk about flexible administrative arrangements reflected what one critic called 'corporate newspeak designed to hide more than it explains.'

Above all, activists zeroed in on changes in the language of social policy debate. In their view, discussions about social assistance in Canada assumed an increasingly hostile, disinhibited, and moralistic tone over time, as talk of personal responsibility, welfare dependence, and individual blame diverted attention from the human costs of spending cuts. Behind what one termed a 'benign facade,' politicians who were nominally on the centre-left lashed out using a discourse that was described in one published account as 'poor bashing.'[44] An interviewee from British Columbia cited the following examples:

> Our provincial New Democratic [social democratic] party used a logo that said, 'making work a better way of life than welfare.' The federal minister who organized the Liberals' social policy review talked about

people abusing the unemployment insurance system when he was responsible for that program. Jean Chrétien spoke about people who stayed at home drinking beer instead of working. The mayor of Toronto insisted he didn't want anti-poverty protesters to demonstrate in a park because they would leave behind used condoms and syringes.

Like many others, this respondent claimed the policy talk of Canadian elites was at least as troubling as their decisions.

Feminist and anti-poverty campaigners noted the ingenious ways in which politicians obscured their punitive actions. According to one observer, Prime Minister Chrétien 'is amazing because he's nasty. He cuts but he doesn't get the Brian Mulroney reputation. Some of the targeted, selective, means-tested strategies introduced by his government – like the National Child Benefit – are actually quite mean-spirited. Yet they are presented as being realistic compromises.' Several activists referred to Chrétien as 'the Teflon man,' a prime minister who could fundamentally restructure the Canadian welfare state, yet escape blame for any negative fallout from his decisions.

Campaigners claimed that Chrétien and many provincial premiers had managed to define social assistance claimants as deficient individuals who failed to contribute to the market economy. In the words of one expert, 'There is an appeal to "working families" that in my view has to do with poor bashing. It is so easy to turn low income working people against the poor, that you hear poor-bashing all the time. Even social democratic politicians in this country talk about poor people not wanting to work.' This emphasis on a narrowly economic valuation of human worth often meant that in most provinces, only paid employed Canadians were considered worthy recipients of Chrétien-era social programs, including the National Child Benefit.

Activists objected as well to what they saw as the socially conservative tenor of leading welfare reform proposals. In the words of one campaigner:

To me, a major point of welfare reform is to get women back with men. Welfare reform often doesn't save much money, and actually can cost more than what we now spend. People say too many women are getting divorced, leaving their kids, and going to school. Welfare reform is one way of stopping this. It stops the state from being the surrogate father. I'm not sure that this is a thought-through, conscious strategy for welfare reform, but it sure seems to be underlying a lot of what is happening.

According to this respondent, single mothers and the organizations representing them found it hard to challenge the notion that lone parents were morally flawed and economically deficient, since 'mothers of young kids just aren't organized to defend their nurturing work.'

Overall, respondents identified four significant consequences of the Chrétien era. The first was an eroded federal presence in the social policy field, which compounded the effects of earlier Conservative decisions. The Mulroney-era ceiling on CAP payments to Alberta, British Columbia, and Ontario began a process that, according to one interviewee,

> forced people into thinking of program costs as our expenditures in this 'have' province, rather than as part of a national framework that was based on cheap 50-cent dollars. This happened at the same time as we saw significant increases in demand for some welfare-umbrella programs that had to be paid for with reduced federal shares. In other words, there was an exponential increase in costs to the provincial purse.

As a consequence of federal fiscal changes, activists maintained, even Canada's better-off provinces, and even those governed by social democratic parties, began to rethink their basic income support programs.[45]

Second, activists claimed that a combination of funding pressures on sub-national governments plus an end to older federal program guidelines led provinces to reorient their social service bureaucracies. In some cases, the names of government departments that delivered welfare programs were altered to reflect more of a pro-work approach. Frontline social service employees became job training and placement advisers who risked seeing their own jobs transferred to private employment agencies. As one close observer of these changes remarked:

> An approach that I would call the 'cop mentality' has taken over the ministry in this province. There's a suspicious us-and-them mentality, which turns waiting rooms into armed camps. We now use an Orwellian language that defines welfare out of existence. Waiting rooms are called participant resource and activity centres, and clients are called participants. We don't have financial assistance workers any longer. Instead, they are known as work placement advisers in what are called employment and benefit centres. The joke is that these places are supposed to be made user-friendly so that when people come in the door, they can be told right away to f--- off.

As evidence to support their claims, campaigners pointed to sharp increases in provincial spending on verifying eligibility for various work-oriented schemes, monitoring compliance with these arrangements, and pursuing vigorous anti-fraud programs. These initiatives often use sophisticated and expensive information technology to track so-called solutions to welfare. According to one critic, 'There are more than six people working in this province on the police side of welfare for every one on the benefits side.'

Third, activists argued that governments in most parts of Canada were unwilling to invest adequately in child-care programs. Many saw an irony between growing public awareness of the need for better child care, on one side, and the emergence of workfare programs that lacked adequate child-care provisions, on the other. As one concluded,

> We confront a number of key problems, including availability of regulated child care, affordability for the vast majority of parents, and quality because the system now is an uneven patchwork. As a devolved set of provincial programs, child care is a mess. I appreciate regional diversity but I believe in national programs. A federal source of leadership is needed to encourage or force national principles using federal funds.

According to this respondent, the Liberals effectively 'buried' their proposal for a national child-care program once they introduced the decentralist and cost-cutting CHST.

For low-income single mothers, the implications of limited child-care provision in an increasingly work-tested social policy environment were very significant. Once the definition of who was an employable social assistance recipient expanded to include all parents of school-age (or, in some provinces, younger) children, the absence of licensed, affordable child care became a crucial issue. As one interviewee reflected, 'Our organization has been calling on the provincial and federal governments for some time to bring in a universal child-care system in this country. How else can you demand that single mothers go to work? The situation now doesn't provide any support other than saying, "Go out and find yourself a babysitter somewhere."' Progressive campaigners viewed the latter approach as both inadequate and unfair, although few believed it would change in the foreseeable future. As one noted, condemning single mothers who relied on welfare meant devaluing the nurturing work of all parents 'to fit with a system that denies everybody's vulnerability.' From this perspective, moralistic attacks against dependency made it difficult to mobilize support for any kind of caring work.

Finally, activists claimed, developments during the Chrétien years left most Canadians unaware of the frayed and balkanized state of their social safety net. Who knew where disappearing welfare caseloads had gone? When would the full consequences of ending shared-cost programs be understood? Only at the worst point of a future recession, interviewees maintained, would the limits of the Chrétien approach likely emerge. The critics' side of the story was rarely heard, since few opportunities existed after 1995 to bring test cases before the courts or to use provincial appeals systems to challenge new directions in welfare reform.[46] Coalition-building problems on the political left were also severe, since groups competed against each other for limited government funds and scarce media attention.

Campaigners argued that at the same time as the gap between rich and poor widened, and as Canadians in the middle feared for their own economic security, it became harder and harder to talk about the people at the bottom of the ladder. In the words of one interviewee, 'We have got people on social assistance with a very limited sense of citizenship. It is hard to talk about improvements without restoring the basic sense of dignity and respect for poor people as citizens. Yet we can't get funding to fight for basic rights, and groups that do oppose governments on this level are threatened with losing their charitable status.' In short, the prospects for effective mobilization against prevailing social policy directions in Canada seemed quite dim by the end of the second Chrétien term.

Assessing the Consequences in Britain

In asking British voters for a second mandate to pursue New Labour's vision of 'economic prosperity and social justice,' Tony Blair laid out his assessment of past accomplishments as well as future challenges.[47] Speaking in May 2001, Blair stated:

> The New Deal has shown that governments can make a difference in the fight against unemployment. Our programme of welfare reform has led to benefit bills falling in real terms for the first time in decades. At the same time, the minimum wage has lifted the pay of hundreds of thousands ... But there are still too many people not working who could be, and so continuing welfare reform will be essential to our second term

> agenda ... We seek a mandate for further reform of the welfare state. To make the tax and benefit system reward work, tackle poverty and penalise irresponsibility.[48]

Blair's speech calling the election, delivered at a school in the same modest neighbourhood of southeast London where he announced the New Deal in June 1997, concluded with a pitch for 'fresh radical change.'[49] According to the prime minister, 'the great issue of this election is opportunity for all, not just the few. This election is about a radical vision of lifting barriers and liberating people's potential in a decent society.'[50]

As the signature social policy of New Labour's first term, the New Deal was presented in official accounts as a major success story. Government reports claimed the take-up rate of Income Support benefits among lone parents by mid-2000 was more than 3 per cent lower than it would have been in the absence of the program. Figures released in October 2000 by the chancellor, Gordon Brown, showed the number of single parents on this particular benefit decreased from more than one million in May 1997 to about 910,000 in May 2000.[51] By February 2001, official data showed 895,000 lone parents on Income Support.[52]

New Labour elites were pleased that the participation rate for lone parents in paid work rose from about 44 to 50 per cent between 1997 and 2000. This level remained below US figures of about 70 per cent, which the chancellor identified as his policy target, and French rates of more than 80 per cent.[53] Clearly, Brown did not believe that the New Deal on its own could transform patterns of paid employment in Britain. In public statements during his first term as chancellor, Brown acknowledged that the surging British economy by itself would have lured about 80 per cent of ex–benefits claimants into paid work, whether or not the New Deal had been in place.[54]

Government data also showed that through 2000, 'only about one in five lone parents approached became full participants' in the voluntary New Deal for Lone Parents.[55] This rate of participation in the 20 per cent range was widely attributed to limited child-care availability in the UK, where studies reported 'only one child care place for every 6.9 children under the age of eight.'[56] By way of comparison, rates of participation in other New Deal programs with larger budgets, notably the youth and long-term unemployed schemes, were much higher. These compulsory New Deals had fewer than one-quarter female participants, in part because eligibility rules attached to them required participants to be claiming Jobseekers' Allowance (unemployment) benefits. Given that British 'women are less likely to be among the registered unemployed' than men, females also tended to be quite scarce among those who qualified for the most generous New Deal schemes.[57]

On the political right, critics of New Labour's welfare reform approach argued that the decline in lone parents claiming Income Support matched the rise in uptake for the Working Families Tax Credit (WFTC) – a work-tested and means-tested supplement introduced in 1999 to replace the Family Credit scheme. The new credit was available to parents, whether single or in couples, who were employed for at least sixteen hours per week.[58] Because it was usually paid via the wage packet, employer groups opposed the WFTC as an administrative burden that, in the words of a leading Conservative, turned private sector firms into 'unpaid benefit offices.'[59]

On the other side of the spectrum, supporters of the WFTC argued that delivery via the wage packet ensured an approximately 60 per cent higher rate of take-up than had been the case under Family Credit. From their perspective, taxified in-work benefits delivered by employers or the national taxation agency (Inland Revenue) were less stigmatizing – and hence more attractive – than older means-tested benefits paid by the social security department. Government- and trade union–sponsored advertising that informed people about the WFTC also helped to raise the take-up rate, as did its relatively generous payments that extended further into the middle class than did Family Credit. Moreover, supporters argued, Labour raised the value of the universal Child Benefit in 1998 and following and (under the terms of the WFTC) offered child-care tax credits of more than £100 per week for the children of employed parents who were enrolled in registered care.[60] These provisions were seen as compelling evidence that the Blair government was more interested than its Tory predecessors in helping low-income families and – above all – in ending child poverty.

Initial reports indicated that about half of the households claiming the WFTC were headed by a single mother, usually in her thirties, who received an average wage supplement of about £77 per week.[61] This payment to supplement earned income meant that the WFTC in effect raised hourly wages from the initial statutory minimum of less than £4 in 2000 toward a £6 or £7 hourly rate. Among observers who were concerned about the ability of low-wage workers to support themselves and their families, both the WFTC and the national minimum wage were viewed as important contributions toward 'making work pay.'

On the eve of the May 1997 elections, anti-poverty and feminist activists described their expectations of New Labour in power as guarded, restrained, and 'not very hopeful.' According to many campaigners, Tony Blair's 'no new spending' pledge was likely to tie the hands of the new government. Interviewees also suspected New Labour had little understanding of the economic realities facing low-income mothers. In fact, some claimed Blairite modernizers were no different from Conservatives in assuming that unemployment was a problem faced only by men, or that child-care provisions were sufficiently abundant and affordable in all regions. In the words of one respondent, 'Lots of women say they want to work part-time, but it's a bit like asking people if they want to fly to the moon. Often, it is asking women about a choice they don't have.' New Labour's talk of creating more choices would only be meaningful, according to another campaigner, if the government invested 'lots and lots of money which just isn't there.'

New Labour clearly wanted to break with Conservative precedents by moving more lone mothers from benefits to paid employment. The questions raised in response by campaigners were numerous and varied. Would adequate supports for job training or child care be provided in order to make work a meaningful option over benefits? Were New Labour elites prepared to recognize, other than at the level of conventional 'family values' rhetoric, nurturing work in the home as socially valuable labour?

Although anti-poverty and feminist activists endorsed many of New Labour's policy proposals, they also wanted the Blair government to go further than it seemed willing to move – both in terms of addressing structural problems in the labour market and valuing the unpaid work of adults outside the formal work force. On the national minimum wage, for example, these interests as well as trade unions tended to see the starting level as pegged too low, at £3.60 for adults, and as rising too slowly, with an increase of only ten pence an hour after eighteen months. Low wages based on a low national minimum meant that the government paid out very large sums in income supplements via the Working Families Tax Credit. From the perspective of campaigners on the left, New Labour's desire for cooperative relations with business groups meant that the Treasury effectively propped up low-wage work, thus offering employers little incentive to pay above the statutory minimum rate. Over time, these observers claimed, the national minimum wage floor would begin to operate as a wage ceiling for the most vulnerable and poorly paid workers.

Another source of concern among campaigners rested in the treatment of children and child care by New Labour. Although they emphasized that far more attention was paid to difficulties facing employed parents after 1997 than before, many believed important challenges remained. For instance, child-care tax credits established under New Labour were capped or limited per week, and were only meaningful if affordable, registered care could be obtained in the same areas where jobs were plentiful. Since credits were not geared under the WFTC to the number of children in a household, it was hardly worthwhile for parents with more than two pre-school children to seek paid employment. As one campaigner noted, 'The take-up on the child-care tax credit is only about 10 per cent, since the ceiling on the credit is way below the actual costs of registered care. People who get the same payments in some cases have vastly different numbers of kids and costs of care. Our preference is a universal, affordable child-care system where you didn't have these cumbersome tax credits.'

Respondents were especially angered by New Labour's very contentious decision in 1997 to cut lone parent premiums for social benefits. At one level, their opposition was linked to frustration with the way Prime Minister Blair carried through on Tory spending estimates, faced a public outcry, and then dumped Harriet Harman as the senior woman in cabinet to prove he was 'responsive' to critics. In the words of one embittered activist, 'Harriet Harman was set up to fail, to take the blame conveniently for things that aren't working.' According to another, 'Harriet Harman was given a job to do, and then she was sacked for doing it.'

Campaigners distrusted Labour's subsequent efforts to compensate for the benefit cuts, and dampen down public as well as backbench outrage. Increases to universal Child Benefit rates announced in 1998 and following were often portrayed as little more than a convenient cover for the government's hotly contested decision on lone parent premiums. According to this view, universal benefits were boosted to divert attention away from other changes, but would be allowed to 'wither on the vine' once more elaborate means-tested and, in the case of the WFTC, work-tested schemes came into effect.[62]

As well, aspects of the various New Deal schemes drew criticism from anti-poverty and feminist campaigners. First, New Deal supports for education were limited to twelve months of assistance with vocational–level high school training, as long as that training led directly to paid employment. Campaigners endorsed this provision, but believed that Labour's decision to introduce university tuition fees would make it more difficult in the future for less advantaged students to learn beyond the secondary school level. Second, activists questioned the Blair government's motives for making a work-focused interview mandatory as of April 2001 for lone parents with children five years and older. Some objected to the switch under the New Deal from treating personal advisers as job counsellors who built up the confidence and self-esteem of lone mothers to using those same advisers as 'cops intent on enforcing sanctions.'

Third, respondents who paid close attention to official reports on New Labour innovations were concerned that the limits of those initiatives were being ignored. For example, many noted that not only was the New Deal program relatively unsuccessful in placing single mothers from minority backgrounds in paid work, but also the take-up rate for the Working Families Tax Credit was low among the same group. In addition, older questions about the valuation of men's and women's work seemed to be swept under the carpet. As one campaigner observed, 'We see little attention devoted to questions like undervalued work. Who does it? Mostly women. The gap between men's and women's wages is as big as ever. Minimum wage rules can only go so far to deal with the pay gap.'

At the level of public discourse, many activists breathed a sigh of relief in May 1997. In their view, Tory government attacks against single mothers stood out as a crucial and extremely harmful legacy of the previous eighteen years. One campaigner recalled Conservative efforts to link single mothers with the rise of lawless behaviour. In her words:

> As I see it, mothers are being blamed for youth crime and it's really hard on women. The more you stigmatize single parents, the more likely women are to remain in abusive relationships. We are feeding the notion of an ideal family as one where there is a male head of household. The feeling is that too much has been given to those who broke with the nuclear family. The idea is to applaud those who conform. Yet the traditional mode was destructive for lots of women.

Other respondents pointed to media claims that working mothers caused British students' standardized test scores to decline. In their view, these assertions proved it did not matter whether mothers were claiming benefits or working for pay; women as a group were simply blamed for a variety of social woes during the Thatcher and Major years.

Yet activists worried that Blairite talk about party modernization and social change was deliberately misleading, since it coexisted with very traditional visual images of the party leader. In particular, efforts by the New Labour media team to present Tony Blair as a contented and conventional family man were profoundly disconcerting to feminist campaigners. As one lamented, 'The Labour leadership still feels it's necessary to distance itself from anything controversial. The norm, the traditional standard, is so crucial. Tony Blair's office always emphasizes how he is happily married with loads of kids. This is all to show how Labour fits the norm.'

Several interviewees claimed that elements of the parliamentary Labour party were prepared to continue the Conservative practice of stigmatizing people on benefits. They cited the 1997 appointment of Frank Field as Harriet Harman's junior colleague at the Department of Social Security as evidence that Labour was prepared, in the words of one activist, 'to do Clintonesque things with welfare mothers.' According to these campaigners, Field imported to Britain the moralistic language of Charles Murray and other American conservatives, in that he elevated individualistic notions of personal responsibility while condemning dependence on state benefits. In the words of an anti-poverty activist:

> Frank Field comes close to saying that people on benefit are fraudulent, and he sees nothing wrong with compelling lone parents to work. He has the moral talk about deserving and undeserving poor. So much negative talk has surrounded social security that we have lost sight of how important benefits are. The stigma is still that of the fraudulent scrounger. Labour's take on the last government seems to be that it wasn't tough enough on scroungers.

Campaigners feared that Field, Harman, and others in New Labour were prepared to outdo the Conservatives in both their policy talk as well as their push to reduce benefits spending and increase rates of paid employment.

The Blair government initially relied on the national minimum wage, more liberal earnings disregards, and the voluntary New Deal for lone parents to lower benefits uptake and raise paid labour force participation. Interviewees feared that, over time, Labour would resort to more coercive measures to press down on benefits uptake, since initial results from the voluntary approach were far from overwhelming. According to campaigners, a more compulsory push into paid employment was likely because, as one pointed out, 'there are lots of people for whom work is really not an option.' Achieving the massive transformation of the British welfare state that Field and others prescribed would, according to many activists, require the importation of US-style mandatory workfare.

In explaining their views of the New Deal, many respondents pointed to the relatively limited resources devoted to the lone parent scheme. These observers believed that because the government defined the criminal consequences of male youth unemployment as a top priority, the bulk of welfare-to-work funding was targeted toward under-25-year-olds.[63] This channelling of scarce public funds meant that the training, education, personal advising, and child-care provisions made available to lone parents were far less generous than were welfare-to-work supports for unemployed youth.

Campaigners also highlighted what they saw as the New Deal's short-term focus on 'getting people jobs fast,' in some cases via privatized job centres that were combined with privatized benefits offices. The language of New Deal administrators focused on 'the move to active benefit management' and 'enhancing employability,' phrases that set off alarm bells among progressives who were familiar with developments on the other side of the Atlantic. Many suspected that Britain was about to import a cheap, quick-fix, US-style approach to welfare reform, perhaps involving large-scale privatization of government services. For example, many respondents wondered if the New Deal's use of the voluntary sector to train unemployed youth, or its willingness to allow private firms to run pilot schemes, reflected the thin edge of the wedge called privatization.

In more general terms, activists questioned whether New Labour leaders understood the consequences of their pro-work orientation for single mother households. As one stated, the New Deal meant 'lone parents will be trapped in low pay rather than in low benefits, as they are now.' Another argued, 'I don't think you deal with poverty by putting people into poverty-level work.' In the words of a third:

> Labour are not willing to redistribute income, only opportunity. It's an American idea that says people might reject opportunity and, when they do, that's their tough luck. But I think people need income to have oppor-

tunities. What good is a training course if you've not got the bus fare to get to the college? What good is a laptop computer for every child when, in many cases, they have not had a decent breakfast?

These concerns reflected a widely held sense among campaigners that even though New Labour constituted an improvement over the Conservatives, the Blair government's outlook on work and welfare was full of blind spots.

Unlike their counterparts in North America, activists in Britain generally supported New Labour efforts to decentralize the delivery and design of welfare-to-work programs. Most viewed the highly centralized practices that had evolved under the Conservatives as out of step with wide regional variations in the availability of jobs, for example. To the extent that campaigners did express scepticism about decentralization, they questioned whether a highly centralized New Labour elite would go far enough in devolving British social policy.

The parallels between activists in North America and Britain were perhaps clearest with respect to their shared sense of limited influence. Respondents questioned during the Blair years referred consistently to the greater openness of New Labour elites as compared with their Conservative predecessors. Campaigners remarked about 'freer access to government' after 1997, and noted that they faced the unusual prospect of 'a government that *wants* to consult.' Some organizations seemed overwhelmed by endless requests for submissions to official policy commissions, task forces, and reviews. This greater ease of access after nearly two decades of policy isolation led anti-poverty and feminist interests to express their initial public statements about the Blair regime in very cautious terms, in the belief that New Labour was at least willing to listen to careful, well-reasoned interventions.

As time passed, however, the strategy described as 'softly, softly' by one campaigner gave way to a more vocal approach, as activists realized that physical access to New Labour elites could not be construed as policy influence over cabinet decision-making. The disconnect between contact and impact was particularly demoralizing for groups that focused on social benefits for low-income people who did not work for pay. Unlike interests that championed in-work benefits and a decent minimum wage – which arguably won significant improvements after 1997 – organizations with a traditional social benefits orientation sensed they had virtually no effect on decision-making. In the words of one close observer, 'Those groups that talk about security have got far less from the government than those that talk about work. People who can't work are being left behind, as are the groups that represent them.'

One anti-poverty activist framed a growing sense of frustration in the following terms: 'We are concerned that the nurturing work of lone moms is being ignored. Why should a single mom pay a child minder if she is working at McDonald's – especially if her kids are less than five years old?' According to another, 'There is all this rhetoric about "work for those who can, security for those who can't." Yet how can the government claim that this increasingly punitive side of the New Deal offers security to carers and the cared-for, for example? We know that people have dropped off benefits rather than trying to deal with all of this policing.'

Campaigners overwhelmingly linked the creation of a New Deal for lone parents to the influence of Harriet Harman. Yet her demotion following the lone parent benefits fiasco led many to conclude that Labour party women were, like feminist and anti-poverty interests, ineffective in challenging the discursive and social policy directions of the first Blair government. Some activists argued that politically ambitious women were simply too concerned about their prospects for promotion to the front benches to adopt any controversial positions. Others believed that female MPs led lives that were so different from those of women on benefits that the former could not speak credibly about issues relevant to the latter. For a variety of reasons, in short, New Labour women were viewed as an unlikely source of progressive pressure on benefit issues.

In general, anti-poverty and feminist campaigners were hopeful about their ability to shape the broad contours of New Labour social policy, but realistic about the limits of that influence. Activists who pressed for supports to assist people in low-wage employment seemed more optimistic than those who focused on improving the prospects of people who did not work for pay. Relieved that the Thatcher/Major years were at last over, these interests sought new ways to present their claims to a government whose 'doors are open.' As one respondent reflected, 'We still need to make our point. We wanted this government, we helped elect this government, and now we need to hold their feet to the fire so they do what we are all committed to seeing them do.' The looming question was quite simple: Would feminist and anti-poverty campaigners in Britain retain some influence through a second

Blair term? Could they avoid becoming as marginalized as their counterparts in North America?

Conclusions

The consequences of Third Way social policy can be evaluated using a variety of different measures, which in turn produce disparate conclusions. Quantitative data suggest that the uptake of 'passive' income support benefits tended to decline during the Clinton, Chrétien, and Blair years. Caseloads under the AFDC/TANF regime in the United States, social assistance programs in major Canadian provinces, and the Income Support scheme in Great Britain all dropped after Third Way leaders came to office. At the same time, public investments in a variety of new or, in the American case, newly enriched work-tested payments increased over time, whether measured through US spending on the Earned Income Tax Credit, Canadian expenditures on the National Child Benefit, or British investments in the Working Families Tax Credit. As taxified or fiscalized benefits that were also means-tested, the EITC, NCB (as delivered in most provinces), and WFTC were all linked to concerted campaigns to move more single mothers off traditional means-tested income supports, and to 'make work pay' using in-work supplements. One of the most obvious consequences, then, of Third Way leadership in the welfare field rested in a cross-national shift away from older social benefits not tied to paid work, toward a growing emphasis on in-work credits designed to make paid employment more attractive.

Third Way political executives used a variety of methods to pursue these changes. In North America, work-tested benefit schemes generally relied on individual parents who were employed for pay to file a personal income tax return. In Britain, the New Labour approach relied on employers to deliver a government tax credit to parents via the wage packet.[64] The extent to which these in-work credits or benefits extended up the income ladder also varied. Comparative accounts suggested the National Child Benefit in Canada as well as the Working Families Tax Credit in Britain crept further into the middle classes of those countries than did the Earned Income Tax Credit in the United States.[65]

Less quantifiable aspects of Third Way welfare reform include the consequences of these changes for campaigning interests in all three countries. Data drawn from interviews with anti-poverty and feminist activists and experts suggest that two Clinton administrations in the US and two Chrétien governments in Canada first raised and then dashed the expectations of many progressives. In North America, respondents reported a sense of frustration, marginalization, and powerlessness vis-à-vis Third Way social policy. By way of contrast, campaigners in Britain who pressed the government to improve supports for low-wage employees were reasonably pleased with New Labour's first term record, while others who sought to improve benefits for those not in paid employment seemed disheartened by their lack of policy influence. In all three countries, activists seemed discontent with the tone of Third Way social policy rhetoric. Many maintained that even though 'post-conservatives' were somewhat more muted in their language than conservatives, the former still invoked elements of the latter's hot button discourse on welfare and single motherhood.

What were the larger implications of welfare reform as pursued by Bill Clinton, Jean Chrétien, and Tony Blair? Chapter 6 pursues this compelling question of 'So what?'

CHAPTER SIX

The Rise of the Duty State

Of what larger importance is the comparative study of conservative and Third Way welfare reform? Who cares if the rhetoric and actions of Bill Clinton, Jean Chrétien, and Tony Blair were fundamentally consistent with, or divergent from, those of their predecessors?

This chapter presents a broad-ranging argument in response to the 'so what' question. We propose that the willingness of Third Way leaders to pursue and, above all, extend the main lines of conservative discourse and policy will likely prove extremely significant to the evolution of American, Canadian, and British welfare states. In particular, we suggest, the trajectory from conservative to Third Way approaches set in motion a series of changes that could, over time, replace the embattled social citizenship and entitlement groundings of Anglo-American welfare states with a more rigid, obligations-based orientation. As a result of these shifts, the post-war, rights-oriented but still residual liberal welfare state is gradually being transformed into a responsibility-obsessed duty state that demands specific quid pro quo undertakings from individuals seeking support.

From this perspective, Third Way leaders were very important because they helped to tip an already precarious balance between collective responsibility and individual obligation in Anglo-American social policy toward a seemingly inexorable focus on duties owed. During an earlier period, the work of T.H. Marshall, Richard Titmuss, and other scholars emphasized notions of universal – albeit predominantly male – entitlement as the basis for meaningful civic participation. The social contract they envisaged was clearly a two-way street, where reciprocal ties between state and society meant that collective responsibilities were at least as significant as individual ones. Their contributions and the struggles of women's movements in many advanced industrialized countries helped to shape an increasingly egalitarian, collectivist, and rights-based understanding of social belonging, not just in expansive continental European welfare states but also in the more bare-bones, residual schemes of the Anglo-American world.

As conservative critics of these schemes assumed an increasingly vocal role, particularly in the US and UK following the late 1970s, organized opposition to prevailing welfare arrangements began to seep well beyond its traditional confines. Charles Murray, Lawrence Mead, and other proponents of vast cuts to social spending or, alternately, vastly increased regulation of potential welfare claimants began to shape an emergent public consensus that said prevailing welfare policies were normatively bad, administratively broken-down, and fundamentally backward in their effects. Thanks to their interventions, the reciprocal aspect of state/society relationships came to be vastly overshadowed by a unidirectional focus on what individuals owed other individuals, all in the context of a highly fragmented social unit. What states owed individuals, therefore, became transitional or temporary in nature in some emergent duty states (notably the United States), and remained conditional or contingent on tightly scripted norms of behaviour.

Conservative political elites, especially in the US and UK, helped to fuel the general argument that older, reciprocity-based social policies had been a costly, misguided mistake. Yet their equally important legacy rested in small incremental changes that, taken together, helped to undermine the fragile liberal welfare states that had been built in North America and Great Britain. Three crucial elements of the conservative imprint, reinforced by the rhetoric and actions of Third Way leaders, are explored here. The first concerned a narrowing of social benefits eligibility, which worked over time to erode notions of universal entitlement. A second aspect involved the elevation or, indeed, glorification of paid work by responsible individuals, in effect further weakening ideas about social rights. A third element entailed the growth of a highly directive public administration or private contractor presence in the lives of poor citizens, which served to impose and enforce specific quid pro quo obligations to the emergent duty state.

In the field of social assistance, budgetary and rules changes imposed during the Reagan/Bush, Mulroney/Campbell, and Thatcher/Major years served to alter in important ways the meaning of social rights in each of these countries. Punitive talk about 'welfare queens' and 'scroungers,' particularly in the US and UK, helped to turn public attitudes sharply against not just poor people, but also the social programs established in the 1930s and following to assist them. The emphasis on reduced spending, spending wisely, and, especially in Canada, targeting benefits to those 'most in need' created a policy environment in which austerity and selectivity were trumpeted as wise responses to waste and universality.

This trend continued to reverberate through the Third Way years in the United States, Canada, and Britain, as 'post-conservative' leaders stressed the importance of making tough decisions in light of both fiscal problems and the presumed failures of the welfare state. Bill Clinton's arguments about 'ending welfare as we know it,' Jean Chrétien's effort to slay the federal deficit dragon by restructuring social transfers to the provinces, and Tony Blair's adoption of a Mulroney-style language of 'real need' each reflected a conflation of fiscal austerity and policy change issues. In North America, the effects of this confluence were easy to identify in the elimination of any national entitlement to income support based on need as of 1996.

Arguably the most significant consequence of austerity arguments as a basis for greater targeting or selectivity, and hence tighter eligibility regimes, rested in their effects on social rights. Whether formally or informally, any narrowing of the grounds of entitlement to social assistance whittled away at what was an already compromised social citizenship regime in the United States, Canada, and Great Britain. The fact that access to unemployment insurance schemes tended to narrow during the same decades as welfare benefits also became harder and harder to obtain meant that two fundamental safety net programs were being simultaneously transformed. As Robert Henry Cox writes, austerity measures can

> fundamentally change the idea of social rights in a welfare state. Instead of codifying formal claims that individuals can legally press against their governments, programmes are becoming more exclusive rather than inclusive, they are placing a greater emphasis on needs rather than rights as the basis of the claim to assistance, and they often mark a shift from universal to selective assistance.[1]

In countries where social rights were far from fulsome to begin with, the pro-austerity discourse and policies of both conservative and Third

Way leaders were bound to reverberate well beyond the picayune details of welfare or unemployment insurance eligibility.

Second, the emphasis of conservative and especially Third Way elites on paid employment as the unambiguous answer to what was called 'welfare dependency' set off a significant round of policy innovations. The enrichment of the Earned Income Tax Credit in the United States, the implementation of the National Child Benefit in most parts of Canada, and the establishment of the Working Families Tax Credit in Britain reflected a view that paid work was the *sine qua non* of responsible individual behaviour. Third Way talk about 'making work pay' reinforced older messages coming from changes to eligibility rules and budget cuts, so that a clear picture emerged. Traditional welfare programs had failed, and would be gradually supplanted by work-tested benefits operating for the most part via the tax system in North America and the wage packet in Britain.

The attendant normative cues were obvious. Paid work is what matters. Individuals should take care of themselves via the labour market and investments for their personal futures. Individual responsibility holds higher political valuation than do social rights. Older welfare programs grounded in notions of collective entitlement will disappear as selective, work-tested approaches that reward paid employment are set in place to assist responsible individuals.

Clearly, the use of tax-based credits and benefits to assist low-income workers in an age of shrinking welfare programs was preferable to the complete absence of such supports. Yet the something-is-better-than-nothing argument should not obscure a number of fundamental limitations of taxified, work-tested social policies. Even though tax-based payments seemed defensible in an age of 'making work pay,' since they helped employed adults with children, these same credits also created a convenient escape hatch for low-wage employers. As Jared Bernstein points out in his assessment of the United States,

> the EITC is not perfect. Some of its benefits surely end up subsidizing employers, who would likely have to raise their wage offers in the absence of the program. More important ..., relying solely on tax policy to raise the incomes of low-wage workers is a serious mistake. We also need policies that focus directly on raising pretax wages. Otherwise, we face the likelihood of a perpetually expanding low-end labor market, with jobs

> that fail to pay a living wage and thus require ever-increasing taxpayer subsidy.[2]

Given that no other systematic effort to help low-wage workers, especially single mothers coming off welfare, was in play, the probability seemed high that government subsidies to supplement low incomes would become new fixtures of Anglo-American social policy. In Bernstein's words, the expenses associated with 'repairing the damage caused by market outcomes' were far from insignificant and, over time, these costs 'shifted from employers to taxpayers.'[3]

The third element of change in Anglo-American systems involved the growing popularity of directive or supervisory approaches to dealing with low-income people. Consistent with the erosion of social rights and the celebration of paid work, both conservative and Third Way policies pushed hard on rules, directions, and administrative oversight as critical to reshaping individual behaviour in a manner that was ostensibly more responsible and consistent with middle-class norms. Whether through the use of myriad so-called Learnfare, Bridefare, and workfare schemes at the state level in the United States, the implementation of varied work-for-welfare programs in Canadian provinces, or compulsory New Deal welfare-to-work counselling rules in Britain, the introduction of supervisory approaches was an obvious common thread across the three cases.

The United States arguably advanced the furthest down this path. In the state of Wisconsin, a model for Canadian provinces including Ontario as well as for British New Deal architects, Republican governor Tommy Thompson pioneered a Learnfare program that withheld social benefits from households where children had uneven school attendance records. Under his watch, Wisconsin sharply cut the value of welfare payments and experimented with 'hard' time limits so that at the end of a fixed period on welfare, recipients' social assistance payments simply ended. Thompson's W-2 workfare program defined employable adults as mothers whose children were twelve weeks of age or older. People who declined three offers to participate in W-2 compulsory work schemes were denied cash benefits. To cope with the strains of running this program, Wisconsin subcontracted the administration of W-2 to outside organizations including Goodwill Industries.[4]

Supporters of a moralistic approach applauded the terms of Wisconsin's child exclusion rule known as the 'family cap,' under which women who conceived while on benefits were refused additional payments for new babies. A related set of initiatives aimed to increase child support payments from non-custodial fathers (thus replacing public funds going to mothers) and encourage the formation of traditional rather than single-parent households. Hospitals, for example, were awarded money each time they persuaded a new mother on social assistance to identify the father of her baby. As well, genetic testing was permitted for the purposes of establishing paternity.[5]

What made supervisory or 'paternalist' strategies notable at a political level was their reliance on complex, highly rule-based administrative schemes to govern the treatment of low income individuals.[6] Especially in the United States, lone mothers applying for cash benefits became subject to public sector or, alternatively, confessional or 'faith-based' and private sector subcontractor oversight of the minute details of their lives. The withdrawal of rights-based entitlements to income support based on need and the introduction of work-tested benefits in their place were thus accompanied by the growth of increasingly detailed and moralistic regulatory strategies for governing the 're-socialization' of individual welfare claimants.

Progressive observers of welfare reform dynamics in the Anglo-American world raised a variety of questions about this pattern. Writing from the perspective of human liberty and individual rights, sociologist Ralf Dahrendorf remarked that there was something unsettling about Third Way leaders who said the state 'will no longer pay for things but will tell people what to do.'[7] His claim was grounded in a larger argument about the primacy of social cohesion over individual rights in the world view of Bill Clinton and Tony Blair, but one could go farther and ask whether paternalist regulation would not in fact worsen problems of cohesion. As Robert Henry Cox pointed out, the decline of fixed, rights-based entitlements was accompanied by the rise of discretionary administrative options. Under highly individualized welfare regimes, responsible individuals had to 'present the case and persuade officials' about their own needs. According to Cox, '[T]he potential for inequality in implementation increases ... The brazen fare better than the meek in such a welfare state.'[8] It is difficult to see how social cohesion could be enhanced, then, by competition among the least advantaged for scarce public, confessional, and private resources that are seen as bestowed by the more advantaged.

Taken together, austerity arguments that pushed narrow targeting and the erosion of social rights meshed neatly with work-based 'alternatives' to welfare and with highly regulatory approaches to social policy. Their combined upshot was the Anglo-American duty state, under which individual obligations trumped social rights and administrative discretion rewarded 'responsible behaviour.' For poor women, the crucial irony within this scenario was stark and sharp. Surely among society's most dutiful members were mothers who cared for their children in the absence of a spouse or partner, in the absence of measurable financial assets, and in the absence of supportive social norms that said caring work mattered. Yet it was precisely lone mothers at the bottom of the income scale who were singled out under the terms of the emergent duty state to find paid work, or a husband, in order to conform to moralistic norms about 'self-sufficiency,' 'self-reliance,' or 'family values.' Just as older social rights–based claims or entitlements were giving way to a nascent regime grounded in ideas about duties owed, women who thought they were fulfilling their obligations were assigned yet more responsibilities and stripped of the rights they might have used to contest those additional burdens.

In the United States, arguably the most advanced duty state case of the three examined in this study, feminist campaigners mobilized in the late 1990s under the banner of the Women's Committee of One Hundred. This group brought journalists and academic experts together with political activists to press for a government-sponsored caregivers' allowance. As initially conceived, this cash benefit would be paid by the state to single mothers as a formal recognition of the valuable labour entailed in caring for children, and would not be work-tested in the sense of requiring paid employment outside the home.[9]

Although the idea of a caregivers' allowance offered an innovative approach from an American perspective, it was far from clear that such a strategy would fit well within the larger scenario laid out in this discussion. At one level, any proposal to spend scarce state resources on new benefits in an age of social policy austerity would be a very tough sell among both government elites and the general public. Efforts over time to tighten eligibility rules, narrow benefits access (including through the use of time limits and child exclusion rules), and eliminate universal rights-based entitlements had already created an extremely thin funnel for access to cash social assistance payments in the United States.

It seemed highly unlikely that a caregivers' allowance proposal could break out of the constraints imposed by this long-term policy legacy, since the allowance idea was grounded in notions of restoring an older and more accessible scheme of lone mothers' pensions – albeit under a different name. Allowances would cost money, thus violating the austerity principle; open up the channels of eligibility, hence pushing against systematic moves in the opposite direction; and attempt to reinstil a social rights–based view of access to income support, in effect challenging the argument that entitlement-based welfare programs had failed miserably.

Where caregivers' allowance proposals seemed somewhat more promising was in their use of the rhetoric of work to sustain claims for income support. In an age of work-tested benefits, after all, was it not logical to tailor a new program around the nurturing labour of single mothers? Rewarding what had been unpaid work in the home via a government-administered caregivers' allowance scheme seemed to offer American campaigners a magic formula for winning long-elusive social policy gains.

Yet the history of payments to carers in other political contexts, especially in other Anglo-American systems, suggested that this strategy offered a less than perfect solution. First, care allowances were often meagre in subsistence terms and highly restrictive at the level of eligibility. The British Invalid Care Allowance, introduced in 1975, was created as a modest program to recognize individuals who gave up paid work (or reduced their hours of work) in order to care for elderly, sick, or disabled people. The framers of that allowance assumed that married men would be the primary claimants, since it was only following a 1986 European Court of Justice decision that married women were even considered eligible.[10] At no point was the British allowance structured in such a way as to replace foregone earnings in their entirety. Instead, it provided a small financial recompense for carers and a huge fiscal savings for governments, since allowances paid to carers were far less costly than institutional provisions for elderly, sick, and disabled people.

Second, for care allowances to offer more generous payments as work-tested benefits in a highly regulatory duty state, they would likely be recast in entirely different terms from those envisaged by the Women's Committee of One Hundred. Rather than being constructed as feminist supports for independent households headed by single mothers, they would probably be reconstituted by social conservatives as financial incentives or requirements to form traditional households. Particularly in the United States, it was difficult to imagine how a supportive constituency for lone parent caring benefits could be built, just as it was hard to know how the feminist language about care and nurturing would remain distinct from the 'family values' rhetoric that employed the same terms for very different purposes.

Third, caregiving subsidies delivered via Anglo-American tax systems were likely to pay little attention to the devaluation of women's work in the marketplace, and hence would do little to challenge entrenched patterns of pay inequality, job segregation, and so on. As well, providing tax relief for carers at home only reinforced traditional assumptions that female family members belonged in the home where, according to the terms of the new market-driven duty state, they would be assigned 'responsibility' for any other members who needed assistance.[11]

Finally, the caring allowance idea ran afoul of duty state assumptions about supervision, rules, and obligations owed. Even if a public consensus and elite consensus were reached to establish lone mother caring payments at a reasonable level, the question of how the success of state investment might be measured would remain. In a highly supervisory social policy context, who would determine which lone mothers had met their directive targets, and hence should be paid a caring allowance? The idea of monitoring, supervising, and directing care in the home echoed far older social welfare practices that were not only invasive and stigmatizing, but also not necessarily effective or attractive from the perspective of people living in low income households.

Probably the most damning critique of a care allowance approach followed from its failure to challenge traditional divisions of labour in the home. If one of the core goals of second-wave liberal feminism in the United States was to offer equal employment opportunities to women and men, and to valorize and redistribute the unpaid labour traditionally done by women, then it was difficult to see how a state-sponsored scheme paying poor mothers for their work at home could advance those basic objectives. Indeed, it seemed more likely that care allowances in an Anglo-American setting would further reinforce the exploitation and labour market segregation of low-income, and oftentimes minority women, by paying them very modest sums to remain in an isolated job ghetto at home. Given the declining availability of decent, affordable housing in many cities in the United States, Canada, and Great Britain, this approach would conflate difficult living and working conditions – and it was hard to believe that on their own, caregiving stipends would do much about the urban housing crisis.[12]

A somewhat more promising avenue for political engagement in the age of the duty state rested in the realm of labour market reforms. Campaigns to raise the minimum wage to the level of a meaningful 'living wage' to ensure that high-quality child care was available and affordable to all families, and to insist on subsidized parental leaves during the early stages of each child's development, offered realistic challenges to the conservative and Third Way legacy. Each demand implied that Clintonesque talk about 'making work pay' failed to go far enough in establishing basic supports for not just paid employment, but also human development in a globalizing world. If 'investing in people' was to hold any substantive resonance at all, then clearly it required far more buoyant public provisions than existed in these three countries for workers, parents, and children across the class spectrum.

From the perspective of low-income mothers, probably the most crucial labour market reforms were those involving equal pay and job segregation issues. Justice at work for women was thus an essential platform that demanded attention in the age of the duty state, since it brought to light the obligations owed by government to paid employed women who played by a biased set of rules and could not get ahead under a degendered approach to pay, benefits, and job security. If the work available to females generally paid less, offered fewer opportunities for advancement, and was more likely to be of a part-time, insecure, and non-standard variety than that available to males, then no amount of neutered talk about 'making work pay' would make much difference to lone mother households in an age of welfare reform.[13]

It was at this crucial intersection where issues of work and gender met social policy that progressive campaigners had at least some hope of altering the harsh face of the Anglo-American duty state. Given the differing welfare traditions that had evolved in each country, the chances of exerting some critical influence were perhaps somewhat greater in Canada and Britain than in the United States. If the US was the most individualistic, market-driven, and work-obsessed society of the three under consideration, then it obviously presented the hardest challenge for campaigners who wanted to 'make work pay' in gender-sensitive, humane terms. The success of locally based efforts to introduce what was termed a living wage in a number of major US cities, however, indicated that it was possible to contest the duty state at the level of work, pay, and the real-world effects of ending welfare.[14]

Although Canada was strongly influenced by its neighbour to the south, the country remained somewhat more open to arguments for universal child care access, paid parental leave provisions, and so on than was the case in the United States. This variation emerged in provincial-level efforts beginning during the 1990s in Canada, notably in Quebec and British Columbia, to provide high-quality, heavily subsidized, non-profit care for the children of working parents.[15] As well, decisions to extend parental leaves and to ensure that parents' jobs were held or reserved for longer periods after childbirth occurred across a wide ideological spectrum, from the Liberal federal government to hard right Conservative provincial regimes in Ontario and Alberta.[16]

It was arguably in Great Britain that the prospects for humanizing the emergent duty state were most promising. As the most tightly woven social safety net of the three under consideration, Britain's first-generation welfare state simply required more effort to unravel than was necessary in North America. Moreover, the power of social conservative interests was far weaker there than in Canada or certainly the United States, which meant that the constituency for many varieties of 'faith-based' or confessional approaches to welfare reform was considerably smaller. Geographic proximity to continental Europe also offered British campaigners for improved child care, sturdier equal pay, and enhanced parental leave provisions a handy source of models that remained quite distant from their counterparts on the other side of the Atlantic.

As welfare reform experimentalists worked away in the busy duty state laboratories of the United States, Canada, and Great Britain, progressive critics confronted an important juncture of their own. Elections to the top political executive ranks produced differing outcomes in these countries: Al Gore lost the highly contentious presidential race in the same period as the Chrétien Liberals were elected to a third term, and just before Blair's New Labour won a strong second term mandate. How would a George W. Bush administration shape the contours of US social policy and influence developments among America's closest allies? Would the widening gap between rich and poor, reflecting the emergence of what some observers termed a 'drawbridge society,' continue to grow in each of these countries? Or would the more secular, cohesive, and, in the Canadian case, egalitarian strands of political culture outside the US provide leverage for interests that sought a different approach?

By comparing the ways that receding welfare states and emergent duty states evolve in future years, analysts will learn more about how convergent or divergent these Anglo-American countries are, and how successful progressive campaigners have been in advancing their perspectives. The severe obstacles that faced these interests under conservative as well as Third Way political executives suggested their prospects were far from rosy.

Appendix: Interview Schedules

A. United States Interview Schedule

1. Can you tell me about the background to your work on social assistance issues? How long have you been involved and in what policy debates?
2. What is the membership base of your organization? Staff size? Budget per year? Main sources of funding?
3. How would you describe the Clinton years with respect to issues of social policy, especially social assistance? How has the presence of a Democratic president affected your work?
4. What strategies has your group used to gain policy influence since the 1992 presidential elections? Would you say those strategies were different from those used during previous Republican administrations? Previous Democratic administrations?
5. Has your organization operated primarily on a pro-active or re-active footing during the Clinton years? What have you initiated, and who or what have you responded to?
6. What were the main strengths and weaknesses of social welfare policy in the United States before the 'reforms' of the last ten years? In your view, what are the advantages and disadvantages of changes introduced during the Reagan, Bush, and Clinton administrations?
7. From your perspective, what would an ideal social assistance system look like?

8. Has there been any progress from your perspective on income maintenance or social assistance policies during the Clinton years? In what areas? How did progress occur?
9. How would you assess changes in policy access, including participation in policy making by your organization, during the years since 1992?
10. In conclusion, what would you say has been the most lasting legacy of the Clinton administration with respect to social policy?

B. Canada Interview Schedule

1. Can you tell me about the background to your work on social assistance issues? How long have you been involved and in what policy debates?
2. What is the membership base of your organization? Staff size? Budget per year? Main sources of funding?
3. How would you describe the Chrétien years with respect to issues of social policy, especially social assistance? How has the presence of a Liberal government at the federal level affected your work?
4. What strategies has your group used to gain influence since the 1993 federal elections? Would you say those strategies were different from those used during previous Conservative federal governments? Previous Liberal governments?
5. Has your organization operated primarily on a pro-active or reactive footing during the Chrétien years? What have you initiated, and who or what have you responded to?
6. What were the main strengths and weaknesses of social welfare policy in Canada before the 'reforms' of the last ten years? In your view, what are the advantages and disadvantages of changes introduced during the Mulroney and Chrétien years?
7. From your perspective, what would an ideal social assistance system look like?
8. Has there been any progress from your perspective on income

maintenance or social assistance policies during the Chrétien years? In what areas? How did progress occur?

9. How would you assess changes in policy access, including participation in policy making by your organization, during the years since 1993?
10. In conclusion, what would you say has been the most lasting legacy of the Chrétien government with respect to social policy?

C. British Interview Schedule

1. Can you tell me about the background to your work on social assistance issues? How long have you been involved and in what policy debates?
2. What is the membership base of your organization? Staff size? Budget per year? Main sources of funding?
3. How would you describe the Blair years with respect to issues of social policy, especially social assistance? How has the presence of a Labour government affected your work?
4. What strategies has your group used to gain influence since the 1997 elections? Would you say those strategies were different from those used during previous Conservative governments? Previous Labour governments?
5. Has your organization operated primarily on a pro-active or reactive footing during the Blair years? What have you initiated, and who or what have you responded to?
6. What were the main strengths and weaknesses of social welfare policy in Britain before the 'reforms' of the last ten years? In your view, what are the advantages and disadvantages of changes introduced during the Thatcher, Major, and Blair years?
7. From your perspective, what would an ideal social assistance system look like?
8. Has there been any progress from your perspective on income maintenance or social assistance policies during the Blair years? In what areas? How did progress occur?

9. How would you assess changes in policy access, including participation in policy making by your organization, during the years since 1997?
10. In conclusion, what would you say has been the most lasting legacy to date of the Blair government with respect to social policy?

Notes

1. Introduction

1 For one account of this 'family panic' atmosphere, see Mimi Abramovitz, 'Poor Women in a Bind: Social Reproduction without Social Supports,' *Affilia: Journal of Women and Social Work* 7:2 (Summer 1992), 23–43.

2 Kent Weaver refers to social conservatives in the United States who opposed what they viewed as a 'moral meltdown' caused in part by the policy interventions of the 'single mother's lobby.' See R. Kent Weaver, *Ending Welfare as We Know It* (Washington: Brookings Institution, 2000), 212, 213. With reference to British debates, see Ruth Levitas, *The Inclusive Society? Social Exclusion and New Labour* (London: Macmillan, 1998).

3 For an elaboration of this thesis, see Sylvia Bashevkin, *Women on the Defensive: Living through Conservative Times* (Chicago: University of Chicago Press, 1998). The argument is consistent with the approaches of Levitas, *The Inclusive Society*; as well as of Ruth Lister, 'Equality and Welfare Reform in Blair's Britain,' in Edward Broadbent, ed., *Democratic Equality: What Went Wrong?* (Toronto: University of Toronto Press, 2001), 162–94.

4 For assessments of dependency from a feminist perspective, see Wendy Sarvasy, 'Reagan and Low-Income Mothers: A Feminist Recasting of the Debate,' in Michael K. Brown, ed., *Remaking the Welfare State: Retrenchment and Social Policy in America and Europe* (Philadelphia: Temple University Press, 1988), 253–76; Martha A. Ackelsberg, 'Feminist Analyses of Public Policy,' *Comparative Politics* 24:4 (July 1992), 486, 490; Nancy Fraser and Linda Gordon, '"Dependency" Demystified: Inscriptions of Power in a Keyword of the Welfare State,' *Social Politics* 1:1 (Spring 1994), 4–31; Rickie Solinger, 'Dependency and Choice: The Two Faces of Eve,' in Gwendolyn Mink, ed., *Whose Welfare?* (Ithaca, NY: Cornell University Press, 1999), 7–35;

and Eva Feder Kittay, 'Welfare, Dependency, and a Public Ethic of Care,' in Mink, ed., *Whose Welfare?* 189–213.

5 For accounts of this rhetoric, see Levitas, *The Inclusive Society*; Gwendolyn Mink, *Welfare's End* (Ithaca, NY: Cornell University Press, 1998); and Meg Luxton and Leah Vosko, 'Where Women's Efforts Count: The 1996 Census Campaign and "Family Politics" in Canada,' *Studies in Political Economy* 56 (1998), 43–82.

6 Kathryn Edin and Christopher Jencks, 'Welfare,' in Christopher Jencks, *Rethinking Social Policy: Race, Poverty, and the Underclass* (Cambridge: Harvard University Press, 1992), 204.

7 See Gerard William Boychuk, *Patchworks of Purpose: The Development of Provincial Social Assistance Regimes in Canada* (Montreal: McGill-Queen's University Press, 1998). In Canada, critiques of decentralization were most strongly voiced outside Quebec.

8 See T.H. Marshall, 'Citizenship and Social Class,' in T.H. Marshall and Tom Bottomore, *Citizenship and Social Class* (London: Pluto, 1992). The point of this argument was to suggest the constructive potential of an enlarged social citizenship for women and men, rather than to advocate a return to traditional male breadwinner assumptions.

9 According to Thatcher's 1987 comment, 'There is no such thing as society. There are individual men and women and there are families'; as quoted in Wendy Webster, *Not a Man to Match Her: The Marketing of a Prime Minister* (London: Women's Press, 1990), 57.

10 This phrase was used by Tony Blair's Third Way guru, Anthony Giddens. See Anthony Giddens, 'Better than Warmed-Over Porridge,' *New Statesman*, 12 February 1999, 25; and Anthony Giddens, *The Third Way: The Renewal of Social Democracy* (Cambridge: Polity, 1998), 8.

11 Gary Bryner, *Politics and Public Morality: The Great American Welfare Reform Debate* (New York: Norton, 1998), 114–15.

12 For an elaboration of this argument, see Mink, ed., *Whose Welfare?*; Mink, *Welfare's End*; Sanford F. Schram, *After Welfare: The Culture of Postindustrial Social Policy* (New York: New York University Press, 2000); Max B. Sawicky, ed., *The End of Welfare? Consequences of Federal Devolution for the Nation* (Armonk, NY: M.E. Sharpe, 1999); and Joel F. Handler and Lucie White, eds., *Hard Labor: Women and Work in the Post-Welfare Era* (Armonk, NY: M.E. Sharpe, 1999).

13 *Creating Opportunity: The Liberal Plan for Canada* (Red Book; Ottawa: Liberal Party of Canada, 1993), 39.

14 Tony Blair, *New Britain: My Vision of a Young Country* (London: Fourth Estate, 1996), 142–3.

15 See, for example, Weaver, *Ending Welfare as We Know It*.

16 See Paul Pierson, *Dismantling the Welfare State? Reagan, Thatcher, and the Politics of Retrenchment* (Cambridge: Cambridge University Press, 1994). By implication, we also question the view that Canadian social assistance standards have been remarkably resilient and distinctive in the face of social policy changes in the US. For an overview of this position, see Sylvia Bashevkin, 'Rethinking Retrenchment: North American Social Policy during the Early Clinton and Chrétien Years,' *Canadian Journal of Political Science* 33:1 (March 2000), 7–36.

17 Pierson's view could prove more convincing in longitudinal research on health care or education policy, where the preferences of middle-class interests for some state presence may have operated as a brake on ideological and institutional change.

18 Ramesh Mishra, *Globalization and the Welfare State* (Cheltenham: Edward Elgar, 1999).

19 On concepts of symbolic and substantive representation, see Hanna Fenichel Pitkin, *The Concept of Representation* (Berkeley: University of California Press, 1967). For empirical applications of this thesis, see Shelah Gilbert Leader, 'The Policy Impact of Elected Women Officials,' in Louis Maisel and Joseph Cooper, eds., *The Impact of the Electoral Process* (Beverly Hills, CA: Sage, 1977), 265–84; Sirkka Sinkkonen and Elina Haavio-Mannila, 'The Impact of the Women's Movement and Legislative Activity of Women Members of Parliament on Social Development,' in Margherita Rendel, ed., *Women, Power, and Political Systems* (London: Croom Helm, 1981), 195–215; and Debra L. Dodson, ed., *Gender and Policymaking* (New Brunswick, NJ: Center for the American Woman and Politics, 1991).

20 See Giddens, *The Third Way*; and Anthony Giddens, *The Third Way and Its Critics* (Cambridge: Polity, 2000).

21 Ruth Lister, *The Exclusive Society: Citizenship and the Poor* (London: Child Poverty Action Group, 1990), 68.

22 On the child poverty discourse of Canadian and British elites in particular, see Armine Yalnizyan, 'How Growing Income Inequality Affects Us All,' in Broadbent, ed., *Democratic Equality*, 130–1; and Lister, 'Equality and Welfare Reform in Blair's Britain,' 187.

23 Gøsta Esping-Andersen, *Politics against Markets: The Social Democratic Road to Power* (Princeton: Princeton University Press, 1985); and Esping-Andersen, *The Three Worlds of Welfare Capitalism* (Princeton: Princeton University Press, 1990).

24 Much of the literature on this subject addresses the growth of the National Welfare Rights Organization in the United States during the 1960s. See, for example, Frances Fox Piven and Richard A. Cloward, *Poor People's Movements: Why They Succeed, How They Fail* (New York: Random

House, 1977), chap. 5; and Martha F. Davis, 'Welfare Rights and Women's Rights in the 1960s,' *Journal of Policy History* 8:1 (1996), 144–65. On the growth of a federally funded welfare rights presence in Canada, see Rodney Haddow, 'The Poverty Policy Community in Canada's Liberal Welfare State,' in William D. Coleman and Grace Skogstad, eds., *Policy Communities and Public Policy in Canada* (Toronto: Copp Clark Pittman, 1990), 221–3.

25 Over time, the federal share of AFDC costs increased so that it reached 50 to 80 per cent by the 1990s. See Weaver, *Ending Welfare*, 20.

26 See Stephen M. Teles, *Whose Welfare? AFDC and Elite Politics* (Lawrence: University Press of Kansas, 1998), chap. 6.

27 Weaver, *Ending Welfare*, 19.

28 The province of Quebec retained its own family allowance after the federal program was eliminated. See Maureen Baker, *Canadian Family Policies: Cross-National Comparisons* (Toronto: University of Toronto Press, 1995), 129.

29 See Martha Jackman, 'Poor Rights: Using the *Charter* to Support Social Welfare Claims,' *Queen's Law Journal* 19:1 (Fall 1993), 65–94.

30 On Canadian benefits relative to measures of the poverty line, see Maureen Baker and David Tippin, *Poverty, Social Assistance, and the Employability of Mothers: Restructuring Welfare States* (Toronto: University of Toronto Press, 1999), 81. On levels of social assistance payment in Canada versus the US, see Rebecca Blank and M. Hanratty, 'Responding to Need: A Comparison of Social Safety Nets in the United States and Canada,' in David Card and R.B. Freeman, eds., *Small Differences That Matter* (Chicago: University of Chicago Press, 1993), 191–231.

31 See Baker and Tippin, *Poverty, Social Assistance, and the Employability of Mothers*, 108, 198. Housing Benefit was administered by local governments in Britain but subsidized by the central government.

2. Conservative Legacies

1 See Frances Fox Piven and Richard A. Cloward, *Poor People's Movements: Why They Succeed, How They Fail* (New York: Random House, 1977), chap. 5; and Martha F. Davis, 'Welfare Rights and Women's Rights in the 1960s,' *Journal of Policy History* 8:1 (1996), 144–65.

2 Vaughn Palmer, 'Varmint-Hunting with a Credible Minister,' *Vancouver Sun*, 21 January 1994, A16. Premier Harcourt also referred to fraudulent claimants as 'cheats and deadbeats.'

3 Margaret Thatcher, inaugural lecture to the George Thomas Society, Janu-

ary 1990, as quoted in Joan Isaac, 'The Politics of Morality in the UK,' *Parliamentary Affairs* 47:2 (April 1994), 184.

4 Keith Joseph, as quoted in Beatrix Campbell, *The Iron Ladies: Why Do Women Vote Tory?* (London: Virago, 1987), 160.

5 Ronald Reagan, *An American Life* (New York: Simon and Schuster, 1990), 190; emphasis in original.

6 Ibid., 185.

7 Ibid., 189.

8 As quoted in David Zucchino, *Myth of the Welfare Queen* (New York: Simon and Schuster, 1997), 65. See also Lou Cannon, *President Reagan: The Role of a Lifetime* (New York: Simon and Schuster, 1991), 518. For a press account of Reagan's speech, see '"Welfare Queen" Becomes Issue in Reagan Campaign,' *New York Times*, 15 February 1976.

9 Zucchino, *Myth of the Welfare Queen*, 65.

10 See Charles Murray, *Losing Ground: American Social Policy, 1950–1980* (New York: Basic Books, 1984), 227–8; George Gilder, *Wealth and Poverty* (New York: Basic Books, 1981); and Lawrence Mead, *Beyond Entitlement* (New York: Free Press, 1986).

11 Mimi Abramovitz, 'Poor Women in a Bind: Social Reproduction without Social Supports,' *Affilia: Journal of Women and Social Work* 7:2 (Summer 1992), 35; emphasis in original.

12 Reagan, *An American Life*, 188. Experts have long debated whether jurisdictions like California in the United States or British Columbia in Canada operate as 'magnets' because of their nice weather and fine scenery and, indeed, whether welfare recipients can be considered a geographically mobile population in North America. See Gerard William Boychuk, *Patchworks of Purpose: The Development of Provincial Social Assistance Regimes in Canada* (Montreal: McGill-Queen's University Press, 1998), 100–1.

13 Reagan, *An American Life*, 201.

14 Ibid., 189.

15 On Clinton and the Family Support Act, see Gary Bryner, *Politics and Public Morality: The Great American Welfare Reform Debate* (New York: Norton, 1998), 73–4.

16 For example, the 1981 OBRA denied AFDC benefits to pregnant women until their third trimester if they had no dependent children. See Jean Stefancic and Richard Delgado, *No Mercy: How Conservative Think Tanks and Foundations Changed America's Social Agenda* (Philadelphia: Temple University Press, 1996), 83; and Wendy Sarvasy, 'Reagan and Low-Income Mothers: A Feminist Recasting of the Debate,' in Michael K. Brown, ed.,

Remaking the Welfare State: Retrenchment and Social Policy in America and Europe (Philadelphia: Temple University Press, 1988), 257, 259.

17 On the provisions of the 1981 OBRA, see Peter Gottschalk, 'Retrenchment in Antipoverty Programs in the United States: Lessons for the Future,' in B.B. Kymlicka and Jean V. Matthews, eds., *The Reagan Revolution?* (Chicago: Dorsey Press, 1988), 138. The pattern whereby many single mothers collecting AFDC worked for pay but failed to reveal their earnings to officials is documented in Kathryn Edin and Christopher Jencks, 'Welfare,' in Christopher Jencks, *Rethinking Social Policy: Race, Poverty, and the Underclass* (Cambridge: Harvard University Press, 1992), 205–21.

18 On changes to unemployment insurance schemes, see R. Kent Weaver, 'Social Policy in the Reagan Era,' in Kymlicka and Matthews, eds., *The Reagan Revolution?* 152. OBRA also narrowed the terms of eligibility for food stamps and partially de-indexed their value. See ibid., 153.

19 This position was consistent with Reagan's embrace of supply-side or trickle-down economic theories. See Gottschalk, 'Retrenchment in Antipoverty Programs,' 140.

20 Catherine S. Chilman, 'Welfare Reform or Revision? The Family Support Act of 1988,' *Social Service Review* 66:3 (September 1992), 359.

21 Bryner, *Politics and Public Morality,* 74, 75.

22 This figure on child support collections is drawn from Sarvasy, 'Reagan and Low-Income Mothers,' 263.

23 Among the most outspoken critics of funding limitations under the FSA was Senator Daniel Patrick Moynihan, Democrat of New York. See Bryner, *Politics and Public Morality,* 75, 77, 78; Chilman, 'Welfare Reform or Revision'; and Jamie Peck, 'Workfare in the Sun: Politics, Representation, and Method in US Welfare-to-Work Strategies,' *Political Geography* 17:5 (1998), 548.

24 Reagan, as quoted in Bryner, *Politics and Public Morality,* 75.

25 One of Quayle's most memorable political interventions was his attack on the television character Murphy Brown for her decision to have a child as a single woman.

26 As quoted in Stephen M. Teles, *Whose Welfare? AFDC and Elite Politics* (Lawrence: University Press of Kansas), 132.

27 See Thomas J. Corbett, 'Welfare Reform in Wisconsin: The Rhetoric and the Reality,' in Donald F. Norris and Lyke Thompson, eds., *The Politics of Welfare Reform* (Thousand Oaks, CA: Sage Publications, 1995), 23, 25.

28 See Teles, *Whose Welfare?* 139.

29 See R. Kent Weaver, *Ending Welfare as We Know It* (Washington: Brookings Institution, 2000), 413.

30 As quoted in Brooke Jeffrey, *Breaking Faith: The Mulroney Legacy of Deceit, Destruction and Disunity* (Toronto: Key Porter, 1992), 175.

31 As quoted in Louise Dulude, 'The Status of Women under the Mulroney Government,' in Andrew B. Gollner and Daniel Salée, eds., *Canada under Mulroney* (Montreal: Véhicule Press, 1988), 258.

32 As quoted in John Sawatsky, *Mulroney: The Politics of Ambition* (Toronto: Macfarlane, Walter and Ross, 1991), 539.

33 Mulroney, in ibid., 541.

34 As Mulroney stated in his famous 'open for business' speech to the Economic Club of New York in 1984, 'Today's reality ... is that government in Canada has become much too big. It intrudes too much in the marketplace. It inhibits and distorts entrepreneurial activity. Some industries are overregulated, others are overprotected' (as quoted in Lawrence Martin, *Pledge of Allegiance: The Americanization of Canada in the Mulroney Years* [Toronto: McClelland and Stewart, 1993], 70). In his 1988 comments to the Pan American Society in New York, Mulroney claimed that 'the driving force behind growth and job creation is a dynamic private sector' (as quoted in Martin, *Pledge of Allegiance*, 147).

35 As quoted in Andrew B. Gollner and Daniel Salée, 'A Turn to the Right? Canada in the Post-Trudeau Era,' in Gollner and Salée, eds., *Canada under Mulroney*, 14.

36 As quoted in Sawatsky, *Mulroney*, 547.

37 Among the most notable of these lurches forward and back was the 1985 announcement by Finance Minister Michael Wilson of a partial de-indexing of seniors' pensions, meaning payments would no longer increase automatically with the cost of living. After sustained protest by seniors' groups, including an on-camera confrontation between Mulroney and an elderly demonstrator from Ottawa named Solange Denis, the proposal was withdrawn. See Michel Gratton, *So, What Are the Boys Saying? An Inside Look at Brian Mulroney in Power* (Toronto: PaperJacks, 1988), chap. 12. On the Mulroney government's social policy strategy, see Ken Battle, 'The Politics of Stealth: Child Benefits under the Tories,' in Susan D. Phillips, ed., *How Ottawa Spends, 1993–1994* (Ottawa: Carleton University Press, 1993), 417–48.

38 The Mulroney government also froze federal transfers for health and postsecondary education in their 1990 budget. See Susan D. Phillips, 'The Canada Health and Social Transfer: Fiscal Federalism in Search of a Vision,' in Douglas M. Brown and Jonathan W. Rose, eds., *Canada: The State of the Federation, 1995* (Kingston, ON: Queen's University Institute of Intergovernmental Relations, 1995), 69.

39 Brian Mulroney, speaking in November 1984, as quoted in Jeffrey, *Breaking Faith*, 190.
40 Jake Epp, minister of health and welfare in the Mulroney cabinet, said, 'Canadians are a caring people: we hold it to be a fundamental aspect of our national character that we will help our neighbours who are in need.' As quoted in Gollner and Salee, 'A Turn to the Right?' 267.
41 The Mulroney government introduced a 7% national consumption (goods and services) tax, at the same time as it created a $500,000 lifetime tax exemption for capital gains.
42 See Murray Dobbin, *The Politics of Kim Campbell* (Toronto: Lorimer, 1993), 158; and Roger Gibbins, *Conflict and Unity: An Introduction to Canadian Political Life*, 3rd ed. (Toronto: Nelson, 1994), 217.
43 House of Commons Debates, 9 May 1989, as quoted in Dobbin, *The Politics of Kim Campbell*, 159.
44 Employment and Immigration Canada document as quoted in Robert Mullaly, 'The Politics of Workfare: NB Works,' in Eric Shragge, ed., *Workfare: Ideology for a New Under-Class* (Toronto: Garamond Press, 1997), 36.
45 Federal minister of national health and welfare, as quoted in Andrew F. Johnson, 'Canadian Social Services beyond 1984: A Neo-Liberal Agenda,' in Gollner and Salée, eds., *Canada under Mulroney*, 275–6.
46 Jonathan Murphy, 'Alberta and the Workfare Myth,' in Shragge, ed., *Workfare*, 116.
47 See Boychuk, *Patchworks of Purpose*, 85–7; and Eric Shragge and Marc-André Deniger, 'Workfare in Quebec,' in Shragge, ed., *Workfare*, 64.
48 This figure is based on a calculation using data in Mullaly, 'The Politics of Workfare,' 38.
49 On Canadian self-sufficiency experiments and their relevance to reforms in the US, see Philip K. Robins and Charles Michalopoulos, 'Using Financial Incentives to Encourage Welfare Recipients to Become Economically Self-Sufficient,' *Economic Policy Review* 7:2 (September 2001), 105–23. Canadian self-sufficiency programs defined full-time employment as thirty hours or more per week of waged work.
50 The report was about 600 pages long and contained 274 recommendations. See Thomas Walkom, *Rae Days: The Rise and Follies of the NDP* (Toronto: Key Porter, 1994), 196.
51 See Leonard Shifrin, 'Budget Batters the Poor,' *Toronto Star*, 26 February 1990, A17; and Ronald Melchers, 'The Cap on CAP: Ottawa Plans to Put on a Lid on Its Money for Social Assistance and Social Services,' *Perception* 14:4 (Fall 1990), 19–23.
52 The cap on CAP was later extended through the April 1996 dismantling of

the entire program. See Phillips, 'The Canada Health and Social Transfer,' 71.

53 As quoted in Walkom, *Rae Days*, 196.

54 As quoted in ibid., 198; and in Margaret Jane Hillyard Little, *'No Car, No Radio, No Liquor Permit': The Moral Regulation of Single Mothers in Ontario, 1920–1997* (Toronto: Oxford University Press, 1998), 162.

55 See Little, *'No Car,'* 162.

56 Ontario, Alberta, and Manitoba supported the British Columbia challenge, which was grounded in arguments that the federal government had unilaterally and without consultation changed the terms of a shared-cost program, and had failed to offer the required one-year notice to the provinces of its intention to do so. The BC Court of Appeal ruled unanimously in June 1990 that the federal government could not renege on its obligations. The Supreme Court of Canada overturned that judgment in August 1991 on the basis of federal arguments that the House of Commons could not be constrained in its management of Canada's fiscal affairs. See *Reference Re. Canada Assistance Plan (B.C.)*, 1991, 2 S.C.R.

57 As quoted in Justine Hunter, 'NDP Steals Page from the Socreds to Bash the Poor,' *Vancouver Sun*, 23 September 1993. Harcourt removed Joan Smallwood from the social services portfolio, and appointed Joy Macphail in her place.

58 Ontario's Proposal for a Social Charter in Canada, published as appendix II in Joel Bakan and David Schneiderman, eds., *Social Justice and the Constitution: Perspectives on a Social Union for Canada* (Ottawa: Carleton University Press, 1992), 163.

59 Consensus Report on the Constitution – Charlottetown Final Text, published as appendix IV in Bakan and Schneiderman, eds., *Social Justice and the Constitution*, 172.

60 See Bruce Porter, 'The Social and Economic Union: The Social Charter That Wasn't,' *Perception* 16:4 (1992), 11–12.

61 See Derek P.J. Hum, 'Compromise and Delay: The Federal Strategy on Child Care,' in Ronald L. Watts and Douglas M. Brown, eds., *Canada: The State of the Federation 1989* (Kingston: Queen's University Institute of Intergovernmental Relations, 1989), 158. It is important to note that this Tory proposal was more ambitious in terms of total numbers of new spaces than the 1993 Liberal Red Book proposal.

62 The acronym R.E.A.L. stood for Realistic, Equal, Active, for Life.

63 See Hilary Grammar, 'Social Policy by Stealth,' *Canadian Dimension* 25:4 (June 1991), 19. This drop was accounted for by decisions including the de-indexation of health and education transfers to the provinces, the cap on

CAP, changes to family allowance schemes that eliminated universality, and changes to pension supplements that eliminated universality.

64 Margaret Thatcher, 'Time for a Change,' in Brian MacArthur, ed., *The Penguin Book of Twentieth-Century Protest* (London: Penguin, 1998), 360.

65 Margaret Thatcher, *The Path to Power* (New York: HarperCollins, 1995), 554.

66 Keith Joseph's comments were published in the *Times* (London) on 21 October 1974 and are reprinted in many sources, including Campbell, *The Iron Ladies*, 159–60; Isaac, 'The Politics of Morality in the UK,' 184; and Elizabeth Wilson, 'Thatcherism and Women: After Seven Years,' in Ralph Miliband et al., *Socialist Register 1987* (London: Merlin, 1987), 224.

67 As quoted in Campbell, *The Iron Ladies*, 160, 162. These class categories refer to the unskilled lower end of the British working class.

68 See Martin Durham, *Moral Crusades: Family and Morality in the Thatcher Years* (New York: New York University Press, 1991), 13; and Thatcher, *The Path to Power*, 547.

69 As quoted in Durham, *Moral Crusades*, 13.

70 Thatcher, *The Path to Power*, 560.

71 Ibid., 562.

72 Ibid., 574.

73 Thatcher, 'Time for a Change,' 362; emphasis in original.

74 Conservative Party Manifesto, 1979, as quoted in Thatcher, *The Path to Power*, 447.

75 Ibid., 447.

76 Ibid., 551.

77 See ibid., 120–1.

78 Ibid., 549.

79 See Paul Pierson, *Dismantling the Welfare State? Reagan, Thatcher, and the Politics of Retrenchment* (Cambridge: Cambridge University Press, 1994), 105–7.

80 Fran Bennett, 'The Conservatives' Diary: Policies Affecting Poor Families, June 1979–August 1996,' in Alan Walker and Carol Walker, eds., *Britain Divided: The Growth of Social Exclusion in the 1980s and 1990s* (London: CPAG, 1997), 295.

81 These loans were offered beginning in 1988 under the rubric of the Social Fund. See Pierson, *Dismantling the Welfare State?* 112.

82 Council rents increased by an average of 21 per cent in 1980, 45% in 1981, and 19% in 1982 according to Bennett, 'The Conservatives' Diary,' 290–1. Another important goal of Tory housing policy was reducing the influence of local authorities, which remained crucial to Thatcher's efforts to centralize political power further and undermine the legitimacy of what she portrayed as 'loony left' local councils.

83 See Thatcher, *The Path to Power*, 562; as well as Margaret Thatcher, *The Downing Street Years* (New York: HarperCollins, 1993), 629.

84 As quoted in Mavis Maclean and John Eekelaar, 'Child Support: The British Solution,' *International Journal of Law and the Family* 7 (1993), 213.

85 On the use of US models in Britain, see Maclean and Eekelaar, 'Child Support.' In rare cases where fathers had child custody and mothers failed to pay maintenance, the state would deduct from mothers' wages.

86 Thatcher, *The Path to Power*, 563. On the significance of the Child Support Act to British social policy, see Ruth Lister, 'The Family and Women,' in Dennis Kavanagh and Anthony Seldon, eds., *The Major Effect* (London: Macmillan, 1994), 359. On the use in Britain of child support models imported from the United States, see David P. Dolowitz, 'Welfare: The Child Support Agency,' in David P. Dolowitz with Rob Hulme, Mike Nellis, and Fiona O'Neill, *Policy Transfer and British Social Policy: Learning from the USA?* (Buckingham, Eng.: Open University Press, 2000), 38–58.

87 See Maclean and Eekelaar, 'Child Support,' 223.

88 Jonathan Bradshaw and Christine Skinner, 'Child Support: The British Fiasco,' *Focus* (University of Wisconsin, Madison) 21:1 (Spring 2000), 80.

89 See Lister, 'The Family and Women,' 359.

90 Ibid., 357.

91 Thatcher, *The Path to Power*, 545.

92 See Vicky Randall, 'The Politics of Childcare Policy,' *Parliamentary Affairs* 49:1 (January 1996), 185–6, and Lister, 'The Family and Women,' 358.

93 See Maclean and Eekelaar, 'Child Support,' 226. According to David Willetts, 'The Family,' in Dennis Kavanagh and Anthony Seldon, eds., *The Thatcher Effect* (Oxford: Oxford University Press, 1989), 270, one purpose of Family Credit under the 1986 Social Security Act was to ensure that working families were always better off than those on social benefits. This was not necessarily the case under the old Family Income Supplement introduced in 1971, under which working households were sometimes worse off than those on benefits.

94 These quotations are from statements by Tory members of parliament William Hague, Peter Lilley, and Michael Portillo, respectively, as reported in William Lawton, 'The State of the Welfare State in Canada and Britain,' paper presented at the Canadian Political Science Association meetings, Montreal, 1995, 11.

95 See ibid., 12; and Lister, 'The Family and Women,' 360.

96 This percentage included health, education, and social security expenditures. See Lawton, 'The State of the Welfare State,' 11.

97 Dennis Kavanagh, *Thatcherism and British Politics: The End of Consensus?* 2nd ed. (Oxford: Oxford University Press, 1990), 216.

98 Lister, 'The Family and Women,' 352.

99 Ibid., 353; and Ivor Crewe, 'Values: The Crusade That Failed,' in Kavanagh and Seldon, eds., *The Thatcher Effect*, 244.

100 This British phrase was directed in particular to households headed by homosexual adults. See Maclean and Eekelaar, 'Child Support,' 205; and Sylvia Bashevkin, *Women on the Defensive: Living through Conservative Times* (Chicago: University of Chicago Press, 1998), 137.

101 See Katherine Teghtsoonian, 'Neo-Conservative Ideology and Opposition to Federal Regulation of Child Care Services in the United States and Canada,' *Canadian Journal of Political Science* 25 (1993), 97–121; and Randall, 'The Politics of Childcare Policy.'

102 Lister, 'The Family and Women,' 363.

103 See Bashevkin, *Women on the Defensive*, chap. 2.

104 For a more detailed statement of this argument as applied to the British case, see Joni Lovenduski and Vicky Randall, *Contemporary Feminist Politics: Women and Power in Britain* (Oxford: Oxford University Press, 1993), 38, 266–9.

3. Promises, Promises

1 *Creating Opportunity: The Liberal Plan for Canada* (Red Book; Ottawa: Liberal Party of Canada, 1993), 21.

2 Ibid., 39.

3 See Richard Layard, *What Labour Can Do* (London: Warner Books, 1997), 72–3.

4 Ibid., 58.

5 This phrase was first used by Clinton in a 1991 campaign speech written by Bruce Reed of the Democratic Leadership Council. Reed went on to assume a major domestic policy role in the Clinton White House. See Joel Handler, *The Poverty of Welfare Reform* (New Haven: Yale University Press, 1995), 110, 113.

6 Clinton, as quoted in David Maraniss, *First in His Class: A Biography of Bill Clinton* (New York: Simon and Schuster, 1995), 329–30.

7 Bill Clinton, 1992 presidential nomination acceptance speech, as quoted in Paul J. Quirk and Joseph Hinchliffe, 'Domestic Policy: The Trials of a Centrist Democrat,' in Colin Campbell and Bert A. Rockman, eds., *The Clinton Presidency: First Appraisals* (Chatham, NJ: Chatham House, 1996), 279.

8 The Clinton plan envisaged providing either subsidized private sector

work or government-funded community service jobs at the end of the two-year time limit.

9 See Robert B. Reich, *The Next American Frontier* (New York: Times Books, 1983); Reich, *The Work of Nations* (New York: Knopf, 1991); Lester Thurow, *The Zero-Sum Society: Redistribution and the Possibilities for Economic Change* (New York: Basic Books, 1980); and Thurow, *The Zero-Sum Solution: Building a World-Class American Economy* (New York: Simon and Schuster, 1985).

10 *Putting People First*, as quoted in Robert B. Reich, *Locked in the Cabinet* (New York: Vintage, 1998), 31.

11 *Putting People First*, as quoted in John MacArthur, 'Commentary,' *Globe and Mail*, 16 May 1997.

12 As quoted in Quirk and Hinchliffe, 'Domestic Policy,' 279.

13 David T. Ellwood, *Poor Support: Poverty in the American Family* (New York: Basic Books, 1988), 11.

14 See ibid., 12.

15 According to Ellwood's *Poor Support*, 'Currently the EITC is low enough that it roughly offsets only the taxes a working person will pay into the Social Security system' (115).

16 Ibid., 115.

17 See ibid., 116–17, 177–8. The advantage of a refundable tax credit like the EITC was that it was payable even to individuals who owed no personal income taxes.

18 Garfinkel also pressed the idea of government-assured child support payments. See Handler, *The Poverty of Welfare Reform*, 153.

19 Ellwood, *Poor Support*, 12.

20 Ibid., 13.

21 See Mary Jo Bane and David T. Ellwood, *Welfare Realities: From Rhetoric to Reform* (Cambridge: Harvard University Press, 1994).

22 Ibid., 157.

23 Ibid., 158.

24 Ibid.

25 Ibid.

26 Ibid., 160.

27 Ibid.

28 David Ellwood, as quoted in Reich, *Locked in the Cabinet*, 158; emphasis in original. This same figure is cited in Robert Reich, 'We Must Still Tax and Spend,' *New Statesman*, 3 May 1999, 20.

29 As quoted in Bob Woodward, *The Agenda: Inside the Clinton White House* (New York: Simon and Schuster, 1995), 17.

30 Handler, *The Poverty of Welfare Reform*, 113–14.

31 Ibid., 115.

32 See E.J. Dionne Jr, *They Only Look Dead: Why Progressives Will Dominate the Next Political Era* (New York: Simon and Schuster, 1996), 30.

33 As quoted in Quirk and Hinchliffe, 'Domestic Policy,' 267.

34 As quoted in ibid., 267.

35 'Investing in People' was the title of chapter 2 of *Creating Opportunity*, popularly known as the Red Book. This policy document was co-authored by Paul Martin, who became federal minister of finance, and Chaviva Hošek, who became a policy adviser in the Prime Minister's Office.

36 Ibid., 9.

37 See Edward Greenspon and Anthony Wilson-Smith, *Double Vision: The Inside Story of the Liberals in Power* (Toronto: Doubleday, 1997), 43, 64, on Paul Martin's reliance on the ideas of Robert Reich.

38 *Creating Opportunity*, 73, 74. On the evolution of an approach to social policy in Canada that collectively pools risk, see Pat Armstrong, 'The Welfare State as History,' in Raymond B. Blake, Penny E. Bryden, and J. Frank Strain, eds., *The Welfare State in Canada: Past, Present, and Future* (Concord, Ont.: Irwin Publishing, 1997), 54–61.

39 *Creating Opportunity*, 16–20.

40 Jean Chrétien, *Straight from the Heart* (Toronto: Key Porter, 1985), 115.

41 Ibid., 114.

42 Ibid.

43 As quoted in Greenspon and Wilson-Smith, *Double Vision*, 98.

44 See Thomas J. Courchene and Arthur E. Stewart, 'Financing Social Policy: Observations and Challenges,' in Terrance M. Hunsley, ed., *Social Policy in a Global Economy* (Kingston, Ont.: Queen's University School of Policy Studies, 1992), 129–54.

45 *Creating Opportunity*, 24.

46 Ibid., 21.

47 Ibid., 40.

48 Ibid., 39.

49 Ibid., appendix A, 111.

50 As quoted in Patrick Doyle, 'Canadians Want Work, Not Pogey,' *Toronto Star*, 21 September 1993, A1.

51 As quoted in ibid.

52 This phrase was frequently invoked by both Chrétien and McKenna, and struck a responsive chord in the right-wing press. See Peter Stockland, 'Work for Welfare: Liberal Boss Favors Employment Scheme,' *Toronto Sun*, 21 September 1993, 37.

53 As quoted in David Vienneau, 'Activists Criticize Politicians' "Workfare" Ideas,' *Toronto Star*, 22 September 1993, A12.
54 See, for example, the comments of federal NDP leader Audrey McLaughlin in 'Welfare Recipients "Crying" for Work, Chrétien Says,' *Hamilton Spectator*, 22 September 1993, A7; and in Jill Vardy and Alan Toulin, 'Consensus Building on Tying Welfare to Work Plan,' *Financial Post*, 22 September 1993, 11.
55 See Vardy and Toulin, 'Consensus Building on Tying Welfare to Work Plan.'
56 See Faron Ellis and Keith Archer, 'Reform: Electoral Breakthrough,' in Allan Frizzell, Jon H. Pammett, and Anthony Westell, eds., *The Canadian General Election of 1993* (Ottawa: Carleton University Press, 1996), 62–3.
57 See Sylvia Bashevkin, *Women on the Defensive: Living through Conservative Times* (Chicago: University of Chicago Press, 1998), 221, 225.
58 Ellis and Archer, 'Reform,' 59–63, 69–70.
59 Vienneau, 'Activists Criticize Politicians' "Workfare" Ideas.'
60 Edward Greenspon, 'These Liberals Are Different,' *Globe and Mail*, 23 October 1993, A1.
61 See 'The Final Vote,' *Globe and Mail*, 27 October 1993, A14.
62 *Social Justice: Strategies for National Renewal, The Report of the Commission on Social Justice* (London: Random House, 1994), i.
63 Ibid., 1.
64 Ibid., 221, 21.
65 Ibid., 8; see also 224.
66 Ibid., 1, 20.
67 Ibid., 9; see also 239–40.
68 Ibid., 37; emphasis in original.
69 Ibid., 207, 5.
70 Ibid., 104.
71 Their model was the Australian Jobs, Education, and Training program, known as JET. See ibid., 178.
72 Ibid., 238.
73 Ibid., 251, 384.
74 Ibid., 245.
75 Ibid., 245–9.
76 Ibid., 264.
77 Ibid., 262, 264.
78 Ibid., 311.
79 Ibid., 312.
80 Ibid.; emphasis in original.

81 Tony Blair, as quoted in Paul Anderson and Nyta Mann, *Safety First: The Making of New Labour* (London: Granta, 1997), 23.
82 Blair, as quoted in ibid., 244.
83 As quoted in ibid., 263.
84 Tony Blair, 'Valuing Families,' in Blair, *New Britain: My Vision of a Young Country* (London: Fourth Estate, 1996), 249, 250.
85 See Frank Field, *Making Welfare Work: Reconstructing Welfare for the Millennium* (London: Institute for Community Studies, 1995); and Field, *How to Pay for the Future: Building a Stakeholders' Welfare* (London: ICS, 1996). During the 1970s, Field served as director of the Child Poverty Action Group.
86 Blair, 'Social Justice,' in Blair, *New Britain*, 142, 143.
87 Blair, 'The Stakeholder Economy,' in Blair, *New Britain*, 302, 293; and 'New Labour, New Economy,' in ibid., 116.
88 Tony Blair, January 1997 conference speech, as quoted in Anderson and Mann, *Safety First*, 224.
89 Blair, *New Britain*, 293; and Blair, as quoted in Jon Sopel, *Tony Blair: The Modernizer* (London: Bantam, 1995), 212.
90 Labour policy documents, as quoted in Stephen Driver and Luke Martell, *New Labour: Politics after Thatcherism* (Cambridge: Polity, 1998), 109.
91 See John Rentoul, *Tony Blair* (London: Warner Books, 1997), 436–7; and Andy McSmith, *Faces of Labour: The Inside Story* (London: Verso, 1996), 357–8.
92 See Ruth Levitas, *The Inclusive Society? Social Exclusion and New Labour* (London: Macmillan, 1998), 141.
93 Tony Blair, 'New Labour, New Britain,' in Blair, *New Britain*, 43.
94 See Anderson and Mann, *Safety First*, 60, 104.
95 See Leo Panitch and Colin Leys, *The End of Parliamentary Socialism: From New Left to New Labour* (London: Verso, 1997), 252–6; Patrick Seyd, 'Tony Blair and New Labour,' in Anthony King et al., *New Labour Triumphs: Britain at the Polls* (Chatham, NJ: Chatham House, 1998), 60–2; Nick Jones, *Campaign 1997: How the General Election Was Won and Lost* (London: Indigo, 1997), 185–9; and Layard, *What Labour Can Do*.
96 See McSmith, *Faces of Labour*, 295; and Sopel, *Tony Blair*, 143–4.
97 Bill Clinton, *Between Hope and History: Meeting America's Challenges for the 21st Century* (New York: Random House, 1996), 117; emphasis in original.
98 For a classic account, see T.H. Marshall, 'Citizenship and Social Class,' in T.H. Marshall and Tom Bottomore, *Citizenship and Social Class* (London: Pluto, 1992).

4. 'Post-Conservative' Developments

1 As quoted in House of Commons Library Research Paper 19/1999 at www.parliament.uk/commons/lib/research/rp99/rp99.htm.
2 As quoted in *The Guardian*, 11 December 1997; quoted in Simon Duncan and Rosalind Edwards, *Lone Mothers, Paid Work and Gendered Moral Rationalities* (London: Macmillan, 1999), 289.
3 Progressive critics in Britain opposed New Labour decisions to shorten the period under which people could appeal a denial of benefits, and to appoint one or two employees of government agencies rather than three independent laypersons to appeals tribunals (which operated under a new appeals service within the benefits agency). They also pointed to an increased backlog of appeals cases after 1997.
4 See Bob Woodward, *The Agenda: Inside the Clinton White House* (New York: Simon and Schuster, 1995).
5 Robert B. Reich, *Locked in the Cabinet* (New York: Random House, 1998), 65.
6 See Theda Skocpol, *Boomerang: Health Care Reform and the Turn against Government* (New York: Norton, 1997), 41; Jacob S. Hacker, *The Road to Nowhere: The Genesis of President Clinton's Plan for Health Security* (Princeton: Princeton University Press, 1997); and Haynes Johnson and David S. Broder, *The System: The American Way of Politics at the Breaking Point* (Boston: Little, Brown, 1996).
7 See Johnson and Broder, *The System*.
8 See Gary Bryner, *Politics and Public Morality: The Great American Welfare Reform Debate* (New York: Norton, 1998), 80; Skocpol, *Boomerang*, 101; Johnson and Broder, *The System*, 347; and R. Kent Weaver, 'Ending Welfare as We Know It,' in Margaret Weir, ed., *The Social Divide: Political Parties and the Future of Activist Government* (Washington: Brookings Institution, 1998), 381–2.
9 See Bryner, *Politics and Public Morality*, 83.
10 As Joseph Califano, a veteran of the Jimmy Carter cabinet, reflected in early 1993, 'welfare reform is the Middle East of domestic politics'; as quoted in Paul J. Quirk and Joseph Hinchliffe, 'Domestic Policy: The Trials of a Centrist Democrat,' in Colin Campbell and Bert A. Rockman, eds., *The Clinton Presidency: First Appraisals* (Chatham, NJ: Chatham House, 1996), 281.
11 On the background to these proposals, see Mary Jo Bane and David T. Ellwood, *Welfare Realities: From Rhetoric to Reform* (Cambridge: Harvard University Press, 1994). As Clinton administration appointees, Bane and Ellwood co-chaired the White House task force on welfare reform.

12 On the 'deficit-neutral' approach of the administration task force on welfare reform, see Quirk and Hinchliffe, 'Domestic Policy,' 280. According to Robert Reich, the May 1994 cabinet debates focused on where to find an additional $2 billion to finance job training and child-care expenses for ex-AFDC recipients who sought paid employment. See Reich, *Locked in the Cabinet*, 180, 329.
13 See Bryner, *Politics and Public Morality*, 84–5.
14 Newt Gingrich et al., *Contract with America* (New York: Times Books, 1994), 66.
15 See Bryner, *Politics and Public Morality*, 115.
16 As quoted in Bryner, *Politics and Public Morality*, 119.
17 HHS web document, 'Major Provisions of the PRWORA of 1996,' www.acf.dhhs.gov/news/welfare/aspesum.htm, dated April 1997, 1.
18 See Bryner, *Politics and Public Morality*, 175–81.
19 Text of the Personal Responsibility and Work Opportunity Reconciliation Act, as quoted in Mary Jo Bane, 'Welfare as We Might Know It,' *The American Prospect* 30 (January–February 1997), http://www.prospect.org/print/v8/30/jbane-m.html, 4. For one account of the history of US welfare rights law, see William H. Simon, 'The Invention and Reinvention of Welfare Rights,' *Maryland Law Review* 44:1 (1985), 1–37.
20 Bane, 'Welfare as We Might Know It,' 5.
21 Gwendolyn Mink, *Welfare's End* (Ithaca, NY: Cornell University Press, 1998), 2. Mink's argument foreshadows the discussion in chapter 6, below, about the rise of a duty state to replace the welfare state.
22 See Loretta A. Kane, 'Activists Go "Hungry for Justice" in Welfare Fight,' www.now.org/nnt/11–96/hungry.html.
23 Smeal was at the time president of the Fund for the Feminist Majority. See *Feminist News*, 22 August 1996, www.feminist.org/news/newsbyte/august96/0822.html.
24 See Mink, *Welfare's End*.
25 Estimates suggested at least one-half of women collecting AFDC were fleeing violent situations. Pressure from NOW and other groups led to the introduction of a hardship or violence exemption in TANF, under which up to 20 per cent of state assistance recipients could be exempted from the five-year lifetime limit for cash benefits. The hardship exemption applied to persons who had been battered or otherwise cruelly abused. See *Feminist News*, 22 August 1996, www.feminist.org/news/newsbyte/august96/0822.html; and *Feminist Majority Newsletter*, 8:2, www.feminist.org/cgi-bin/fmf/AT-fmf_sitesearch.cgi
26 On US public attitudes toward welfare policy, see R. Kent Weaver, *Ending*

Welfare as We Know It (Washington: Brookings Institution, 2000), chap. 7; and Steven M. Teles, *Whose Welfare? AFDC and Elite Politics* (Lawrence: University Press of Kansas, 1998), chap. 3.

27 See Mink, *Welfare's End*, 120; and Bryner, *Politics and Public Morality*, 12.

28 Frances Fox Piven, 'Was Welfare Reform Worthwhile?' in Frances Fox Piven and David Ellwood, 'Controversy,' *The American Prospect* 27 (July–August 1996), http://epn.org/prospect/27/27-cnt.html, 2.

29 See Reich, *Locked in the Cabinet*, 330. Morris claimed a presidential veto of the Republican welfare reform legislation would eliminate Clinton's 15-point electoral edge in November 1996.

30 As quoted in Paul J. Quirk and William Cunion, 'Clinton's Domestic Policy: The Lessons of a "New Democrat,"' in Colin Campbell and Bert A. Rockman, eds., *The Clinton Legacy* (New York: Seven Bridges Press, 2000), 220.

31 Reich left his post as labor secretary after one term. On his views about Clinton's decision to sign PRWORA, see Reich, *Locked in the Cabinet*, 329–31.

32 Peter Edelman, 'The Worst Thing Bill Clinton Has Done,' *Atlantic Monthly* 279:3 (March 1997), 43.

33 The study was conducted by the Urban Institute, a middle-of-the-road think tank based in Washington. See Quirk and Cunion, 'Clinton's Domestic Policy,' 219; Edelman, 'The Worst Thing;' Reich, *Locked in the Cabinet*, 331; Bane, 'Welfare as We Might Know It,' 7; and Bane, 'Stand By for Welfare Casualties,' *New York Times*, 10 November 1996.

34 Edelman, 'The Worst Thing,' 49.

35 Ibid., 51.

36 As Frances Fox Piven noted in a commentary on Ellwood's article, 'He seems not to understand that he helped unleash the political maelstrom that is producing escalating welfare cutbacks.' See Piven, 'Was Welfare Reform Worthwhile?' 2.

37 David Ellwood, 'Welfare Reform as I Knew It: When Bad Things Happen to Good Policies,' *The American Prospect* 26 (May–June 1996), http://epn.org/prospect/26/26ellw.html, 9.

38 Bane, 'Welfare as We Might Know It'; 6.

39 Edelman, 'The Worst Thing,' 57.

40 See Weaver, 'Ending Welfare as We Know It'; and Joel F. Handler, 'Low-Wage Work "As We Know It,"' in Joel F. Handler and Lucie White, eds., *Hard Labor: Women and Work in the Post-Welfare Era* (Armonk, NY: M.E. Sharpe, 1999), 15.

41 See Weaver, 'Ending Welfare as We Know It,' 380; and John Myles and Paul Pierson, 'Friedman's Revenge: The Reform of "Liberal" Welfare States in Canada and the United States,' *Politics and Society* 25 (1997), 461–4.

42 Weaver, *Ending Welfare as We Know It*, 81.
43 Weaver, 'Ending Welfare as We Know It,' 398.
44 See John Scholz, 'Tax Policy and the Working Poor: The Earned Income Tax Credit,' *Focus* 15:3 (1993–4), 3–4.
45 Canada, Ministry of Human Resources Development, *Improving Social Security in Canada: A Discussion Paper* (Ottawa: Minister of Supply and Services, 1994), 7.
46 See William Low, 'Wide of the Mark: Using "Targeting" and Work Incentives to Direct Social Assistance to Single Parents,' in Jane Pulkingham and Gordon Turnowetsky, eds., *Remaking Canadian Social Policy* (Halifax: Fernwood, 1996), 198.
47 See James J. Rice, 'Redesigning Welfare: The Abandonment of a National Commitment,' in Susan Phillips, ed., *How Ottawa Spends, 1995–1996* (Ottawa: Carleton University Press, 1995), 188.
48 As David Ellwood, assistant secretary of Health and Human Services in the first Clinton administration, observed, '[W]e got hit by a freight train, in part, of course, because our own train moved too sluggishly'; see Ellwood, 'Welfare Reform as I Knew It,' 9.
49 See Keith G. Banting, 'The Social Policy Review: Policy Making in a Semi-Sovereign Society,' *Canadian Public Administration* 38:2 (Summer 1995), 283–90.
50 See Susan D. Phillips, 'The Canada Health and Social Transfer: Fiscal Federalism in Search of a Vision,' in Douglas M. Brown and Jonathan W. Rose, eds., *Canada: The State of the Federation, 1995* (Kingston: Queen's University Institute of Intergovernmental Relations, 1995), 65–96; Alan M. Maslove, 'The Canada Health and Social Transfer: Forcing Issues,' in Gene Swimmer, ed., *How Ottawa Spends, 1996–97* (Ottawa: Carleton University Press, 1996), 283–301; and Daniel Cohn, 'The Canada Health and Social Transfer: Transferring Resources or Moral Authority between Levels of Government?' in Patrick C. Fafard and Douglas M. Brown, eds., *Canada: The State of the Federation, 1996* (Kingston: Queen's University Institute of Intergovernmental Relations, 1996), 167–87.
51 See Douglas Durst, 'Phoenix or Fizzle? Background to Canada's New National Child Benefit,' in Douglas Durst, ed., *Canada's National Child Benefit* (Halifax: Fernwood, 1999), 13.
52 Edward Greenspon and Anthony Wilson-Smith, *Double Vision: The Inside Story of the Liberals in Power* (Toronto: Doubleday, 1996), 230.
53 Phillips, 'The Canada Health and Social Transfer,' 66.
54 See Phillips, ibid., 71; Allan Moscovitch, 'The Canada Health and Social Transfer,' in Raymond B. Blake, Penny E. Bryden, and J. Frank Strain, eds.,

The Welfare State in Canada: Past, Present and Future (Toronto: Irwin, 1997), 107; and Margaret Jane Hillyard Little, *'No Car, No Radio, No Liquor Permit': The Moral Regulation of Single Mothers in Ontario* (Toronto: Oxford University Press, 1998), 185–6.

55 For a sympathetic account of this calculus, see Thomas J. Courchene, 'CHASTE and Chastened: Canada's New Social Contract,' in Blake et al., eds., *The Welfare State in Canada*, 16.

56 See Alan Toulin, 'Public Solidly Behind Axworthy's Reforms,' *Financial Post* (Toronto), 22–24 October 1994, A1. Another source reported that 86% of Canadians endorsed workfare. See Patricia M. Evans, 'Linking Welfare to Jobs: Workfare, Canadian Style,' *Policy Options* 16:4 (May 1995), 6.

57 See Therese Jennissen, 'Implications for Women: The Canada Health and Social Transfer,' in Blake et al., eds., *The Welfare State in Canada*, 222, 224; and Shelagh Day and Gwen Brodsky, *Women and the Equality Deficit: The Impact of Restructuring Canada's Social Programs* (Ottawa: Status of Women Canada, 1998).

58 CAP had also contained a provision prohibiting the use of work requirements as a condition for receiving social assistance. According to Jennissen, the only CAP welfare principle that remained in the terms of the CHST involved mobility rights, meaning 'the right to an income based on need regardless of what province the person is from' ('Implications for Women,' 226). See also Moscovitch, 'The Canada Health and Social Transfer,' 107; and Keith G. Banting, 'The Welfare State as Statecraft: Territorial Politics and Canadian Social Policy,' in Stephan Leibfried and Paul Pierson, eds., *European Social Policy: Between Fragmentation and Integration* (Washington: Brookings Institution, 1995), 292. It is notable that while health care standards embodied in the Canada Health Act continued under the terms of the CHST, four out of five social assistance principles contained in CAP were discarded under the new regime. For an argument that the CAP-based social assistance system entailed limited national uniformity, see Gerard Boychuk, 'Reforming the Canadian Social Assistance Complex: The Provincial Welfare States and Canadian Federalism,' in Brown and Rose, eds., *Canada: The State of the Federation 1995*, 115–42.

59 Compare, for example, data in Cynthia Costello and Anne J. Stone, eds., *The American Woman, 1994–95: Where We Stand* (New York: Norton, 1994) with those in *Women in Canada: A Statistical Report* (Ottawa: Minister of Industry, 1995).

60 The Ontario government reduced welfare rates by 21.6% effective 1 October 1995. See Little, *'No Car, No Radio, No Liquor Permit,'* 186.

61 Leah F. Vosko, 'Mandatory "Marriage" or Obligatory Waged Work: Social

Assistance and the Single Mother's Complex Roles in Wisconsin and Ontario,' paper presented at the International Political Science Association meetings, Quebec City, August 2000, 14.

62 On the history of social assistance provisions in Ontario, see Little, *'No Car, No Radio, No Liquor Permit.'*

63 Ontario Works Act, Statutes of Ontario, 1997, chapter 25, schedule A, sec. 1.

64 The Ontario legislation explicitly preventing unionization was later deemed 'a "clear violation" of the United Nations Covenant on Economic, Social, and Cultural Rights.' See Valerie Lawton, 'U.N. Condemns Canadian Poverty,' *Toronto Star*, 5 December 1998, A11.

65 See Little, *'No Car, No Radio, No Liquor Permit,'* 187–8; and Margaret Philp, 'Woman Cut Off Welfare for Fraud Challenges Provincial Ban in Court,' *Globe and Mail*, 16 May 2001, A9. On the death of Kimberly Rogers, a pregnant woman in Sudbury, Ontario, who had been sentenced to six months' house arrest because of welfare fraud, see Richard Mackie and Keith Lacey, 'Inquest Sought in Welfare Case,' *Globe and Mail*, 16 August 2001, A6.

66 See Little, *'No Car,'* 187; and Vosko, 'Mandatory "Marriage,"' n. 38. On efforts to mount a court challenge against spouse-in-the-house provisions in Ontario, see Brenda Cossman, 'Family Feuds: Neo-Liberal and Neo-Conservative Visions of the Reprivatization Project,' in Brenda Cossman and Judy Fudge, eds., *Privatization, Law, and the Challenge of Feminism* (Toronto: University of Toronto Press, 2002).

67 See Maureen Baker and David Tippin, *Poverty, Social Assistance, and the Employability of Mothers: Restructuring Welfare States* (Toronto: University of Toronto Press, 1999), 100.

68 *Ontario Works Act*, 1997, Ontario Regulation 134/98, s. 13 (1). As of 1997, the Ontario government also began to suspend drivers' licences for non-custodial parents (mostly fathers) who failed to keep up with maintenance payments. See Judy Rebick, 'Scapegoats,' *Elm Street*, April 2001, 75.

69 Vosko, 'Mandatory "Marriage,"' 16.

70 On municipal-level reactions to the Ontario Works scheme, see Jamie Peck, *Workfare States* (New York: Guilford, 2001), 240–3.

71 See, for example, Ken Battle, 'The National Child Benefit,' in Durst, ed., *Canada's National Child Benefit*, 38–60. Because 8 of 10 provinces chose to withhold social assistance payments by the same amount as the value of the National Child Benefit, the latter was effectively a work-tested benefit in most of Canada.

72 Little, *'No Car, No Radio, No Liquor Permit,'* 151.

73 Durst, 'Phoenix or Fizzle?' 15.

74 Little, *'No Car, No Radio, No Liquor Permit,'* 151.

75 The promise was stated in *Creating Opportunity: The Liberal Plan for Canada* (Ottawa: Liberal Party of Canada, 1993), 40.

76 See Sandra Bach and Susan D. Phillips, 'Constructing a New Social Union: Child Care Beyond Infancy?' in Gene Swimmer, ed., *How Ottawa Spends, 1997–98* (Ottawa: Carleton University Press, 1997), 235–58. During the Chrétien years, the federal government did lengthen parental leaves and increase funding for child-care tax credits. See Campbell Clark, 'Tories New TV Ads Don't Add Up to 101 Liberal Lies,' *Globe and Mail*, 7 November 2000, A9.

77 Fran Klodawsky and Aron Spector, 'Renovation or Abandonment? Canadian Social Housing at a Crossroads,' in Swimmer, ed., *How Ottawa Spends, 1997–98*, 273.

78 In important respects, these decisions paralleled earlier efforts by the Mulroney government to establish narrower terms of unemployment insurance eligibility, lower benefit levels, and shorter benefit periods. See Peter Stoyko, 'Creating Opportunity or Creative Opportunism? Liberal Labour Market Policy,' in Swimmer, ed., *How Ottawa Spends, 1997–98*, 85–110; and Rodney Haddow, 'How Ottawa Shrivels: Ottawa's Declining Role in Active Labour Market Policy,' in Leslie A. Pal, ed., *How Ottawa Spends, 1998–99* (Toronto: Oxford University Press, 1998), 99–126.

79 See Michael J. Prince, 'From Health and Welfare to Stealth and Farewell: Federal Social Policy, 1980–2000,' in Leslie A. Pal, ed., *How Ottawa Spends, 1999–2000* (Toronto: Oxford University Press, 1999), 182. Only about one-tenth of Canadian workers were employed by the federal government or federally regulated industries.

80 James J. Rice and Michael J. Prince, 'Lowering the Safety Net and Weakening the Bonds of Nationhood: Social Policy in the Mulroney Years,' in Susan D. Phillips, ed., *How Ottawa Spends, 1993–94* (Ottawa: Carleton University Press, 1993), 381.

81 See Michael J. Prince, 'Canada's Multiple Welfare States: Social Policies and the Social Union in a Pluralist Age,' paper presented at Institute for Research on Public Policy conference, 'Back to the Table: A New Social Union for 2002?' (Montreal, March 2001).

82 This phrase was used with reference to Clinton by a former leader of the federal New Democratic party, Ed Broadbent, in a letter to the editor of the *Globe and Mail* (Toronto), 6 July 1999.

83 Moscovitch, 'The Canada Health and Social Transfer,' 107; emphasis in original.

84 As quoted in Paul Anderson and Nyta Mann, *Safety First: The Making of New Labour* (London: Granta, 1997), 205–6.

85 The education or training option was only available to applicants who lacked appropriate qualifications, including high school completion, at the point they entered the New Deal program.
86 On employer subsidies and New Deal income levels, see Stephen Driver and Luke Martell, *New Labour: Politics after Thatcherism* (Cambridge: Polity, 1998), 108, 113.
87 In particular, Gordon Brown frequently invoked this phrase. See Driver and Martell, *New Labour*, 113; and Peck, *Workfare States*, 302.
88 See Driver and Martell, *New Labour*, 108. Pregnant women and parents of dependent children were defined as 'vulnerable' and hence faced lower penalties. See Joel Krieger, *British Politics in the Global Age: Can Social Democracy Survive?* (New York: Oxford University Press, 1999), 26.
89 Driver and Martell, *New Labour*, 108.
90 Ibid.
91 See *DfEE Employment News*, no. 265, July/August 1998, 1.
92 Jon Hibbs, '£200 Million "New Deal" to Steer Lone Parents Back to Work,' *Daily Telegraph*, 3 July 1997, 1.
93 Labour Party, *New Labour: Because Britain Deserves Better* [1997 Labour party manifesto], as quoted in Nick Ellison, 'From Welfare State to Post-Welfare Society? Labour's Social Policy in Historical and Contemporary Perspective,' in Brian Brivati and Tim Bale, eds., *New Labour in Power* (London: Routledge, 1997), 54. The estimated yield on the windfall profits tax was for the years 1997–2002.
94 Email communication from Richard Exell, Trades Union Congress, 26 October 1998.
95 See Christopher Warman, 'Delphine Gets the Call to Work,' *The Times*, 22 June 1999.
96 This was the official figure provided in *DfEE News*, 26 August 1999. An earlier report in Tony Dawe, 'Mr. Jobs Unveils His Crusade,' *The Times*, 22 June 1999, cited a figure of 160,000. In 'Labour Policy Mix Won't Be Diluted,' *Globe and Mail*, 23 June 1999, A15, Tony Blair is quoted as saying that 100,000 youths found jobs during the first two years of the New Deal.
97 Duncan and Edwards, *Lone Mothers, Paid Work and Gendered Moral Rationalities*, 288, report a success rate of about 5%. See also Glenda Cooper, 'One Family in Four Now Lone Parent,' *The Independent*, 30 September 1998, 9.
98 Antony Barnett and Patrick Wintour, 'It's a New Deal, but Will It Be a New Dawn?' *The Observer*, 4 January 1998, 17.
99 Peter Brown, 'A Good Deal or a Bad Deal for the Jobless?' *The Times*, 22 June 1999, 2.

100 Rodney Hobson, 'Slow Start to Brighter Future,' *The Times*, 22 June 1999.

101 See Peter Brown, 'But the New Deal Isn't a Good One for Everybody,' *The Times*, 22 June 1999, 10.

102 Small business owners noted this disparity in their dealings with New Deal staff. See Rodney Hobson, 'Present Imperfect,' *The Times*, 22 June 1999, 8.

103 Tony Blair, 'Introduction: My Vision for Britain,' in Giles Radice, ed., *What Needs to Change: New Visions for Britain* (London: HarperCollins, 1996), 3, 6.

104 Ibid., 11.

105 Duncan and Edwards, *Lone Mothers, Paid Work and Gendered Moral Rationalities*, 286. See also Bill Jordan, *The New Politics of Welfare: Social Justice in a Global Context* (London: Sage, 1998), 36.

106 As one close observer recalled, 'Harriet Harman was mortally wounded by the lone parents fiasco.' On the fall 1997 lone parents debate, see Anthony Bevins, 'Rage, Resignations and Rebellion: Blair Breaks His Party's Heart,' *The Independent*, 11 December 1997; Philip Webster and Jill Sherman, 'Minister Goes in Revolt on Lone Parents,' *The Times*, 11 December 1997; and George Jones and Joy Copley, 'Two Quit as Labour Hit by Revolt,' *Daily Telegraph*, 11 December 1997, 1. For accounts of Harman and welfare reform in the first Blair government, see Sylvia Bashevkin, 'From Tough Times to Better Times: Feminism, Public Policy, and New Labour Politics in Britain,' *International Political Science Review* 21:4 (October 2000), 417–19; and Robert Walker, 'The Americanization of British Welfare: A Case Study of Policy Transfer,' *International Journal of Health Services* 29:4 (1999), 691–5.

Harman had been at the centre of an intense Labour controversy during the opposition years, when a decision to send her son to a grant-maintained grammar school outside the Labour party area she represented as an MP became public knowledge. Harman's supporters insisted she had earlier informed the party leader's office of this choice, and claimed Blair's staff were unaware of how politically charged the issue would become in 1996 and following.

107 *The Guardian*, 11 December 1997, quoted in Duncan and Edwards, *Lone Mothers, Paid Work and Gendered Moral Rationalities*, 289.

108 Patrick Wintour, 'Kinnock's Aide Savages Harman,' *The Observer*, 4 January 1998, 1. The full text of the private letter leaked to the press was reproduced in Charles Clarke, 'Almost Everyone in the Party Is Outraged at the Cuts,' *The Observer*, 4 January 1998, 17.

109 As quoted in House of Commons Library Research Paper 19/1999 at www.parliament.uk/commons/lib/research/rp99/rp99.htm.

110 On protests against the legislation, see Phillip Inman, 'No Benefit in Welfare Reform,' *The Guardian*, 1 May 1999; David Brindle, 'Charities Quit Forum over Disability Cuts,' *The Guardian*, 13 May 1999; and Andy McSmith and Richard Thomas, 'Wheelchair Warriors Target Blair,' *The Guardian*, 16 May 1999.

111 Philip Cowley, Department of Politics, University of Hull, 'Disability Benefit Revolt' message to British Politics Group Discussion List (bpg-l@listserv.uc.edu), 21 May 1999.

112 The Working Families Tax Credit was scheduled to go into effect in October 1999. The 1998 budget raised the value of the universal child benefit by about 20%, and established a ceiling of £105 per week that could be claimed for registered child care by working parents under the terms of the WFTC.

113 See Katherine Rake, 'Delivering for Women? The Next Steps,' unpublished paper for the Fawcett Society, London, 2000.

114 Lone parents who had recently left an abusive relationship were permitted a three-month deferral of the interview requirement. New Labour initially set no fixed target or quota on the number of deferrals it would permit.

115 Budget Statement, House of Commons Hansard Debates, 21 March 2000, col. 864.

116 These changes were proposed in the 1998 National Minimum Wage Act, the 1998 Fairness at Work white paper, the 1998 Human Rights Act, and the 1999 Employment Relations Act. Data collected by the Labour government–appointed Low Pay Commission indicated that more than one million of the 1.9 million employees earning below the proposed minimum wage level in 1998 were women in part-time work.

117 Driver and Martell, *New Labour*, 103–4.

118 Ibid., 89. Field was removed from Blair's cabinet in the same July 1998 shuffle that also dropped Harriet Harman. Harman was later appointed Solicitor General in June 2001.

119 See Driver and Martell, *New Labour*, 88.

120 As quoted in Jordan, *The New Politics of Welfare*, 100, 170.

121 See Anderson and Mann, *Safety First*, 227.

122 See Jill Sherman and Philip Webster, 'Middle-Class State Benefits May Be Taxed,' *The Times* (London), 8 December 1997; Michael White, Ewen MacAskill, and Anne Perkins, 'Benefit Cuts Spark Rebellion,' *Manchester Guardian Weekly* 157:25 (21 December 1997), 9; and Andrew Grice and Christopher Morgan, 'Brown Plans to Put Tax on Child Benefit,' *The Times* (London), 28 December 1997.

123 See Frank Field, *How to Pay for the Future: Building a Stakeholders' Welfare* (London: Institute of Community Studies, 1996); and Duncan and Edwards, *Lone Mothers*, 287.
124 See estimates in Duncan and Edwards, *Lone Mothers*, 288.
125 On the tie between Third Way ideas and new communitarianism, see Ruth Levitas, *The Inclusive Society? Social Exclusion and New Labour* (London: Macmillan, 1998), esp. chap. 5; and Anderson and Mann, *Safety First*, 244–7.
126 Ralf Dahrendorf, 'The Third Way and Liberty,' *Foreign Affairs*, September/October 1999, 16. In a 1998 review of Anthony Giddens's *The Third Way*, radical Labour MP Ken Livingstone argued that New Labour's third way provided 'a cloak for social authoritarianism.' See Ken Livingstone, 'There Are More than Three Ways,' *New Statesman*, 25 September 1998, 84.

5. Charting the Consequences

1 In the United States, a total of 9 interviews were conducted in March 1994, 9 in March 1995, 13 in December 1996 and January 1997, and 7 between December 1998 and May 1999. Although most respondents were based in Washington, DC, or New York City, many had been active in or close observers of social policy development in other regions of the United States.
2 Canadian interviews took place in Ottawa and Toronto in Ontario, and Vancouver and Victoria in British Columbia. Many respondents had been activists or close observers in other regions of the country. The breakdown in terms of primary locations was as follows: 12 in Ontario, 26 in British Columbia, and one in Quebec.
3 In Great Britain, a total of 16 interviews were conducted in 1997, 18 in 1998, 2 in 1999, and 9 in 2000. Five of the 1997 interviews took place in February, when New Labour's victory seemed close to certain, and 11 took place in August, after the party had won its first majority government. Although all respondents were questioned in London, many had worked on social policy campaigns in other parts of England as well as in Scotland and Northern Ireland.
4 White House press releases along with those from the Department of Health and Human Services lauded declining welfare rolls and lowered spending on 'passive' benefits. See, for example www.hhs.gov/news/press/1997pres/970822.html, as well as www.acf.dhhs.gov/news/welsum21.htm. Clinton's speech to the Democratic National Convention in Los Angeles in August of 2000 argued that welfare rolls had been cut in half since 1993 (see www.dems2000.com/Clinton speech.htm).

5 See Demetra Smith Nightingale and Robert H. Haveman, eds., *The Work Alternative: Welfare Reform and the Realities of the Job Market* (Washington: Urban Institute, 1995); and Joel F. Handler and Lucie White, eds., *Hard Labor: Women and Work in the Post-Welfare Era* (Armonk, NY: M.E. Sharpe, 1999).

6 R. Kent Weaver, 'Ending Welfare as We Know It,' in Margaret Weir, ed., *The Social Divide: Political Parties and the Future of Activist Government* (Washington: Brookings Institution, 1998), 403.

7 www.dems2000.com/Clinton speech.htm, p. 4 of 11.

8 Ibid., p. 9 of 11.

9 R. Kent Weaver, *Ending Welfare as We Know It* (Washington: Brookings Institution, 2000), 343. See also Michael Massing, 'Ending Poverty as We Know It,' *The American Prospect* 11:15 (19 June–3 July 2000), as well as the special issue of *Economic Policy Review* 7:2 (September 2001) titled 'Welfare Reform Four Years Later: Progress and Prospects.'

10 Weaver, *Ending Welfare*, 343.

11 Stephen M. Teles, *Whose Welfare? AFDC and Elite Politics* (Lawrence: University Press of Kansas, 1998), 185.

12 Daniel J.B. Mitchell, 'Foreword,' in Handler and White, eds., *Hard Labor*, vii.

13 Julia R. Henly, 'Barriers to Finding and Maintaining Jobs: The Perspectives of Workers and Employers in the Low-Wage Labour Market,' in Handler and White, eds., *Hard Labor*, 49. On the problem of more job-seekers than jobs, see Joel F. Handler, 'Low-Wage Work "As We Know It": What's Wrong / What Can Be Done,' in Handler and White, eds., *Hard Labor*, 5.

14 Handler, 'Low Wage Work,' 6.

15 Ibid., 8, 9.

16 Max B. Sawicky, 'The New American Devolution: Problems and Prospects,' in Max B. Sawicky, ed., *The End of Welfare? Consequences of Federal Devolution for the Nation* (Armonk, NY: M.E. Sharpe, 1999), 6.

17 Howard Chernick and Andrew Reschovsky, 'State Fiscal Responses to Block Grants: Will the Social Safety Net Survive?' in Sawicky, ed., *The End of Welfare?* 168.

18 See Weaver, *Ending Welfare*, 352.

19 Weaver, 'Ending Welfare,' 398.

20 Richard M. Daley, mayor of Chicago, letter to the editor of *USA Today*, 16 April 2001, 14A.

21 See Teles, *Whose Welfare?* chap. 7.

22 See Chernick and Reschovsky, 'State Fiscal Responses,' 165.

23 Weaver, *Ending Welfare*, 79.

24 Teles, *Whose Welfare?* 183.

25 Weaver, *Ending Welfare*, 345.

26 On public opinion toward welfare issues, see Weaver, *Ending Welfare*, chap. 7; Teles, *Whose Welfare?* chap. 3; and Martin Gilens, *Why Americans Hate Welfare: Race, Media, and the Politics of Antipoverty Policy* (Chicago: University of Chicago Press, 1999).

27 As quoted in John Gray, 'Riding High in Polls, Grits Leave Rivals Scrambling to Catch up,' *Globe and Mail*, 23 October 2000, A8.

28 For one spirited critique of Chrétien's first term, see Maude Barlow and Bruce Campbell, *Straight through the Heart: How the Liberals Abandoned the Just Society* (Toronto: HarperCollins, 1995).

29 About 1.3 million Ontario residents received social assistance payments in 1995 (see Ernie S. Lightman, 'It's Not a Walk in the Park: Workfare in Ontario,' in Eric Shragge, ed., *Workfare: Ideology for a New Under-Class* [Toronto: Garamond, 1997], 93), compared with only about 467,000 in September 2000. See 'Ontario Welfare Rolls Down Again,' *Globe and Mail*, 10 October 2000, A21. The Ontario government reported in October 2000 that caseloads had consistently declined for 32 consecutive months.

In British Columbia, 'the number of children on welfare decreased by 37 per cent' between 1996 and 2001, while the number of adults on social assistance dropped by 120,000 during this period. See Paul Sullivan, 'Just Call Me a Bleeding Heart,' *Globe and Mail*, 13 November 2001, A19.

30 Michael J. Prince, 'From Health and Welfare to Stealth and Farewell: Federal Social Policy, 1980–2000,' in Leslie A. Pal, ed., *How Ottawa Spends, 1999–2000* (Toronto: Oxford University Press, 1999), 178.

31 According to Prince, 'From Health and Welfare,' 178, Liberals decided to prop up the cash floor for federal transfers to avoid being accused of damaging public health care. According to journalist André Picard, the 'new money pumped into medicare has pretty well made up for the previous cuts,' even before the pre-election infusion was announced in fall 2000. See Picard, 'Health-care Spending Raised by $15 Billion in Past Three Years,' *Globe and Mail*, 12 October 2000, A4. As announced in the February 1998 budget, the Millennium Scholarship Fund was intended to help 100,000 individual students from low- and middle-income backgrounds with scholarships of about $3000 per year.

32 Changes made to unemployment insurance rules in 2000 to assist seasonal workers were primarily designed to improve Liberal electoral prospects in Atlantic Canada, rather than to lessen in a systematic way the fallout from spending reductions among lower-income Canadians. See Shawn McCarthy, 'Chrétien Backtracks on EI Rules,' *Globe and Mail*, 22 September 2000,

A5; and Shawn McCarthy, 'Liberals to Restore Cuts to EI,' *Globe and Mail*, 27 September 2000, A4.

33 See Bruce Little, 'Welfare Has Endured the Biggest Cuts,' *Globe and Mail*, 11 January 1999, B5.

34 See Armine Yalnizyan, 'How Growing Income Inequality Affects Us All,' in Edward Broadbent, ed., *Democratic Equality: What Went Wrong?* (Toronto: University of Toronto Press, 2001), 130–47.

35 Graham Fraser, 'Poverty Rates Rising, Report Says,' *Globe and Mail*, 12 May 1998, A4.

36 See, for example, R. Brian Howe and Katherine Covell, 'Children's Rights in Hard Times,' in Raymond B. Blake, Penny E. Bryden, and J. Frank Strain, eds., *The Welfare State in Canada* (Toronto: Irwin, 1997), 230–45.

37 Jamie Peck, *Workfare States* (New York: Guilford, 2001), 248.

38 Report by the University of Toronto Child Care Research and Resource Unit, as quoted in André Picard, 'Past Decade Shows Little Progress on Child Care: Report,' *Globe and Mail*, 1 May 2000, A3.

39 Quebec pioneered a system of $5/day regulated child care and British Columbia piloted a scheme for $7/day child care, in both cases with long waiting lists for spaces. Quebec and British Columbia were also exceptional in that they were the only two provinces to retain a commitment to social housing through the 1990s.

40 Report by the University of Toronto Child Care Research and Resource Unit, as quoted in Picard, 'Past Decade,' A3.

41 See Jonathan Murphy, 'Alberta and the Workfare Myth,' in Shragge, ed., *Workfare*, 116; and Maureen Baker and David Tippin, *Poverty, Social Assistance, and the Employability of Mothers: Restructuring Welfare States* (Toronto: University of Toronto Press, 1999), 243.

42 On employability rules, see Baker and Tippin, *Poverty, Social Assistance*, 243; and Margaret Jane Hillyard Little, *'No Car, No Radio, No Liquor Permit': The Moral Regulation of Single Mothers in Ontario* (Toronto: Oxford University Press, 1998), 188. On cuts to provincial child-care spending, see Margaret Philp, 'Canada's Child Care Rated Mediocre,' *Globe and Mail*, 26 September 2000, A1.

43 See Margaret Philp, 'UN Committee Lambastes Canada on Human Rights,' *Globe and Mail*, 5 December 1998. On provincial and federal government defences of their records before the UN Committee on Economic, Social, and Cultural Rights, see Margaret Philp, 'Canada Evasive in Report on Social Issues,' *Globe and Mail*, 12 November 1998.

44 Jean Swanson, *Poor-Bashing: The Politics of Exclusion* (Toronto: Between the Lines, 2001).

45 Both British Columbia and Ontario had NDP governments at the time that the cap on CAP came into effect and when the CHST was announced in the 1995 federal budget.

46 Activists claimed that campaigning groups lost their leverage once national standards or guidelines, including the guarantee of provincial appeals processes, disappeared in the shift from CAP to the CHST.

47 Tony Blair, 'A Mandate for Radical Change' [2001 election announcement], http://politics.guardian.co.uk/election2001/story/0,9029,487681,00.html, 2.

48 Ibid., 3, 4.

49 Sarah Hall, 'Blair Preaches Lesson of Trust and Change,' *The Guardian*, 9 May 2001. For a partial text of Blair's 1997 speech at the Aylesbury housing estate in Southwark, see Peck, *Workfare States*, 261.

50 Blair, 'A Mandate for Radical Change,' 5.

51 Larry Elliott and Charlotte Denny, 'Brown Reforms Lone Parent Aid,' *Guardian*, 9 October 2000. See also Edward Heathcoat Amory, 'Brown Hails Fall in Lone Parents Claiming Benefit,' *Daily Mail*, 10 October 2000.

52 'Income Support Statistics: February 2001 Quarterly Statistical Enquiry,' at www.dss.uk/mediacentre/pressreleases/2001/may/01187.pdf.

53 See Jenny Percival, 'Concern for Children as Labour Sends Lone Parents Back to Work,' *The Scotsman*, 10 October 2000.

54 These data were revealed in an analysis commissioned by the Department of Social Security. See Amory, 'Blair Hails Fall'; and Ruth Lister, 'The Responsible Citizen: Creating a New British Welfare Contract,' unpublished manuscript. Official sources suggested that about 80 per cent of the lone parents who found work after they met with a New Deal adviser would have located those jobs without assistance.

55 Lister, 'The Responsible Citizen,' 26.

56 Percival, 'Concern for Children.'

57 Katherine Rake, 'Delivering for Women? The Next Steps,' paper prepared for the Fawcett Society, London, 2000, 11.

58 According to the WFTC rules, qualified parents had to be responsible for at least one child under the age of 16, or under the age of 19 if the child was in full-time education for university entrance.

59 David Willetts, as quoted in Richard Reeves, 'Go to Work or I'll Freeze Your Giro, Warns Brown,' *Observer*, 5 November 1999. Official Treasury sources suggested the average employer paid about 70 pence per employee per week to administer the Working Families Tax Credit.

60 Government child-care tax credits were also delivered for the most part via employers, a design that drew the same criticisms from business groups as

did the Working Families Tax Credit. Universal Child Benefit rates were raised more than 25% during the first New Labour term.

61 'Working Families Tax Credit Statistics,' Inland Revenue Analytical Services Division, May 2000.

62 Gaby Hinsliff, 'Get Off Benefits and Get Down to Business,' *Daily Mail*, 10 November 1999.

63 On New Labour's emphasis on law and order issues, see Paul Anderson and Nyta Mann, *Safety First: The Making of New Labour* (London: Granta, 1997), chap. 7.

64 Feminist groups noted that the new Working Families Tax Credit might well go to the (man's) wallet rather than the (woman's) purse in couple households. This argument led the government to permit women in couples to collect their WFTC via the tax agency, Inland Revenue, whereas lone parents could only receive it from employers.

65 For a comparison of income supplements in all three countries, see Michael Mendelson, 'The WIS That Was: Replacing the Canadian Working Income Supplement,' Caledon Institute of Social Policy, Ottawa, November 1997.

6. The Rise of the Duty State

1 Robert Henry Cox, 'The Consequences of Welfare Reform: How Conceptions of Social Rights Are Changing,' *Journal of Social Policy* 27:1 (1998), 8.

2 Jared Bernstein, 'Two Cheers for the EITC,' *The American Prospect* 11:15 (19 June–3 July 2000), www.prospect.org/archives/V11-15/bernstein-j.html, p. 1 of 6.

3 Ibid., 3, 5.

4 For an overview of developments in Wisconsin, see Thomas J. Corbett, 'Welfare Reform in Wisconsin: The Rhetoric and the Reality,' in Donald F. Norris and Lyke Thompson, eds., *The Politics of Welfare Reform* (Thousand Oaks, CA: Sage, 1995), 19–54.

5 See Leah F. Vosko, 'Mandatory "Marriage" or Obligatory Waged Work: Social Assistance and Single Mothers in Wisconsin and Ontario,' in Sylvia Bashevkin, ed., *Women's Work Is Never Done: Comparative Studies in Care-Giving, Employment, and Social Policy Reform* (New York: Routledge, 2002).

6 See Lawrence Mead, ed., *The New Paternalism: Supervisory Approaches to Poverty* (Washington: Brookings Institution, 1997).

7 Ralf Dahrendorf, 'The Third Way and Liberty,' *Foreign Affairs*, September/October 1999, 16. In a 1998 review of Anthony Giddens's *The Third Way*, radical Labour MP Ken Livingstone portrayed New Labour's Third Way as

'a cloak for social authoritarianism.' See Ken Livingstone, 'There Are More than Three Ways,' *New Statesman*, 25 September 1998, 84.

8 Cox, 'The Consequences of Welfare Reform,' 11.

9 For a defence of the care allowance proposal, see Gwendolyn Mink, 'Violating Women: Rights Abuses in the American Welfare Police State,' in Bashevkin, ed., *Women's Work Is Never Done*.

10 See Sylvia Bashevkin, *Women on the Defensive: Living through Conservative Times* (Chicago: University of Chicago Press, 1998), 56.

11 See Lisa Philipps, 'Tax Law and Social Reproduction: The Gender of Fiscal Policy in an Age of Privatization,' in Brenda Cossman and Judy Fudge, eds., *Privatization, Law, and the Challenge of Feminism* (Toronto: University of Toronto Press, 2002).

12 See Kristine B. Miranne and Alma H. Young, eds., *Gendering the City: Women, Boundaries, and Visions of Urban Life* (Lanham, MD: Rowman and Littlefield, 2000).

13 See Naomi Barko, 'The Other Gender Gap,' *The American Prospect* 11:15 (19 June–3 July 2000).

14 On the introduction of 'living wage' ordinances in Baltimore and elsewhere since 1994, see David Moberg, 'Martha Jernegon's New Shoes,' *The American Prospect* 11:15 (19 June–3 July 2000); and Robert Pollin and Stephanie Luce, *The Living Wage: Building a Fair Economy* (New York: New Press, 1998).

15 In September 1997, the Quebec provincial government announced that regulated weekday child-care services would be made available at a cost of $5 per day per child for four-year-olds. This offer was extended to three-year-olds as of September 1998, two-year-olds as of September 1999, and one-year-olds as of September 2000, and was scheduled to go into effect for children less than one year old as of September 2001. Policy discussions in Quebec also addressed the extension of these provisions to weekend and evening child care, especially for children of shift workers. In January 2001, the British Columbia NDP government announced its intentions to offer regulated child-care spaces at a cost of $7 per day per child.

16 In February 2001, for example, Alberta announced plans to guarantee the jobs of birth mothers for up to one year, and to offer unpaid parental leaves of 37 weeks' duration to new mothers, new fathers, and adoptive parents. See Dawn Walton, 'Alberta to Expand Parental-Leave Laws,' *Globe and Mail*, 8 February 2001.

Index